EMDR and Dissociation
The Progressive Approach

Anabel Gonzalez & Dolores Mosquera

info@itradis.com

EMDR and Dissociation: The Progressive Approach.

Copyright © 2012 Anabel Gonzalez & Dolores Mosquera.

First edition (revised).

Revision: Miriam Ramos Morrison.

ISBN-13: 978-84-615-9170-1.

ISBN-10: 84-615-9170-4.

To all the colleagues who collaborated in this project, thank you for your effort, for sharing your ideas and experience. It was fun "to think together."

To our patients, thank you for teaching us such important lessons and for being so generous allowing us to share your experiences with our readers.

To Luis and Pachi, for everything.

Preface

It is a privilege for me to accompany this book by a preface. I consider this work essential for all practitioners who work in the context of psychotherapy, as it deals with two main issues in psychopathology: trauma and dissociation.

During the past two decades, EMDR has become the elective choice in treating post-traumatic stress disorders related to the exposure to traumatic events such as accidents, natural or human made disasters. Meanwhile, practicing clinicians have found the application of EMDR to be useful in treating patients who have experienced emotionally traumatic events, which they described as distinctive of their family-of-origin, their personal life history, and their attachment relations. Extensive research and publications have examined in depth EMDR's effectiveness in this fieldwork of psychotherapy. Therefore, EMDR has become more frequently used by clinicians, when facing individuals suffering from chronic traumas and tied to traumatic interpersonal relations.

It is a known fact that in the first childhood years, interactions with others develop important connections in the brain, which progressively influence the inner sense of Self and the capacity to have healthy relationships with the outside world. Experiences of relations with attachment figures during the first childhood years can help develop emotional self-regulation and contribute to the formation of cognitive, behavioral, and emotional patterns. Research on attachment has proven that it is these relationships that influence the development of the ability to rebalance emotions, establish interpersonal intimacy, as well as the ability of self-reflection and mentalizing. In addition, it is quite clear that interpersonal and emotional communication within the family-of-origin can set the foundation for developing resources, feeling worthy, and resiliency when under strong emotional distress, hence fostering mental health.

It is for this reason that when a patient begins psychotherapy, it is inevitable that an EMDR clinician will supplement the treatment plan with the application of EMDR to those memories linked to attitudes, behaviors, and messages from the patient's family. After a thorough and complex reprocessing of the traumatic memories, clinicians will gain access to the information related to those parts of the personality rooted in some traumatic experiences.

Whether the patient suffers from a "small-t trauma" or a "large-T trauma" as a result of early relations within the family, clinical application of EMDR can help in finding more effective ways of functioning and in creating a more integrated and secure attachment style. This is one of the major contributions that EMDR can provide to the field of psychotherapy.

When working with EMDR, the life history unfolds memories of events that either need to be further developed and reinforced if positive and functional, or reprocessed if negative or traumatic. Events, experiences, and characteristics of the family system are interwoven in every dysfunctional memory of an event. The elaboration process of every EMDR session helps the patient not just to reprocess the memory in a more functional and evolutionary way, but also to become more aware of previous or present family dynamics. Therefore, within the context of a therapeutic impact, EMDR results as an added advantage, facilitating the therapeutic process of individualization and differentiation.

In 2011, there are more than 120.000 EMDR licensed psychotherapists and most of these have been able to deeply examine their clinical practice within the fieldwork of psychotraumatology and structural dissociation. The authors of this book have shown us that it is possible to integrate the EMDR treatment from a progressive and complex perspective.

Through the various chapters of this book, the authors guide us toward understanding how EMDR can contribute not just in reprocessing trauma, but also in creating insight that can lead to new personality assets and to a more coherent and healthier functioning.

Isabel Fernandez, PhD.

President of EMDR Italy.

Table of Contents

EMDR and Dissociation: The Progressive Approach.

Chapter 1: Introduction

Anabel Gonzalez & Dolores Mosquera

Frequent difficulties in working with EMDR in complex trauma and dissociation are described, introducing modifications and alternative procedures to overcome them that will be further described in the following chapters. This introduction sets the general tone of this book: from clinical situations to the theoretical model and practice oriented proposals.

Chapter 2: The A-B-C of Severe Traumatization

Anabel Gonzalez & Dolores Mosquera

Concepts and terms necessary to understand the authors´ proposals are explained in this chapter.

Chapter 3: AIP Model and Structural Dissociation: A Proposal to Extend the Framework   21

Anabel Gonzalez, Dolores Mosquera, Andrew M. Leeds, Jim Knipe, & Roger Solomon

The theoretical model of EMDR, the Adaptive Information Processing model (AIP), is analyzed, integrating relevant concepts related to severe and early traumatization, attachment theory, and recent neurodevelopmental findings, in order to provide a comprehensive model to guide EMDR case-conceptualization in cases of structural dissociation.

Chapter 4: The Dissociative Language   43

Dolores Mosquera, Anabel Gonzalez, & Natalia Seijo

The treatment of severely traumatized patients goes beyond using protocols and procedures. The therapist needs to combine skills with attunement and mindsight and consider indirect and non-verbal communication, patient ambivalence, and many other issues that the authors have called "dissociative language."

Chapter 5: Enhancing High Order Mental Functions: Beyond Resource Installation

Anabel Gonzalez, Dolores Mosquera, & Andrew M. Leeds

Strengthening the patient is a main goal in the treatment of structural dissociation. Some approaches outline the need for working with the inner system of dissociative parts, but this is not the only aspect that should be considered for an effective therapy with this clinical group. Some authors have highlighted the importance of enhancing different high order mental functions such as mentalization, metacognitive procedures, mindfulness, and others. The relevance of these aspects for EMDR therapy will be described.

Chapter 6: Introducing Healthy Patterns of Self-Care

Anabel Gonzalez, Dolores Mosquera, Jim Knipe, & Andrew M. Leeds

Therapy is caring. The patient may come to our office without a clear motivation to get better or to learn to take care of himself. A neglectful or traumatic early environment influences the individual's self-care. The authors propose exploration and work on self-care patterns as part of the preparatory phase of EMDR therapy.

Chapter 7: Working Toward Integration: Co-consciousness and Connection

Anabel Gonzalez, Sandra Baita, & Dolores Mosquera

Dual attention is not easily achieved in structural dissociation. The authors propose different procedures to enhance dual attention or co-consciousness, understanding them as a part of a continuous journey toward the healthy integration of the personality.

Chapter 8: Overcoming Dissociative Phobias

Anabel Gonzalez & Dolores Mosquera

The concept of dissociative phobias comes from the Theory of Structural Dissociation of the Personality, and it gives the EMDR therapist a comprehensive map to plan the therapy with these patients. Here, phobias are understood by the authors as layers to progressively approach traumatic memories, in order to access and process them in a safe and effective way.

Chapter 9: Working on Blockages or Stuck Points

Dolores Mosquera, Anabel Gonzalez, & Andrew M. Leeds

Sometimes, dissociation presents a blurred picture, with unclear targets difficult to identify. This situation does not imply the need to wait for years until the patient is ready to begin standard EMDR trauma processing. As part of the progressive approach that the authors propose, a dynamic way of processing unspecific points of blockage is illustrated with case-descriptions.

Chapter 10: Working on Therapeutic Relationship Problems with EMDR Therapy

Dolores Mosquera, Anabel Gonzalez, & Andrew M. Leeds

Developing the therapeutic relationship in severe traumatization presents many challenges that are often related to enmeshed relationships in early traumatic and neglectful scenarios. How to identify and connect with different relational situations and "where the patient has learned them" is described and illustrated with clinical vignettes.

Chapter 11: Working on Ambivalence, Defenses and Motivation for Therapy

Dolores Mosquera, Anabel Gonzalez, & Andrew M. Leeds

Motivation for therapy cannot be a pre-condition for working with these clients. By doing this, we risk leaving aside the most damaged clients, who do not believe that they deserve to get better, who blame themselves for being abused, or who have damaged capacities for self-care. Ambivalence, defenses, and lack of motivation are symptoms of early traumatization. The authors present some proposals to deal with these issues.

Chapter 12: Trauma Processing in Structural Dissociation   229

Anabel Gonzalez, Dolores Mosquera & Janina Fisher

Trauma processing is a crucial aspect of EMDR therapy in complex trauma, but it needs many adaptations in standard procedures. Far from an all-or-nothing perspective, where trauma processing is a specific and discrete stage of therapy, the authors propose a progressive introduction of trauma processing, which constitutes the core of the "progressive approach" presented in this book.

Chapter 13: The Meeting Place Procedure for EMDR Therapy   253

Anabel Gonzalez, Dolores Mosquera, & Roger Solomon

The meeting place offers a central conjunction of procedures where different approaches proposed in this book can be performed. In this particular way of working from the meeting place, self-care patterns are installed, high order mental functions are enhanced, dissociative phobias and blockages are processed, and many other procedures may be included. The idea of working from the meeting place introduces an integrative perspective from which to work with the inner system.

Chapter 1
Introduction

Anabel Gonzalez & Dolores Mosquera

EMDR was developed for the treatment of PTSD. It is a structured approach that follows 8 phases including history taking (phase 1), preparation and stabilization (phase 2), reprocessing of traumatic memories (phases 3 to 7), and reevaluation (phase 8). In EMDR therapy, past, present, and future elements are approached in chronological order. When there is simple trauma, following these phases can be quite easy, but when there is complex trauma, clinicians encounter many difficulties with standard procedures. In this book, we will try to describe some of the basic aspects that EMDR therapists must understand in order to adequately apply EMDR in the most severe cases. We will also describe some of the variations we have found useful when treating people with dissociative disorders and complex trauma.

In order to understand most of the procedures explained in the following chapters, the reader should be familiarized with the theory of Structural Dissociation of the Personality (Van der Hart, Nijenhuis, & Steele, 2006). We think it is very useful to keep this map in mind since not having a clear and complete framework when treating complex trauma may cause different problematic situations. In chapter 2, we will briefly explain some of the basic concepts that will be mentioned in this book.

When dealing with severe cases (complex trauma clients, dissociative disorders, personality disorders, and other diagnoses included in the category of severe traumatization), problems may emerge along the different phases of the EMDR standard protocol. Reactions to these difficult situations may evoke different responses in novice and experienced therapists. In the following sections, we will describe some of the difficulties we have observed in each one of the EMDR standard protocol´s phases when treating complex trauma.

Phase 1: History Taking

A client refers a single traumatic episode during the past year as the origin of his problems. He explains that, after a car collision, he is afraid of many situations and has become very paranoid regarding other people, especially when it comes to getting close to others or establishing intimate relationships. He does not refer any problems before this incident and describes his childhood as "happy" without giving any details. He remarks that everything was okay before the accident, but the real consequences of the recent trauma were not enough to justify such an intense and broad present problem (he did not suffer any physical injuries and the car had a slight scratch on the side since they were only cruising at 20 mph).

Novice EMDR therapist: The client says his childhood was fine. This is a "simple trauma" case.

Experienced therapist: The client's description of his "wonderful" family makes me be cautious with this client. EMDR must wait while I gather more information.

Understanding that some memory networks may be stored in a different part of the personality (Van der Hart, Nijenhuis, & Steele, 2006) gives us a more comprehensive map and a good way of approaching these clients. A certain group of memories may simply not be accessible in the first phase of the EMDR protocol (amnesia).

In some cases, the individual may be aware that "there are missing pieces" in his autobiographical memories, but in other cases, he may not be aware at all. At times, the client remembers, but is so ashamed or scared that he cannot say anything, at least until a trusting therapeutic relationship is established or becomes stronger.

Another frequent situation we have encountered is that some clients do not realize how traumatic issues are connected to their present symptoms. Some have difficulties identifying the triggers of their current problems. These could be warning signals for the EMDR therapist, since non-realization of trauma is a crucial aspect in severe traumatization. When a client does not realize how much the trauma is influencing his present problem, the therapist may suspect it is one more post-traumatic consequence.

In some cases, we must be careful and not explore thoroughly these areas in the first sessions. Pacing the process and adapting it to the client's timing is a crucial aspect of therapy in severe traumatization. Nevertheless, it is extremely important to have a map that not only includes the information given by the client, but those aspects that the client does not want (or is not able) to tell us. We will delve further into these aspects in chapter 4, when discussing dissociative language.

Currently, in many European countries there is a tendency to do a long stabilization phase, waiting until the client is "ready" for EMDR reprocessing. We believe the stabilization phase is important, but we are worried about the long periods (sometimes years) that some clinicians are taking. One of the key concepts we want to emphasize is gradual intervention. Step by step procedures can be very useful in severe traumatization. We believe that taking an all-or-nothing perspective with severely traumatized clients is not useful. Waiting until the client can work with a standard procedure for traumatic memories can be equivalent to, "First cure the client, and then do EMDR."

Phase 2: Preparation

In our experience, a specially complicated issue with severely dissociated clients is the safe place installation (SPI), as Mattheβ (2008) and Lanius (2008) report. In fact, we think that the safe place installation could be proposed as a dissociative screening test. It is possible that a person who has experienced repeated abuse in the family environment has never felt safe. In these cases, the same people who are supposed to create safety are frequently the ones who cause the damage. The places where we look for shelter, or build our intimacy, are often directly linked to traumatic experiences in this group of clients. So, it makes sense that, by trying to build a safe place with them, connections with traumatic memories become activated. We have found many situations where the word "safe" per se is a trigger.

> Novice EMDR therapist: I was trying to install a safe place and the client got hyperaroused. It's dangerous to use EMDR.

> Experienced EMDR therapist: I need to work on stabilization for a long time until the client is ready to do EMDR

A client with a diagnosis of dissociative disorder not otherwise specified (DDNOS) begins to imagine her safe place, without using bilateral stimulation (BLS). She initially thinks about her room at home. We ask her to focus on that image, trying to notice if this place would be completely safe for her. The answer is an uncomfortable somatic sensation. We ask her to search for another place, and she chooses a place by the sea. Everything seems to imply safety, but a few minutes later, the word "safe" itself evokes fears, with a monstrous appearance: terrible birds attacking her "safe" place from the air. We are not applying BLS at the moment and, considering the situation, we decide not to. We suggest that she builds a protective glass vault, which she constantly feels as fragile and we need to reinforce again and again in different ways. She finally manages to keep her safe place out of the birds´ reach, but then, from the ground beneath her feet, thousands of horrible insects begin to crawl out. At last, we are able to spread the protective vault under the ground. More than an intervention to generate calm and safety, this safe place exercise turns out to be like a scary movie.

Another client imagined his safe place in the middle of the ocean surrounded by sharks and he did not know how to swim. Although he said this did not bother him, the therapist understood that the word "safe" had a different meaning for him.

This may adopt a more subtle appearance. Clients can present physical symptoms as "My head hurts, my eyes hurt," "I feel a lot of pressure in my head, as if it was going to explode," "I feel dizziness;" or refer a sensation of blockage. These difficulties can be expressed indirectly, such as the client becoming distracted or switching the topic of conversation. Sometimes the procedure apparently works, but the therapist does not feel the client is truly describing emotions or sensations. Other times, the installation seems to go as expected, but after the session the client becomes overwhelmed without a clear reason.

Turkus and Kahler (2006) propose changing the term "safe place" for "healing place" when working with dissociative clients, precisely to avoid these kinds of situations. The authors define this place as an imaginary place where the individual can go during a crisis situation, when he feels overwhelmed, or during the therapeutic work. The client is told something like, "This is the moment to take care of yourself, to facilitate the deep internal caring process. It´s a moment to invite every aspect of the self, every part of your mind and your internal spirit, to create this caring place. This place only exists in your imagination. It is a new space where you can take care of your entire mind, your body, and your spirit." This approach is similar to other aspects that we will describe in chapter 6, where we discuss self-care patterns.

Other authors such as Twombly and Walthan (2008) propose different strategies to overcome the difficulties for the safe place installation with these clients. All these approaches are very helpful, but the great amount of strategies to deal with difficulties during the safe place installation point out the complexity of this intervention with DID clients.

Although, in our experience, resource development and installation (RDI) causes fewer problems than the safe place installation, it should not be considered a simple harmless intervention. Some of the difficulties that can arise during RDI have been described by Leeds, who developed the positive affect tolerance and integration protocol (2007), a procedure for working with clients with attachment disturbances.

Sometimes any positive element (safe place, resource installation) will turn into a negative one, as in the following example:

> Therapist (trying to search for a safe place): It would be interesting if you could resort to an imaginary safe place when you feel bad, do you think you could do that?
>
> Client: No, I can´t, for a simple reason: I can evoke wonderful things, but they turn into nightmares and I can´t get out once I´m there…. I cannot think of an imaginary safe place because, when I try to do that, what begins as pleasant gets deformed and turns unpleasant.
>
> T: So you don´t think it´s possible to find a safe place?
>
> C (agitated): No, I can´t, frankly, I just can´t, I am not trying to be difficult.

When structural dissociation exists, the resources may be locked up in dissociated fragments that contain lost memories. So in many cases, when we reinforce or strengthen the client, we are actually reinforcing the main personality, the host, or the apparently normal personality (ANP) (Van der Hart, Nijenhuis, & Steele, 2003, 2008). If we do this in a competitive internal system, based on fight for control, some dissociative parts may see us as "allied with their enemy," triggering hostile reactions by parts of the personality who feel threatened.

Of course, this does not mean that SPI or RDI are not very useful interventions in clients with structural dissociation. We just want to point out that any intervention (SPI, RDI, or reprocessing dysfunctional elements with BLS) may cause problems for these clients if it is not applied as part of a global therapeutic frame, bearing in mind the particular structure of the internal system in each client.

It is important to understand that this structure is not initially, in many cases, completely evident, and sometimes it only becomes clearer or changes as we move forward in the therapeutic process.

The aspects that need to be reinforced in severely traumatized people will be outlined in this book (chapters 5 and 6): time orientation, separation between past, present, and future and between the inside world and the outside world, the work from the *adult self*, and the installation of healthy *self-care patterns*. Relational problems are very important in these clients, and in chapter 10 we will describe frequent relational situations and specific EMDR procedures to overcome them. Furthermore, we will describe alternative procedures in chapters 5 and 8, where "installation" and "processing" are progressively combined with internal system work, prior to trauma work.

Phases 3-7

Going from phase 2 to phases 3 through 7 can be a complicated issue, so there is a general recommendation of stabilizing the client prior to approaching trauma (Brown, Scheflin, &

Hammond, 1998). Every time we hear or read this type of statement, we ask ourselves "When is the client stable enough for trauma work?"

> Novice EMDR therapist: Should I start with the earliest memory or the worst memory?

> Experienced EMDR therapist: If there are dissociative parts, there should be excellent collaboration and empathy within the internal system before introducing any kind of bilateral stimulation.

The task force advises that the following should be prior to proceeding with trauma processing when a dissociative disorder is present (Shapiro, 2001):

1. Good affect tolerance.
2. A stable life environment.
3. Willingness to undergo temporary discomfort for long-term relief.
4. Good ego strength.
5. Adequate social support and other resources.
6. History of treatment compliance.

This emphasis on security and stabilization before using EMDR for trauma processing in dissociative clients is understandable. But as we mentioned before, in some cases, if we strictly follow these recommendations, clients should be almost completely recovered before working with EMDR on traumatic issues and, by extension, before processing negative aspects. In practice, we should previously connect with each dissociative part, strengthen the ANP, solve the internal conflict, reduce the main symptoms and the present problems of the client, and finally (never before) proceed with EMDR reprocessing of traumatic memories.

In many countries, this is generating a misuse of EMDR. We have a very powerful therapeutic tool, but we cannot use it before the most difficult part of the therapeutic work has been done; a process that may last years. It seems clear that, in these cases, we cannot proceed like we usually do with simple PTSD. In our opinion, it is becoming evident that we need to develop further interventions that allow us to apply our therapeutic tools as soon as possible, in a safe way.

Another question is how and when to approach traumatic contents. The chronologic therapeutic plan that therapists learn in Level I EMDR training is not always adequate for severe traumatization, where trauma is chronic and overwhelming. Different variations have been proposed, such as Hofmann´s inverted protocol (2004) and Leeds´ (2009) alternative ways to plan the therapy in these cases.

The question of "when" to begin with trauma processing is a tricky question that emerges from an all-or-nothing perspective. We defend a progressive approach to deal with traumatic contents, introducing processing elements in the stabilization phase and integrating stabilization resources with trauma work. Like removing onion layers, we will progressively approach the core memories, from the outside to the inside. The hand metaphor is usually employed in describing EMDR processing. In the standard procedure we start from the worst memory (the back of the hand), and the associative process (the fingers) end with two or more neutral or positive associations. In severe traumatization, starting with the core traumatic memory can be overwhelming and re-traumatizing. Our suggestion is to start with the aftermath of early trauma, initially processing the tip of the finger as to progressively approach the most difficult part. We call this intervention the tip of the finger strategy.

Regarding "how" to process, when we have done enough stabilization work and have processed peripheral elements, different modifications have been proposed for the standard protocol. The modifications can be grouped in four types: gradual steps, guidance, fractioning, and synthesis. We will develop these aspects in chapter 12, when discussing trauma processing.

Phase 8: Re-Evaluation

This phase is especially important, as it indicates how the reprocessing has actually worked. We should not judge the effectiveness of a session based only on the appearance of the associations. A session considered apparently unproductive, or far from the usual way in which EMDR works, may lead to a symptomatic or functional improvement in the client. It is necessary to remember this and not change the way of working just because the appearance of the processing does not fit what is usually seen in other type of clients.

Novice EMDR Therapist: What the hell happened in this session? Why did I do EMDR? Things were easier with cognitive behavior therapy!

Experienced EMDR therapist: This session keep looping continuously. We haven't reprocessed anything. Maybe this client is not a good candidate for EMDR.

The reevaluation phase is really a preferential guide to orientate the therapeutic work in these cases (Gonzalez, 2008). Sometimes, an EMDR session that seems negative for the therapist is considered useful for the client, or the results are a dramatic decrease of symptoms such as severe self-harming behavior. On other occasions, an apparently stabilizing and innocuous exercise such as the safe place installation is followed by an increment in anxiety during the following days after the session. There are no two identical clients. We need standards to guide and structure our work, but these standards must be more like a "therapeutic GPS" rather than a set of rigid rules.

As Francine Shapiro (2001) states, "It is better to provide practitioners with a conceptual framework or model to serve as a guide to their clinical practice than merely to give them an inflexible step-by step procedure for implementing EMDR." Phase 8 shows which type of intervention is actually effective in helping a specific client at a specific moment of the therapy process. Using a careful and progressive approach, the client´s AIP (and good clinical judgment) will guide the therapy.

Summary

During reprocessing, the client´s AIP system (Adaptive Information Processing) sometimes does things spontaneously. In a client with secondary or tertiary structural dissociation, while a dysfunctional element is being processed with a single part, a different one might begin to appear in the processing, with its own associations. Both parts are going through the associative process together, and the target can finally become completely desensitized. The therapist just has to make sure that both parts maintain a cooperative style, as the session develops fluently and spontaneously, in order to make important steps in the integration process. But often, the achievement of these results requires more interventions by the therapist, introducing structure and direction proportionally to each client´s needs.

If the AIP system can do the work, our intervention will be minimal. But we must take care of the process and help the client when this is not the case. Interventions for severely traumatized clients often need to be introduced in a gradual way. These clients frequently need guidance and external structure, fractional work, and facilitation of the synthesis process in order to process effectively. Keeping in mind the main characteristics of severely traumatized people, we can work from the EMDR perspective in a holistic way, as we will describe in this book.

The traditional approach of using EMDR just for trauma reprocessing is a powerful intervention, but we consider that EMDR has much more to offer. In this sense, we could consider this approach as Reductionist EMDR, where EMDR processing would only be done in a client who has been able to install the safe place and resources and has good emotional regulation, social support, and so on. There are many clients (the ones that need help the most) who cannot benefit from EMDR procedures if we limit processing to these aspects.

In this book, we propose expanding the application of EMDR procedures to include all the phases of the therapy. In our opinion, in developing EMDR as a comprehensive psychotherapeutic approach, all these aspects should be kept in mind. Different contributions will be explained in the following chapters.

Chapter 2
The A-B-C of Severe Traumatization

Anabel Gonzalez & Dolores Mosquera

Simple Trauma and Complex Trauma

Several authors (Herman, 1992; Van der Kolk, Roth, Pelcovitz, Sunday, & Spinazzola, 2005) have indicated that PTSD symptoms are only adequate to describe the consequences of single traumatic events, but do not include most of the features that derive from early, severe, and chronic maltreatment and neglect. In order to describe these particular clinical presentations, a new category has been proposed for the DSM-V, Disorders of Extreme Stress (DESNOS: Van der Kolk, Roth, Pelcovitz, Sunday, & Spinazzola, 2005). Victims of chronic interpersonal trauma present features that have not been adequately described in the posttraumatic stress disorder criteria. Herman (1992) proposes a different concept, which she has called Complex PTSD. Symptoms are arranged in seven categories: deregulation of (a) affect and impulses, (b) attention or consciousness, (c) self-perception, (d) perception of the perpetrator, (e) relations with others, (f) somatization, and (g) systems of meaning. Other authors (Classen et al., 2006) propose differentiating between posttraumatic personality disorder-disorganized (PTPD-D) and posttraumatic personality disorder-organized (PTPD-O).

Simple trauma would describe only PTSD. The standard EMDR protocol for traumatic memories is oriented towards simple trauma. This is why we will use the term standard EMDR procedure for PTSD to refer to what EMDR therapists call "standard protocol."

Accurately discriminating when a client has "simple trauma" is not always easy, especially for inexperienced EMDR therapists. Some cases of severe traumatization with a highly functioning or very convincing apparently normal part of the personality can be misdiagnosed as "simple trauma."

A client who does not refer problems in childhood, or describes a good relationship with his parents, and does not show any relevant current symptoms might present low scores in the DES (Dissociative Experiences Scale; Bernstein & Putnam, 1986). This can be a very defensive façade of a severe early traumatization, and it is a common presentation of complex trauma and dissociation.

Dissociative Disorders

Dissociative disorders are described in the DSM-IV-TR and include dissociative amnesia, dissociative fugue, depersonalization disorder, dissociative identity disorder (DID), and dissociative disorders not otherwise specified (DDNOS). Although we will not describe dissociative symptoms in depth, we want to highlight some relevant aspects.

The main diagnosis, and the most severe, is DID. In the DSM-IV-TR, amnesia between personality states is a requirement for the diagnosis. However, several relevant authors question this, because many severely disturbed clients do not meet this criterion (Dell, 2002; 2006). These authors propose intrusions (feelings, thoughts, or sensations perceived as "not me," auditory hallucinations, passive influence phenomena, etc.) as key dissociative symptoms.

DDNOS includes some clients that have been labeled as DDNOS type I, which is very similar to DID, but does not meet all the diagnostic criteria (e.g., amnesia between personality states is not present).

Many clients with dissociative amnesia, dissociative fugue, and depersonalization disorder have undetected dissociative parts. When there are symptoms of DID or DDNOS, the diagnosis of amnesia, fugue, or depersonalization cannot be established. They should be considered just symptoms of the main disorder, DID or DDNOS.

The inability to remember part of or their entire childhood history is common in many severely traumatized clients, but it is not enough to diagnose a dissociative disorder, not even dissociative amnesia.

Conversion disorders are classified differently in both international classifications of mental disorders (DSM and CIE). The ICD-10 unifies both diagnoses as dissociative (conversion) disorders, labeling the different conversion disorders as dissociative motor disorders, dissociative convulsions, dissociate anesthesia, sensory loss, and mixed and non-specified forms. The relevance given to DID is not the same in both classifications: While in the DSM-IV-TR, DID is one of the main subtypes of dissociative disorders, multiple personality disorder is included in the ICD-10 as a residual category of "other dissociative (conversion) disorders."

Phases of Treatment

The standard EMDR protocol for PTSD is structured in eight phases. This classification can sometimes generate confusion with what is called the phase-oriented approach for complex trauma disorders (Brown, Scheflin, & Hammond, 1998; Chu, 1998; Courtois, 1999; Gelinas, 2003; Herman, 1992; Kluft, 1993; Steele, Van der Hart, & Nijenhuis, 2001, 2005; Van der Hart, Nijenhuis, & Steele, 2006). Phase-oriented treatment has its origins in the work of Pierre Janet (1898a, 1919, 1925), who described three phases: (1) stabilization and symptom reduction; (2) treatment of traumatic memories; and (3) personality re-integration and rehabilitation. Notice that phase 1 in this phase-oriented treatment is equivalent to phases 1 (history taking) and 2 (stabilization and preparation) in EMDR.

Is Structural Dissociation Synonymous with Dissociative Disorders?

NO. The term dissociative disorder is related to a diagnostic label that includes dissociative identity disorder, dissociative disorders not otherwise specified, dissociative amnesia, conversion disorder, and other dissociative disorders. This diagnosis is categorical and characterized by different symptomatic presentations.

Structural dissociation of the personality describes a mechanism by which trauma generates psychopathology. Notice that we are talking about trauma, this is, not only dissociative disorders - the most severe clinical picture in the posttraumatic spectrum - but also the other end, PTSD. In the middle of this spectrum there are diagnosis such as borderline personality disorder (see Mosquera, Gonzalez, & Van der Hart, 2011), somatization disorder, and disorders of extreme stress or complex PTSD.

Dissociative Parts in Dissociative Disorders, Dissociative Parts in Structural Dissociation, and Ego States

Dissociative Parts in Dissociative Disorders

They have been called alters, alternate personalities, personality states, identities, or dissociated parts. Each one of these distinct identity or personality states has its own relatively enduring pattern of perceiving, relating to, and thinking about the environment and the self. These dissociated parts of the mind are experienced by the client as separate from each other.

Dissociative Parts of the Personality in Structural Dissociation

These dissociative parts include those present in dissociative disorders, but also the psychobiological subsystems that become divided in all posttraumatic conditions, including diagnosis such as borderline personality disorder, somatization disorder, and even posttraumatic stress disorder (simple PTSD). From this perspective, PTSD and DID would be the extremes of a posttraumatic spectrum, characterized by the same underlying psychic phenomena: the structural dissociation of the personality secondary to traumatizing events (Van der Hart et al., 2006).

Ego States

Ego states are those parts of the personality that make up the entire self. The concept of ego states, as defined by John and Helen Watkins, refers not only to dissociative parts of posttraumatic pathology, but also to those that compose each individual´s healthy self. These ego states give us the ability to adapt, think, act, and respond differently in different situations. Watkins and Watkins (1997) propose a therapeutic approach that stems from psychoanalysis and hypnosis. From this perspective, the goal of therapy is not full integration of the personality - because according to them this does not exist - but overcoming inner conflicts between ego states.

In this book, we will use the concept of dissociative parts defined by the Theory of Structural Dissociation of the Personality. In PTSD, dissociative parts frequently have a very rudimentary first person perspective (mental autonomy), but in DID, the first person perspective is highly developed. In both cases, dissociative parts are the pathological consequence of traumatizing events.

Apparently Normal Part (ANP) and Emotional Part (EP) of the Personality

An animal is eating, and suddenly hears a noise. His feeding behavior stops, the alert system is activated, and the animal is now focused on identifying a potential threat. After the noise is identified and labeled as harmless, the alert disappears, and the animal keeps eating its food.

Daily life activities are incompatible with defense. When a traumatizing event occurs, the action system of defense is strongly and recurrently activated, and the personality reorganizes itself in alternating and competing subsystems (Myers, 1940). Defensive subsystems become rigid and fixated in traumatic experiences: that is the **Emotional Part of the Personality (EP)**. To deal with daily life, part of the client´s mind must avoid all that is related to this EP, so it could result in adaptive compromise. This part, focused on daily activities, is different from an integrated personality, but tries to go on with life. Because of this façade of normality, this part is called **Apparently Normal Part of the Personality (ANP).** The next paragraph exemplifies how ANP and EP may present clinically:

> "After that moment, I told myself that I should continue with my life as if nothing had happened. I would never think about that again and, for a while, I was able to do this, but I was just acting (ANP). I went to the office, I did housework, and I went out at night. The only thing I couldn´t do was stop. I was terrified by the idea of having even one free minute. So my usual day was filled with frantic activity. I had many sexual encounters that were becoming more and more damaging to me as time went by. From time to time, I have terrible nightmares (EP). When I wake up, it feels as if I was still there and then."

Action Systems

The Theory of Structural Dissociation of the Personality (TSDP) integrates neurobiological knowledge with a psychological theory of personality. Different adaptive mental and behavioral actions develop along psychobiological action systems, already present in many animal species (Lang, 1995; Panksepp, 1998; Van der Hart et al., 2006).

1. One major action system is focused on survival against an imminent threat (Fanselow & Lester, 1988). It includes defensive subsystems such as flight, freeze, fight, and total submission (Porges, 2001). The **Emotional Part of the Personality (EP)** will be related to these defensive action systems.

2. Other action systems are concerned with functions of daily life (Panksepp, 1998). These systems include energy regulation, attachment and care taking, exploration, social engagement (Porges, 2001), play, and reproduction. They all involve approaching attractive stimuli (Lang, 1995). The **Apparently Normal Part of the Personality (ANP)** will be based on these action systems.

Primary, Secondary, and Tertiary Structural Dissociation

The more severe, early, and chronic the trauma, the more structural dissociation of the personality there will be. Depending on how fragmented the client´s mind is, Van der Hart et al (2006) classify the situation as:

Primary Structural Dissociation of the Personality

There is only one EP, fixated in trauma time, and one ANP, trying to go on with daily life. This situation would be equivalent to simple PTSD.

Secondary Structural Dissociation of the Personality

There is only one ANP, but more than one EP. More severe traumatization implies further subdivisions. Different defensive action systems are activated in a pervasive traumatizing environment, but they must be blocked in order to survive. For example, a child cannot fight against an abusive father or escape (flight) from a dangerous home. Both action systems will become blocked and this will be the basis for different emotional parts (e.g., in the future, an enraged part that blames the client for the abuse and an anxious part that flees from minor stressors). This subtype includes diagnosis such as Dissociative Disorders not Otherwise Specified (DDNOS) and Borderline Personality Disorder (BPD). The dramatic changes in behavior and emotional characteristics of BPD would represent different EPs, but they do not always have a developed first person perspective, nor do they have different names, nor interact with the ANP using a high degree of mental autonomy.

Tertiary Structural Dissociation

It involves not only more than one EP, but also more than one ANP. Division of the ANP may occur as certain aspects of daily life become associated with traumatizing events, so that they tend to reactivate traumatic memories. The client's personality becomes increasingly divided in an attempt to maintain functioning while avoiding traumatic memories. Tertiary structural dissociation refers only to clients with DID.

Dissociative Phobias

Structural dissociation of the personality is generated by trauma, but it is maintained by a series of phobias that characterize trauma survivors and by relational factors (Nijenhuis et al., 2002; Steele et al., 2001, 2005). Here, "phobia" is understood as a mechanism. It does not mean that the client presents a co-morbid diagnosis of phobic disorder.

The personality is divided in ANP and EP, and it is the phobia that the ANP has towards the traumatic memories that prevents the resolution of this initial division and the re-integration of the personality. This is the core **phobia of traumatic memories** (Janet, 1904).

The ANP can avoid not only traumatic contents (trying not to think about trauma) but also all mental activity (trying not to think or feel at all). This is the **phobia of mental actions** that includes inner experiences such as emotions, body sensations, thoughts, images, fantasies, wishes, and needs.

When dissociative parts have a developed first person perspective (mental autonomy), complex interactions can happen in the inner world, generating a mental conflict that consumes a lot of the client's energy. A part which is focused on the fight action system and wants "to be strong" can reject another emotional part that submitted to the abuser in order to survive, blaming this submissive EP for being weak and allowing the abuse to happen. This is the phobia **of dissociative parts**, and overcoming this phobia is necessary before approaching core traumatic events. If we try to work on a traumatic memory with the standard EMDR protocol, without being aware of the presence of these dissociative parts, activation of the traumatic material can activate these parts and the inner conflict between them.

Other relevant phobias in the first stages of the treatment are relational **phobias of closeness, abandonment, loss, and rejection, particularly in regards to the therapist.**

Secondary and tertiary structural dissociation are usually based on early traumatization, in which attachment disturbances are the norm. A person who grows up with dysfunctional caregivers tends to develop different difficulties in relationships, and these will be present in the therapeutic relationship.

Other dissociative phobias usually appear later in therapy, as the **phobia of dissociative parts related to the perpetrator.** The most difficult for trauma survivors to accept is having some personality aspects that are similar to or remind them of the abuser. More **phobias related to attachment** can appear as we approach trauma work, and when current functioning improves the **phobia of normal life**, the **phobias of healthy risk taking and change**, and the **phobia of intimacy**, including sexuality and body image, usually emerge.

Integration in the Theory of Structural Dissociation of the Personality

The goal of therapy is the re-integration of the personality that was divided by trauma. This re-integration involves a basic level (synthesis and differentiation) and a more complex one that allows the traumatic memory to become a narrative autobiographical one: realization (personification and presentification) (Janet, 1904, 1928; Van der Hart et al., 2006).

1. **Synthesis**: Some aspects of the traumatic experience, the most threatening ones, should be shared between different dissociative parts, including the ANP. Other elements should be differentiated, such as the EP that imitates the abuser needing to be properly differentiated from the abuser.

2. **Realization** involves a lot of cognitive and affective work, particularly grieving for how it was and how it cannot be. The client can remain in the present while he recounts a traumatizing event, neither reliving it nor becoming depersonalized. There is **personification** (e.g., this happened to me, and it has influenced me in this way), and there is also **presentification** (e.g. this is my past, now I have options and I can change).

Internal System

This is a descriptive term for all aspects or parts of the mind in an individual with structural dissociation. This includes dissociative parts, memories, feelings, and any other way of describing an individual's dissociated aspects. Understanding the parts as a system rather than as separate personality states provides an important frame of reference for treatment.

Switching

This is the process of changing from one existing part of the personality to another. Switching may be set off by outside stimuli such as an environmental trigger or by internal stimuli, such as feelings or memories. Switching may be observable, such as changes in posture or facial expression, as well as changes in voice tone or speech patterns. Switching may also be observed by changes in mood, regressed behavior, and variable cognitive functioning. Sometimes it can be difficult to identify from the outside.

Dysfunctional Attachment

The concept of attachment describes the relationship dynamics between humans. The term was initially used to describe infant-caregiver interactions. The pioneer of these studies was Bowlby (1969), followed by Mary Ainsworth (Ainsworth et al., 1978), who described secure, avoidant, and anxious subtypes of attachment behavior. Disorganized attachment was described later (Main & Solomon, 1986). In the 1980s, the theory was extended to attachment in adults.

The two main ways of measuring attachment in adults include the Adult Attachment Interview (AAI; George, Kaplan, & Main, 1985) and self-report questionnaires. The AAI and the self-report questionnaires were developed independently and for different purposes.

The following table reflects the relationships between categories from the AAI and the behavior of a 12-month-old baby when he is reunited with his mother after a brief separation in which he is left with a stranger, "The Strange Situation" experiment developed by Mary Ainsworth.

AAI George, Kaplan, & Main (1985)	Strange Situation Ainsworth et al., 1978; Main & Solomon, 1986
Secure/autonomous: Speaks coherently and interactively with the interviewer about his experiences, being favorable or unfavorable. Answers questions with sufficient but not excessive elaboration, and then returns the conversational turn to the interviewer. Provides a coherent narrative that may include even traumatic issues.	**Secure**: Seeks physical contact, proximity, and interaction. If upset after the separation, is readily soothed by parents and returns to exploration and play.
Dismissing: Minimizes the discussion or importance of attachment-related experiences. Typically, responses are internally inconsistent and often excessively short. Relationships with parents are usually described as highly favorable, but without supporting evidence and, when such evidence is given, it tends to contradict the global evaluation.	**Insecure-avoidant**: These infants avoid and ignore parents upon reunion, remaining occupied with toys, and may ignore parents' efforts to communicate.
Preoccupied: The memories aroused by a question seem to draw the subject's attention and guide his speech. This can result in lengthy and angry recounting of childhood interactions with parents, which may inappropriately move into discussions of a present relationship. The speaker may also digress to remote topics, use vague language, and describe a parent negatively and positively in the same sentence.	**Insecure-resistant**: Infants alternate between appearing very independent and ignoring mother and then suddenly becoming anxious while trying to find her. Upon reunion, they cling and cry, but also look away and struggle, and their parents are not able to sooth their distress.

Unresolved or disorganized: Frequently demonstrates substantial lapses in reasoning or discourse. The respondent may express childlike beliefs or lapse into prolonged silence or eulogistic speech.	**Disorganized**: Infants cry for parents at the door and then run away when it opens, approaching parent with head down. Behavioral strategies seem to collapse. They may seem to freeze or engage in stereotyped behavior.

Table 1. Relationships between categories from the AAI and the behavior of a 12-month-old baby when he is reunited with his mother after a brief separation

Emotional Regulation and Window of Emotional Tolerance

Emotional regulation is not only related to hyperarousal, but also to all processes related to emotional awareness, contact, and modulation. This concept is linked to the *window of emotional tolerance*, which is the level of activation that allows productive information processing (Ogden & Minton, 2000). We can see different problems that can present outside this tolerance window:

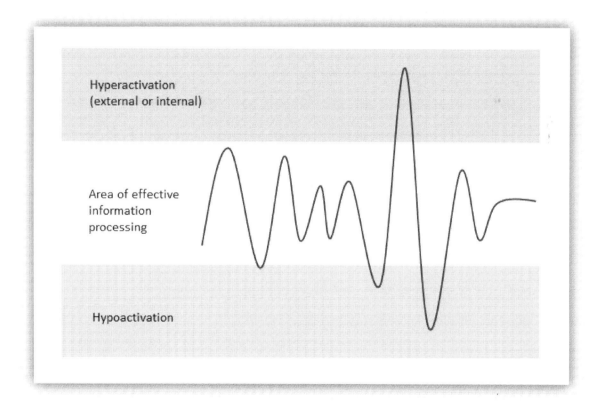

Lack of emotional recognition, understanding one´s own emotions and needs as important, negative interaction between primary and secondary emotions (e.g., being afraid to feel rage), inability to

modulate or overcome distressing emotions, lack of abilities such as change of attentional focus or using cognitive reasoning to modify emotional states, disconnection from some specific emotions, or general detachment, are all possible situations related to emotion regulation that can be disrupted in trauma survivors.

Chapter 3
The AIP Model and Structural Dissociation: A Proposal to Extend the Framework

Anabel Gonzalez, Dolores Mosquera, Andrew M. Leeds, Jim Knipe, & Roger Solomon

The Adaptive Information Processing Model (AIP) is the theoretical model for EMDR therapy proposed by Shapiro (1991, 2001). The AIP model was developed to guide history taking, case conceptualization, treatment planning, and intervention and also to predict treatment outcome and the consistency of the many patterns of response to it.

This model regards most psychic pathologies as derived from earlier life experiences that set in motion a continued pattern of perception, affect, behavior, cognitions, and consequent identity structures. Psychopathology is viewed as configured by the impact of earlier experiences that are held in the nervous system in a state-specific form (Bower, 1981).

With the AIP model we can have a conceptual framework to serve as a guide for clinical practice. In Francine Shapiro´s words, "It is better to provide practitioners with a conceptual framework or model to serve as a guide to their clinical practice than merely to give them an inflexible step-by step procedure for implementing EMDR (Shapiro, 2001)."

This statement becomes especially relevant in disorders involving severe and prolonged neglect and traumatization, which have been named as "complex trauma" (Herman, 1992) or disorders of extreme stress (DESNOS: Van der Kolk et al., 2005), personality disorders, and dissociative disorders; all of them characterized by secondary or tertiary structural dissociation.

To approach the treatment of disorders associated with severe, early, and chronic neglect and traumatization, the AIP model is extending to explain issues related to the effects of chronic, early neglect, and traumatization. Shapiro (2006) describes how lack of attention (neglect) causes failure to thrive and the broad consequences that prevent the development of a sense of self. For this purpose, it is useful to integrate comprehensive theories, which describe phenomena underlying those clinical problems, with the AIP model. We will incorporate elements from the theory of structural dissociation of the personality (Van der Hart, Nijenhuis, & Steele, 2006) and from attachment theory (Bowlby, 1973, 1980; Main, 1996, 1999).

We believe that integrating these theories (and other concepts) enhances the capacities of the AIP model for case formulation, predicting the impact of interventions, and responding therapeutically to survivors of chronic early neglect and traumatization. They often present in therapy not just with post-traumatic stress symptoms, but also psychological defenses, structural dissociation, and different psychopathological presentations.

Three main areas of development will be addressed in this chapter: The first is to understand differences between mental functioning in people with severe traumatization that cannot be explained fully as caused solely by dysfunctionally stored memories. The second is to integrate a conceptualization that describes specific ways in which attachment disruptions are related to psychopathology. And the third is to understand how dysfunctionally stored information is encoded, and how we can access it and therapeutically move it to adaptive resolution, when there is secondary or tertiary structural dissociation of the personality.

Level of Mental Functioning in Severe Traumatization

Chronic and early neglect and trauma damage the course of neural development, at both neuro-anatomic and functional levels.

Schore (2003) suggested that the maternal-infant dyadic communication in the first two years of life, which generates intense positive affective states and high levels of dopamine and endogenous opiates, represents a growth-promoting environment for the prefrontal cortex. Under the influence of a growth promoting early maternal-infant dyadic communication, increasingly complex self-regulatory structural systems develop in the frontal cortex, especially the orbital prefrontal areas (Damasio, 1994; Pribram, 1987). These areas are connected with the limbic forebrain, the sensory areas, the hypothalamus and reward centers, and the ventral tegmental area (Nauta, 1964). The orbitofrontal cortex (OFC) is especially expanded in the right hemisphere (Falk et al., 1990), and more connected with limbic and subcortical regions. This right hemisphere expansion of the OFC occurs because the right cortex is dominant for the processing, expression, and regulation of emotional information, while the left cortex is dominant for language and abstract processing of information.

When a child grows up in adverse or neglectful environments, the development of these cerebral structures is impaired (Teicher et al., 2006). The effect of these circumstances on mental functioning is broader than the dysfunctional effects of adverse (discrete) events initially described by the AIP model. Shapiro (2006) states that "symptoms that are not purely organic in nature, or caused by inadequate information, are based upon stored experiences." Could we think that some experiences related to attachment and emotional neglect, could be better considered as "inadequate information?"

As Shapiro states (Luber & Shapiro, 2009), "When we are dealing with the most debilitated clients, it is most important for us to incorporate the wisdom of other fields. The more we learn from other disciplines, the more efficient and effective we can become. In order for EMDR to be used as a psychotherapeutic approach applicable to the full range of psychopathologic situations, its theoretical model needs to integrate developmental neuropsychology with the effect of cumulative traumatic experiences." An individual who grows up in conditions of trauma and neglect, may not achieve the optimal level of development of brain structures and neurological functions. Some high-order functions of consciousness depend on the conjoint activity of different brain structures. Tirapu-Ustárroz, Muñoz-Céspedes, & Pelegrín-Valero (2003) discuss different concepts that are included under the term "consciousness." We will refer to the more developed ones: The *consciousness of the self* and the *theory of the mind*.

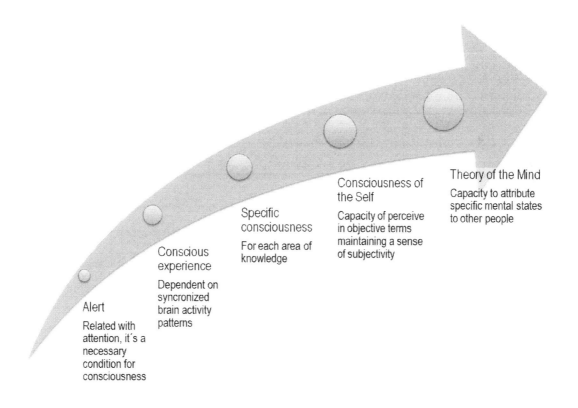

Fig. 1. Levels of consciousness.

Binding of synchronized and distributed activity is crucial for the mechanism of consciousness and its impairment has been described in different mental and neurological disorders such as Schizophrenia (Bob, 2007) and DID (Reinders, Nijenhuis, Paans, et al., 2003).

Putnam (1997) explains the child's developmental process as an evolution of discrete behavioral states toward more flexible and complex states of consciousness, with the development of a reflexive consciousness, which unifies, modulates, and regulates these discrete states. The experience of continuity of consciousness is a complex process and implies an understanding about how information changes and evolves between discrete intervals of experience.

Brain structures important in these integrative processes include the dorsolateral prefrontal cortex (Bodovitz, 2004; 2008) and posterior associative cortices (Reinders, Nijenhuis, Paans, et al., 2003). Other structures that have been associated with integrative functions include superior coliculum of tectum, talamum, cyngulated anterior gyrus, and cerebellum (Strehler, 1991). But probably, the higher mental processes we have called high order mental processes depend on a complex of integrative brain processes.

The sense of agency refers to the experience of oneself as the agent of one's own actions (Newen & Vogeley, 2008). Early adverse environments and emotional deprivation can alter this normal process, with an underdeveloped metaconsciousness or introspective consciousness (Armstrong, 1979) and retention of more primitive ways of functioning. Putnam's description (1997) can be easily related to the brain dysfunctions described by Schore (2003) in relation to people with attachment disturbances. All these references support the hypothesis that severely traumatized people, with early and chronic neglect and relational trauma tend to present a low development of both metaconsciousness and high order mental processes. Some of these traumatized people are still functioning at a high level, but they are probably impaired in more subtle aspects. This underdevelopment is a relevant aspect in many disorders, and in order to understand and successfully address them, the AIP model should offer a framework as comprehensive as possible.

Clinical experience shows us that following successful EMDR therapy, some clients improve their global level of mental functioning, and not just their reaction toward a specific traumatic event. As it is commented in Luber & Shapiro (2009), "The advent of EMDR and the AIP model really shifted the focus to internal growth. The reduction of overt symptoms is viewed as a by-product of the reprocessing as the individual assimilates the new information and expands in terms of awareness and emotional regulation, and the development of all of the different factors that we would be using to define a healthy individual."

As an example: one client showed a primitive thinking modality that could be described from Bateman and Fonagy's mentalization theory (2004) as poor mentalization capacity. After reprocessing a core traumatic issue (emotional maltreatment by her ex-partner) the client spontaneously showed an increase in mentalization. This change probably reflects general consequences of the integration of this previously isolated neuro-network (Shapiro, 2001), which go beyond the effect on the traumatic target. We will describe more about this point while discussing high order mental functions in chapter 5.

However, this spontaneous process often needs to be deliberately enhanced by the therapist in a more active way in cases where developmental neglect and trauma were more severe.

In the standard EMDR procedures, we use interweaves to stimulate effective emotional information processing when the AIP system needs temporary assistance to achieve the results obtained in simpler cases. In these situations, spontaneous movement occurs toward more adaptive capacities and higher levels of consciousness. With severe neglect and traumatization, we have to help the client's mind to evolve toward higher levels of mental functioning (Luber & Shapiro, 2009). With this aim in mind, we will describe self-reflective interweaves, psychoeducational interweaves, core interweaves, and meta-conscious interventions.

We believe that insecure attachment, chronic developmental trauma, and discrete traumatic events have multiplicative effects on consciousness and capacities for mentalization, and should be conceptualized as having different, but intrinsically related, mechanisms. Liotti (2004, 2006) understands disorganized attachment as dissociative symptoms, resulting of an attachment system that is stimulated, but where the needs of the child are not met. This situation would make the person vulnerable to future traumatic events. In clinical practice, we observe how concepts and principles from different approaches: mentalization-based interventions (Bateman & Fonagy, 2004), dialectic-behavioral therapy (Linehan, 1993), Ericksonian hypnosis (Lankton, 1987), the theory of structural dissociation of the personality (Van der Hart, Nijenhuis, & Steele, 2006) and many others, are often mixed with EMDR therapy, but without an underlying comprehensive theoretical model.

Case example

A 36-year-old woman has a childhood history of severe neglect and abuse. She has never had a good attachment figure. After two years of therapy, she explains how this has affected her mental functioning:

> "I never thought, in fact my thoughts were never with me, you know... because talking like this - referring to the way she felt with the therapist - was impossible, to be able to say what I am thinking and feeling... I never had something like that. I never talked to anybody; I thought that was the normal way... the voices in my head. I just changed from one idea to another, but I couldn't do anything about it.
>
> Now I am starting to think about me. I can reflect, I don't just act and feel and think in an automatic way. I can understand now, and you know how many times you had to remind me of this, that when the images of the past were in my mind, they were not happening right now. Before I could understand, everything was mixed up. I can experience an impulse, this still happens, but I can remain focused and don't automatically act on it. I still hear voices, but they are not so intense and they don't control me."

The EMDR procedures used in therapy sessions with this client had to be altered from the standard EMDR procedure. After testing different interventions, working with small fragments and processing them with bilateral stimulation seemed to be the most effective intervention. Targets were images of constant flashbacks that she had. To elicit negative and positive cognitions was simply clinically impossible for this client. The positive cognition - not accessible for her - that needed to be introduced as a constant interweave by the therapist was, "This is a memory, this is not happening right now." After six months of therapy - processing flashback images, working on establishing an optimal therapeutic alliance, and introducing reality orientation with difficulties - the client could start to understand what the therapist was trying to say with this. Until this moment, the client argued, saying, "This is real, It´s present for me. I smell this, I feel the pain in my back…"

The reprocessing seemed to be a constant looping from one traumatic memory to another. Psychoeducational interventions were quite impossible, because the client tended to engage in repetitive answers, explaining that the voices represented the actual abusers, and she was convinced she was possessed by them at that time. The more the therapist tried to explain that this was a consequence of the traumatic experiences, the more early experiences of being ignored and not understood were activated in the client. One day, the client explained the intervention that was needed in these situations, "Just listen to me, nobody has ever listened to me." This client illustrates the importance of "accepting witnessing eyes" as necessary condition for the consolidation of memories. These eyes may initially be "external" (the therapist´s eyes), but at some point it is important for the client´s core self to look at these dysfunctionally stored experiences with the same accepting eyes.

Did this client improve through this modified EMDR processing? During an initial period before introducing BLS, the client showed no evident gains. When modified EMDR procedures were introduced, she developed higher-level mental capacities. Some aspects of these modified EMDR interventions can be understood from the current AIP model, but the relationship with the therapist during these interventions should not be viewed merely as an independent adjunct to memory reprocessing.

The therapeutic relationship and its relevance should be more developed in the EMDR theoretical model. The attachment and social engagement systems are damaged in survivors of early neglect and trauma. To repair these systems through the therapeutic relationship and specific procedures is a separate process, which must be parallel to the reprocessing of dysfunctional memories with modified EMDR procedures. Traumatic memories can be resolved by unblocking the AIP system of the brain. The attachment and social engagement systems can improve by re-learning new patterns.

Shapiro (Luber & Shapiro, 2009) remarked the relevance of "evolving a better grasp on what it is that needs to be incorporated, what experiences the clinician needs to engender over the time of the therapy that can encode the sense of the healthy interaction, and develop the capacity for healthy relationships. Therapeutic experiences where they can feel all that was denied to them in childhood such as positive attachment and connection and unconditional love. These therapeutic experiences can then be firmly encoded and enhanced in their memory networks through focused EMDR processing."

This work on developing high-order mental processes is part of many interventions, but we have not had a theoretical model to explain from the perspective of EMDR theory what we are doing and why it works. As an example, in ego-states therapy, we work by making contact with different mental states, and developing a global understanding of different parts of the internal system. With these interventions, clients are supported in evolving from a fragmented functioning to a more organized, reflexive one. In other words, we help clients learn to "think about what they are experiencing." Even with single episode trauma and the standard EMDR procedure, several elements of the EMDR approach provide indirect ways of reinforcing the capacity for metaconsciousness, including dual attention, mindfulness, metacognitive processes, etc. These include the "mindful approach" with requests to "just notice without judging," direct work on dual attention to the past and the present, and the differentiation between past and present implicit in selecting the negative and positive cognitions.

With some clients, achieving dual attention requires extensive work. In our opinion, for those clients with fundamental impairments in their integrative capacities of consciousness, the development of capacities for metaconsciousness is more than just an accessory element to the "real therapy" (EMDR reprocessing of DSI). It is an essential and foundational part of the therapy. To include these aspects in the theoretical framework will help us design more effective and comprehensive procedures in the field of severe traumatization.

In chapter 5, we will describe procedures to enhance high-order mental processes, like enhancing reflective capacities (metaconsciousness), mentalization interventions, the concept of the adult self, the use of concrete elements to represent mental processes, co-consciousness exercises, etc. These elements are not understood as merely preparation (phase 2) - the "work previous to EMDR therapy" - but as an intrinsic part of EMDR therapy for those with histories of severe and chronic early neglect and abuse. This is a capacity of the mind to observe, know, understand, and accept. It is similar to what psychodynamic therapists refer to as the *observing ego* and Schwartz (1995) calls *the Self*. The presence of this capacity creates the conditions for the operation of the intrinsic, physically-based information processing system that moves disturbing information to adaptive resolution. Dual attention (the oriented self-awareness of past trauma) is an essential element of how EMDR works.

To work on developing high-order mental functions, without first progressively dismantling the dysfunctionally stored information (see next section) that is blocking the system, may be a slower process, and sometimes it will be very difficult to overcome certain "points of blockage" (see chapter 9 for specific interventions with blockages). Yet, attempts to reprocess dysfunctionally stored information, without understanding the specific characteristics of mental functioning in severely traumatized people, are frequently ineffective and sometimes may decompensate the client. To optimize the therapeutic process, we believe it is necessary to simultaneously work on both areas by carefully pacing the therapy and adapting the interventions to the client´s timing.

Dysfunctionally Stored Information (DSI) and Fragmentation: DSI is More than Memories

What do we understand by "memory?" Many clinicians have a limited view of a "memory" as a discrete autobiographical memory. But there are many scholarly definitions of what a "memory" is: implicit, explicit, autobiographical, procedural, conceptual, etc. We could define what the term "dysfunctionally stored memories" means - in a wide sense - but we want to use a different term to indicate that more than memories of external events can be dysfunctionally stored (Van der Hart, Solomon, & Gonzalez, 2010) and targeted with EMDR procedures. Shapiro (2006) describes information processing system as "an intrinsic, physical and adaptive system, geared to integrate external and internal experiences. These experiences are translated into physically stored memories, and these memories are stored in associative memory networks… EMDR focuses on both the reaction and the memory itself… the increase in symptoms because each negative response to a retriggered affect state is also incorporated as another unprocessed memory expanding the network. An example can be the reaction of feeling depressed or of being out of control during an anxiety attack, that are internal responses to a generated affect state triggered in the present." This inclusion of internal experiences broadens the model to incorporate intrapsychic phenomena as dissociative phobias, defenses, and many others.

Therefore, we will use the familiar term "dysfunctionally stored memories" to refer specifically to the memory of traumatic (exteroceptive) events (including implicit and explicit elements) and a new, broader term, "dysfunctionally stored information," to include both autobiographical memories as well as those dysfunctional elements that are generated in the client's intrapsychic experience. The interest in using these terms is more practical than conceptual, because memories include "any information with disturbing affects and sensations that are dysfunctionally stored without appropriate assimilation into larger adaptive networks" (Shapiro, 2006). Interoceptive experiences (e.g., the interaction between two dissociative parts) are actually memories, but in the history of EMDR, more relevance was given to exteroceptive memories (e.g., the memory of an aggression).

The work with defenses, affect tolerance, and many other aspects not focused on external situations implied a broader concept of AIP than the initially described by Shapiro (2002). The terms used in this section can allow us to identify these elements from the same model.

When a traumatic experience cannot be processed by the AIP for different reasons, "the information is frozen in time, isolated in its own neuro-network, and stored in its originally disturbing state-specific form. Because the intensity of the affect has effectively locked the memory into a restricted associative network, the neuro-network in which the old information is stored, is effectively isolated" (Shapiro, 2001; pp 41-42). This definition is very close to this one from Janet (1919, p. 660), "Many traumatized clients seem to have had the evolution of their lives checked, they are attached to an insurmountable obstacle." Intensity of affect is the main cause of an experience becoming dysfunctionally stored, but sometimes there are other causes. For example, the event may threaten the person's idealization of a valuated caretaker, or the person may have learned from past traumatic experiences to quickly dissociate any threatening new event, or quickly activate an avoidance trait in regards to thinking of any new threatening event. Aspects needed to attach to a caregiver and to protect the self can be so incompatible that the co-existence of both phenomena blocks the information processing system.

Let's see the problem of disorganized attachment, characteristic in structural dissociation, from an AIP perspective. If we locate where the dysfunctionally stored information is, we will have relevant targets for processing. The traumatic experience is dysfunctionally stored due to its negative intensity. A frightening/frightened parent, whose availability is inconsistent, unpredictable, and sometimes also tricky (in the sense that the caretaker can elicit the alarm response in the child due to abusive behavior), generates a highly intense experience very difficult to deal with that innate brain systems cannot process. The experience of attachment with the abusive caretaker is also dysfunctionally stored. These experiences may consist of moments where the lack of affection was more painful or when they idealized the few good - or less bad - moments they ever had. In the last case, these memories may be colored with positive affect. Any of these experiences become dysfunctionally stored in different dissociative parts. The repetition and chronicity of these interpersonal traumatic experiences in a critical time for the child's development, facilitates that each of these parts - the one that holds the traumatic experience and the other that holds the attachment experience - adopt a certain level of mental autonomy and first person perspective. These parts relate to each other in a phobic way: the part that holds the memory of damage and the defensive actions in the face of danger rejects the part that needs to keep the attachment to the abuser, considering it weak and also a danger for further survival (phobia of dissociative parts, Van der Hart et al., 2006). The confrontation of these two unconceivable, opposite, and contradictory realities leads to an intolerable emotional burden that is also dysfunctionally stored, thus blocking the system. All this conflict rises in the context of a deficit of integrative capacity and lack of metacognition.

In the next graphic, we can see different points where dysfunctionally stored information (DSI) can be located. To integrate dysfunctionally stored information - contained in these emotional parts - with the remaining experiences of the individual, we need to work on other DSI than the ones directly generated by the traumatizing events - in this case the father being abusive - which would be the traditional target for EMDR standard processing. The memory of the attachment with the abusive father is also dysfunctionally stored information, and sometimes contains idealization defenses that can also be processed (see, Knipe, 2006). In order to approach these points where the experience became blocked in the nervous system, we need to overcome other points of dysfunctionally stored information first. They do not come from a traumatizing experience, but from intrapsychic events, such as the interaction between parts in the internal system, as we have commented in chapter 8 about the dissociative phobias. Also, the co-experiencing of defense against the father and the need to attach to the same abusive father generates its own dysfunctionally stored information. This is due to the disturbing discordance between incompatible realities, and gives us another target for processing.

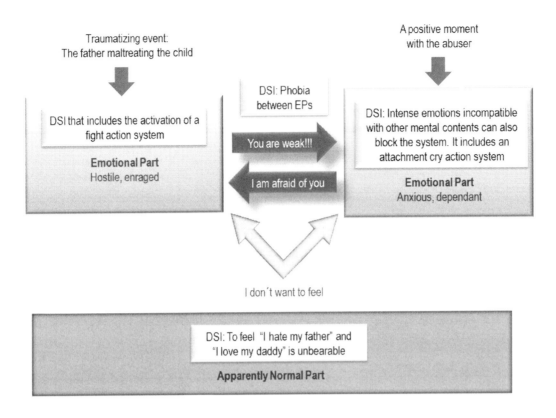

Fig. 2. Dysfunctionally stored information and disorganized attachment.

The earlier, more severe, and chronic is the traumatization, the more there is disorganization and lack of integration. Traditionally, EMDR has considered that traumatic events and neuro-networks are associated in clusters where early-formed maladaptive memory networks subsequently give rise to pathological perceptions, attitudes, and coping responses. Later occurring adverse experiences tend to enlarge these maladaptive memory networks and their associated pathological responses. EMDR theory (Shapiro, 2001, pp 33-34) assumes that different traumatic memories are associated by elements of these maladaptive memory networks: they may share the same emotion, the same belief, can be related to the same people, the same sounds, smells, or physical sensations, etc.

Of these elements, some may be associated within one set of neuro-networks, while other elements derived from the same traumatic event are stored in a separate set of neuro-networks. To understand why some elements of the same memory remain dissociated from each other, it can be useful to consider the concept of action systems (Van der Hart, Nijenhuis, & Steele, 2006) and dissociative parts of the personality. Leeds (1991, 2009) foreshadowed the idea that the AIP includes sets of action tendencies in his proposal to include "acts, urges, and states," as part of the concept of memory network. If we consider that memory networks include action tendencies, which can be held in an adaptive or maladaptive (e.g., developmentally frozen and primitive) form, it helps makes sense of the idea that different memories - or fragments of memories - and intrapsychic events remain rigidly linked and configured as an isolated cluster of dysfunctionally stored information.

Each group of elements could be consolidated around a common point, sharing the same action system. A hypothesis is that different memories or fragments of memories in each cluster are related to the same action system. This grouping of memories does not resemble the linking of memories we observe in people who were raised in less neglectful and traumatizing environments. In people with isolated traumatic events and a secure attachment base, memories can be associated by different elements: they can share the same emotion, the same belief, or any of the same perceptual ingredients of the memory. On the contrary, a child who grows up in a chaotic and neglectful environment fails to develop integration between action systems, so memories for adverse events can be experienced from any of these action systems, or different fragments of the event can remain encoded in different action systems. Clusters of memories or fragments of memories can be stored in an emotional part of the personality, rooted by a specific action system. This could be related to the state-dependant memory (Bower, 1981). With their low integrative capacity, severely neglected and traumatized people cannot reconsolidate memories, which were stored in an emotional part of the personality, with other situations, which were experienced from another emotional part, or with resources stored in the apparently normal part of the personality.

For example, all the elements related to the action system "fight-defense" are linked together. These dysfunctionally stored memories and the action system they are related to, constitute what Van der Hart, Steele, & Nijenhuis (2006) call dissociative parts of the personality, in this case, an emotional part. Each emotional part of the personality stored some aspects of the traumatic event: the memories of aggression from an attachment figure, the emotion of rage, further experiences of damage.

Other action systems and their associated memories cannot coexist with these neuro-networks and the action system of fight. For example, memories related to the attachment with an abusive figure may become associated, and constitute a different cluster of memories related to the action system of attachment. Since dysfunctionally stored elements in each dissociative part of the personality tend to be related to the same action system, some memories are not compatible with others. For example, passive, reactive action tendencies as submission, and the experiences related to it, would be further dissociated from other proactive action tendencies for defense such as flight or fight. In this way, they remain separated and unintegrated with the remaining mental functions. When triggered, they are activated in a mechanical, repetitive, and rigid way because they are disassociated from both other action tendencies for defense and from higher level mental functions that, if developed, might allow for flexible, reflective mentalization on multiple options and selection of the most adaptive action tendency for a specific new situation. Dissociation can be understood as an adaptive response to early neglect and abuse by caretakers. The attachment system must remain separate from action systems such as self-protection. Those behaviors, learned in connection with attachment, develop into the apparently normal part of the personality by looking "normal," which is linked with social acceptance and the maintenance of attachment.

In DID and in many cases of DDNOS, some of these dissociative parts of the personality have gradually acquired some degree of self-person perspective or, in other words, mental autonomy. The origin of these phenomena may lie not in later remembered traumatic experiences, but rather in the absence of an integrative modulation from a safe attachment figure in the first two years of life (Barach, 1991; Dutra, Bureau, Holmes, Lyubchik, & Lyons-Ruth, 2009; Ogawa, Sroufe, Weinfield, Carlson, & Egeland, 1997). While the origin of low metaconsciousness and the tendency toward states of structural dissociation may derive from the absence of early maternal-infant dialogue and early, shared positive affect in states of play, a full understanding of the maintenance of this perception of separateness requires an understanding of additional mechanisms.

In dissociative disorders, intrapsychic events are very relevant. A lot of psychic energy is invested in controlling mental actions, action system activation, etc. This internal control must be maintained during many years, and retraumatization happens not only in the outside world, but also in the intrapsychic world. These aspects must be considered to safely and effectively apply EMDR with these clients.

When a traumatic experience happens within an immature brain, with low meta-consciousness and low self-regulation, both mental flexibility and the possibilities for modulation are very poor. In the absence of a supportive family system and with continuing neglect and abuse, the discrete states of consciousness described by Putnam (1997) can persist in later years. The high emotional activation associated with early neglect and unbearable traumatic experiences does not allow for the reconsolidation of traumatic memories. Together, the lack of general integration with a low order of mental functioning and subsequent traumatic experiences contribute to the persistence of an extreme discontinuity of the mind.

Schore (2003), in *Affect Regulation and Repair of the Self*, described an unhappy pattern that can occur when a mother is unable or unwilling to give eye contact to a baby. It can happen due to illness, addiction, narcissism, etc; but also possibly due to the baby activating the mother's PTSD about her own neglect during childhood. The baby's SNS activation increases because the mother is not soothing the baby, that is, ventral vagal parasympathetic activation is not occurring. At a certain point, the baby activates dorsal vagal parasympathetic response (numbness) as a protection from the damage that would be caused by continual SNS activation. The way in which all these phenomena could block the processing of information is complex, and because it is happening during crucial developmental stages, it may influence how the individual will assimilate new experiences.

Accessing dysfunctionally stored memories of traumatic experiences in a mind that lacks capacities for higher-level integration of consciousness is not a simple task. Because each dissociative part of the personality has a certain degree of self-person perspective, the way to access DSI within one of these parts of the personality is not the same for a different dissociative part of the personality. This is clear in dissociative Identity disorder, where a dissociative part may contain memories not accessible to other parts. This variability in the level of consciousness and self-capacities across different parts of the personality may present many difficulties in developing a therapeutic contract with the therapist and a collaborative attitude within the internal system of parts of the personality. To access a particular traumatic memory and to be able to reprocess it necessitates having an agreement not only from a part that holds certain aspects of this memory, but from the other parts in the system; otherwise, they can block the therapeutic process in many different ways.

To extend the possibility of intervention with specific EMDR procedures, we need to think from a broad conceptualization of the "information" that is dysfunctionally stored. The AIP model outlines the importance of dysfunctionally stored memories, as the core phenomena for maladaptive coping in the aftermath of incompletely processed adverse life experiences. When Shapiro describes AIP in EMDR, basic principles and procedures (2001, p. 31) she says, "When someone experiences a severe psychological trauma, it appears that an imbalance may occur in the nervous system, caused perhaps by changes in neurotransmitters, adrenaline, and so forth. Due to this imbalance, the information-processing system is unable to function optimally and the information acquired at the time of the event, including images, sounds, affect, and physical sensations, is maintained neurologically in its disturbing state."

This paragraph implicitly states that DSI is directly generated by an exteroceptive element (a traumatizing event). But some of the higher order action tendencies that make up the AIP "system" fail to fully develop in cases of severe early neglect. This failure to develop some higher order action tendencies that make up the AIP itself creates vulnerabilities to the later development of a severe dissociative disorder (Dutra et al., 2009) and some personality disorders. Thus while some psychological conditions - such as PTSD - can be viewed from an AIP perspective as resulting from "information... maintained neurologically in its disturbing state," other more severe disorders impair the development of the higher-level action systems that make up the AIP system itself, so the information processing system may not be fully developed. For example, eating disorders can be viewed as resulting from a combination of emotional dysregulation and incomplete development in action tendencies including low-level action systems for feeding, mid-level action systems for body image, and higher order action tendencies for affect regulation and mentalization. Eating disorders are notoriously difficult to treat in general, and cannot be successfully treated without major modifications of standard EMDR procedures (Cooke & Grand, 2009; Forester, 2009; Seubert, 2009; York, 2000; York & Leeds, 2001).

Several proposed protocols which have shown some promise of clinical effectiveness, understand DSI as "more that memories." Interoceptive elements are capable of generating DSI. Some of these protocols are the DeTUR by Popky (1992, 2005), the reprocessing of dissociative defenses by Knipe (1995, 1999, 2006), the management of distress tolerance and positive affect tolerance (PAT) by Leeds (1998, 2011), and CravEX by Michael Hase (2008, 2010).

All these protocols describe elements that can generate DSI because they generate a feeling that the client considers unbearable, like shame in one of the Knipe´s procedures, or the memory of the addiction, as in CravEX. We cannot consider these elements "information acquired at the time of the event." But actually these elements, and many others, can be adequately described by an expanded concept of DSI. The interest in developing this extended concept of DSI is to unify those procedures along with the processing of a traumatic memory within an expanded view of the nature of the AIP, in view of similar observable treatment effects. We proposed to make the DSI definition more inclusive by differentiating between exteroceptively generated (E-DSI: about the relationship between self and environment) and interoceptively generated (I-DSI: about the relationship between different aspects inside the self).

The initial concept of "memories" described by Shapiro (1989, 1991, 1995, 2001) implies an outside-to-inside perspective. This original conceptualization of maladaptive memory networks within AIP minimizes the relevance of interoceptive stimuli not directly connected with the traumatic experience, but this is changing in further developments of the AIP model (Shapiro, 2006). In working with cases of chronic, severe neglect and traumatization, we often focus not on reprocessing the memory of a traumatic experience itself, but on a secondary mental action, which is triggered by an intrapsychic element. Actually, we would not need to use a different term than "memories" if we consider that many forms of memory involve "internal" learning: to self-regulate, to develop a body-map, sensorimotor coordination, etc. Some authors have named these phenomena as psychological defenses (Vaillant, 1992) or affect phobias (McCullough, 1996, McCullough et al., 2003). Many of these aspects can be also described as dissociative phobias (Van der Hart, Nihenjuis, & Steele, 2006). We prefer to use a broad term as "information" to remark that DSI is not restricted to autobiographical memories.

These internally-generated DSI are not always colored by disturbing affect, but often by positive affect, such as relief, idealization, or containment. The DSI originated in an experience of relief or containment of disturbance, and the positive affect maintains the defense, often for the lifetime of the individual. This defense is triggered by any activation of the original disturbing PTSD material and maintained by the positive relief affect. Both types of dysfunctional affect can be processed with appropriate targeting and bilateral stimulation.

In secondary and tertiary structural dissociation of the personality, many complex mental actions result from early neglect and traumatic experiences. Different dissociative parts with sometimes a high degree of self-person perspective interact in the inner world. Some of these mental actions, evolving in the aftermath of neglect and trauma, have enough mental energy and coherence to generate high emotional activation and disrupt the adaptive information processing system, becoming themselves additional sources of dysfunctionally stored information, expanding the traumatic network. Their difficulties in interpersonal relationships increase the propensity of severely traumatized people to be more focused on their inner world. Such internal conflicts consume a large portion of their mental energy and serve as a substitute for "real" relationships on the outside.

DSI for traumatic memories are part of this complex interaction. However, there are other kinds of DSI elements involved with the development and maintenance of psychopathology. If we were to limit the concept of "dysfunctionally stored information" to representations of traumatic experiences (exteroceptively generated DSI), we would limit both our theoretical conceptualization of AIP and potentially limit our use of EMDR procedures to the trauma work phase (phase 2 in the phase-oriented model; Courtois, Ford, & Cloitre, 2009). With such a restrictive understanding of AIP, all the relevant and extended work needed to prepare the client to be able to approach and resolve traumatic experiences (phase 1 in phase-oriented model) would be unable to benefit from the potential power of EMDR interventions.

In our opinion, the concept of dysfunctionally stored information (DSI) in AIP must be viewed as representing more than memories for adverse experiences. We understand unresolved memories as the DSI derived from the direct effect of an external adverse or traumatic (an exteroceptive) element) and the perceptual brain system. Thus, maladaptively encoded memories can be defined as exteroceptively generated dysfunctionally stored information.

Alternately, in chronic, early, and severe traumatization, many DSI elements evolve from early overwhelming interoceptive experiences. The kind of issues that can become overwhelming is much broader when there are chronic failures of caregivers to play a normal part in the development of the person´s capacities for self-regulation.

The development of dissociative parts, which may be sometimes very complex and have a high first-person perspective, is not a simply direct consequence of early traumatic memories. Most crucial here is to understand that accessing and reprocessing these memories is not the first or only goal of EMDR therapy. More complex phenomena are implied, because the antecedent lack of maternal infant dialogue and play are is more relevant to the development of a dissociative disorder than the later or even simultaneous direct effects of trauma (Dutra et al., 2009). The deficits in the early maternal-infant relationship lead to specific difficulties in the therapeutic relationship and in the internal conflict between dissociative parts, and these situations are distinct from experiences of relational trauma. Thus, the relational and self-relational difficulties in those early forming parts of the personality may be enlarged by traumatic memories, but these early forming elements of DSI are not solely or even primarily containers of exteroceptively generated memories. For example, two dissociated parts of the personality (interoceptive elements) may interact (for example, one part submits and another part hates the client for "giving up"), generating high emotional activation and new dysfunctionally stored elements. These elements could be conceptualized as interoceptively generated DSI (I-DSI). Using terms from TSDP we call this I-DSI "phobia of dissociative parts of the personality." This concept from TSDP is central to the development of the therapeutic plan in severely traumatized clients. Another example of I-DSI is the urge to drink alcohol, as a way to regulate shame about having been raped. This is an action related to a phobia (phobia of traumatic memories) but is experienced as a positive anticipation. The client, who is experiencing a strong urge to drink, is focused on wanting something that is experienced as positive. Because of this focus, in therapy, the urge to drink is more accessible to processing. When the urge to drink is processed, the traumatic memory of the rape may emerge into awareness, and if the person can maintain orientation to the safety of the therapist´s office, it becomes more accessible for processing. By following this sequence we can dismantle the onion layers that protect or cover the core trauma.

In Summary, DSI could be Divided into Two Distinct Types:

1. Exteroceptively generated DSI (E-DSI)

Maladaptive memories of unresolved adverse and traumatic experiences are represented as dysfunctionally stored information resulting from an exteroceptive (environmental) element (a traumatic event).

2. Interoceptively generated DSI (I-DSI)

Inner experiences can provoke intense and unbearable emotional activation and block the functioning of the AIP system. The interaction among the different parts of the personality can generate I-DSI which is much more complex than "simple memories." This I-DSI may have different characteristics than E-DSI. Accepting that action systems are facets of memory networks and thus of information which is dysfunctionally stored, these action systems remain in a developmentally primitive and disorganized form in severe and early neglect and traumatization, and tend to be activated in a more rigid, repetitive way. This leads to a different kind of "blockage" in adaptive information processing than is observed in adult onset, single episode traumatic exposure. Among other consequences, this leads to the necessity of providing forms of reprocessing that are much more highly structured by the clinician.

If we fail to keep the impact of I-DSI in mind, standard EMDR reprocessing interventions may present problems, in part because I-DSI itself blocks accessing of E-DSI information. E-DSI and I-DSI are closely related phenomena, and we think that both can be resolved with EMDR procedures. The problem with standard procedure in severe traumatization is that, by using a "big focus" (it would be equivalent to major surgery), many different memory networks and multiple kinds of DSI can be activated at the same time, and one set of DSI blocks others. For example, targeting a traumatic memory, the client experiences fear, but at the same time is afraid of experiencing this reaction, and angry because he experiences his fear as "being weak." Each one of these three elements - fear, fear of being afraid, and anger for being weak - is related to different points of DSI, and the last two prevent the processing of the primary emotion (the initial fear). When we use a "very small focus" (microsurgery) targeting just I-DSI, reprocessing works well. For example, we can reprocess a dissociative phobia by using a modified EMDR procedure, and this will facilitate later access to exteroceptive DSI (a memory of a traumatic event).

The next graph shows an example of both types of DSI in a client with secondary or tertiary structural dissociation. Left circles represent exteroceptive DSI. Right circles represent interoceptive DSI.

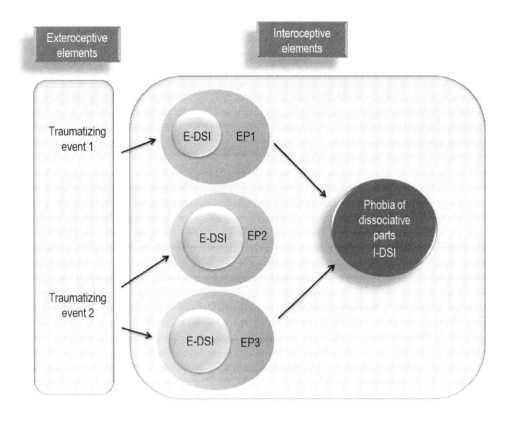

Fig. 3. Exteroceptive and Interoceptive dysfunctionally stored information.

A client experienced the death of her mother (traumatizing event 1) and a sexual abuse by her stepfather (traumatizing event 2). An emotional part (EP1) contains the memory of the mother´s death and contains unmet attachment needs, appearing as a little girl. The sexual abuse is contained in two EPS, one (EP2) related to a submission response, and another (EP3) associated with a fight defense, that appears as an enraged male figure. This male figure attacks the EP1 in the internal world. The EP2 is still not evident in the internal system, because the client as apparently normal part (ANP) cannot realize about the abuse. So, the phobia of the EP3 toward the EP2 cannot be openly expressed. The EP3 blames the EP1 for "being weak" the same way that she rejects the EP2 because of her submissive response. This is just one of many possible examples. The most relevant point is that all these interactions are not associated to an exteroceptive event, all of them are happening in the internal world.

We think this model could allow EMDR therapists to plan interventions in a broader sense. If the therapist just focuses on traumatic memories when dealing with severely traumatized individuals, crucial aspects will be left out. Having a broader conceptualization of AIP can enhance the therapeutic field of intervention for EMDR. Related aspects will be developed in chapter 8.

Insecure Attachment and DSI

Another aspect of AIP we believe needs theoretical development is the conceptualization of how insecure attachment influences psychopathology. Can insecure attachment be understood as DSI? We think this is a question EMDR therapists should reflect on.

Two concepts should be considered before approaching this topic:

1. The differentiation between attachment disruptions and attachment trauma (Ogden, Minton, & Pain, 2006).
2. Disorganized attachment versus insecure-anxious or insecure-dismissing attachment.

Disorganized attachment is a category of attachment disruption associated with highly traumatic environments. Emotional, physical, and sexual abuse is frequent in disorganized attachment. Because of this, when we think about clients with both disorganized attachment and different kinds of abuse in childhood, we commonly find situations where the attachment relationship is related to the overwhelming emotions that characterize discrete traumatic events. When the client remembers these situations, we can see that both the memory of the traumatic experience and information about insecure attachment experiences are held in a distressing, excitatory state-specific form.

Disorganized attachment is characterized by contradictory patterns. But really, this pattern of attachment is not a senseless mixture. Upon deeper examination, we can find orderly patterns of response to the chaos of the historical environment. With a neglectful caregiver, the child's attachment system recurrently remains in a state of hyperarousal, trying to stimulate a caregiver's response that fails to arrive. It eventually lapses into activation of a disconnected submission and withdrawal of energy from the attachment system. Later, when the neglectful caregiver approaches, the caregiver becomes associated with the recurring experience of abandonment, and thus both the attachment and the submission (defense) systems may be activated in parallel. Faced with a frightening caregiver's response (such as yelling to stop crying), the child must simultaneously activate defense systems while faced with a threatening parent (defense) and the attachment system (need for survival) with the only parent he has. Such paradoxical simultaneous activations were the most adaptive responses available at the time of these early disorganizing experiences.

Insecure-dismissing and insecure-anxious attachment represents a more stable pattern of interaction between child and caregiver. The AIP model (Shapiro, 2001, p 30) proposes that, "Information tends to be processed to an 'adaptive resolution.' By adaptive resolution I mean that the connections to appropriate associations are made, and that the experience is used constructively by the individual and is integrated into a positive emotional and cognitive schema." But what is adaptive for a little child is to attach to the caregiver. This same tendency, which in a secure attachment helps wounds heal and resolve negative experiences in the brain, can push the baby to attach to an unsafe caregiver.

The fact that insecure-dismissing and insecure-anxious attachments are quite stable patterns implies that they are formed in a continuous process of learning by the infant. The person develops and experiences their specific attachment pattern(s) as the norm. These attachment-shaping experiences may configure the client's internal working model and personality in a fundamentally different way than discrete traumatic experiences do.

These attachment patterns are based on early, pre-verbal experiences that occur well before the age of the earliest autobiographical memories (Multhaup et al., 2005). When we attempt to reprocess with EMDR later occurring experiences parallel to these early pre-autobiographical attachment-shaping situations, we can see that the responses to the standard EMDR procedure are not the same as with single traumatic events. The level of disturbance is usually lower (especially in dismissing insecure attachment), spontaneous adaptive shifts seldom occur, and much psychoeducation and active interventions are needed. Thus, early, pre-autobiographical, attachment shaping experiences do not seem to be dysfunctionally stored in the same way as discrete traumatic memories (including attachment trauma), and the response to EMDR procedures is also different. With insecure attachment-related experiences (other than disorganized attachment with attachment trauma), sometimes we can find some level of disturbance (especially in preoccupied insecure attachment), but other times there is no disturbance. These situations may correspond in some cases, not to stored experiences, but to "inadequate information" (Shapiro, 2006). So, "adequate information" should be introduced through psychoeducation or the modeling of a healthy therapeutic relationship. The therapist must help the client understand that those experiences were dysfunctional and how they are related to present problems.

BLS may function at this point more as a way of deepening a change of perspective perhaps by decreasing unconscious, defensive anxiety (maybe dysfunctionally stored information contained in a different EP), or by increasing neural connections or integrative capacity. New information can be linked (and reinforced with BLS) to the attachment related experience, which will set up a new foundation for new attachment patterns. These new patterns need to be worked on many times, and this is strikingly different than when we reprocess a traumatic memory. Shapiro (2006) defines reprocessing as "the breaking of old connections and the linking of new associations for more adaptive networks." When we have interoceptive or exteroceptive information associated with high arousal, BLS unblocks this information and fosters new connections. We may also have no disturbance or even hypoactivation associated to dysfunctional information, which remains rigid and unmodified in the system due to repetitive learning or other information preventing the former from evolving. When we apply BLS in this case, this process is not as spontaneous and we need to be more active, enhancing the linking with adaptive information that often should be introduced or reinforced.

When we are reprocessing a traumatic memory, we believe we are using the same emotional information processing mechanisms normally employed by the brain during spontaneous recovery from adverse life experiences. This is one of the central tenants of the adaptive information processing model (see Shapiro, 2001). However, when we incorporate BLS in working on a pattern of insecure attachment derived from what were persistent and preverbal experiences - not a discrete, autobiographical memory for an attachment-related trauma - we believe we must combine the reprocessing of some currently accessed and disturbing emotions with the interactive, intersubjective process of learning. The latter is a natural process in human beings, which typically occurs during the shaping of healthy and secure forms of attachment. This is bringing adaptive, learned information, either encoded or interweaved if not available. The relationship with the therapist creates adaptive memory networks, which can link in during processing.

An interesting speculation concerns the question as to whether the underlying mechanisms are equivalent in both situations. In targeting an attachment-related autobiographical memory, we are reprocessing a specific memory in the same way as in adult onset PTSD. We suppose the underlying mechanisms to be equivalent in reprocessing adult onset experiences and autobiographical attachment-related trauma. But is the mechanism the same in using BLS when reprocessing memories of the early relationship with the caregiver and connecting that information with new adaptive information introduced by psychoeducation? Is the mechanism the same when we use BLS to target intrapsychic elements associated with emotions about current attachment experiences that activate parallel attachment patterns as in early, pre-verbal experience? Is early, pre-verbal information about core patterns of insecure attachment blocked in the same way as for discrete traumatic experiences? Or does the early stored "information" shaping the attachment system remain in the system, not because it is "blocked," nor because it is or was overwhelming, but because these were the earliest patterns of interpersonal and intrapsychic experience shaping the core narrative of self and other and were repeated countless times?

What do we see in clinical observation? Working on insecure attachment issues is often complex with EMDR. Clients often do not recognize these events as dysfunctional. Often they think they are "normal" and have difficulties in relating their childhood attachment experiences to their present problems in current life and relationships. When we ask them to target their earliest recalled attachment experiences with the EMDR standard protocol, the AIP system seldom evolves to an adaptive resolution unless the therapist intervenes extensively and recurrently.

There are two frequent situations. In some cases, clients had an insecure attachment with a primary caregiver but can provide an adequate attachment for their own children, partner, or friends. In this case, we have adaptive information to link in. Nevertheless the linking with this information seldom happens spontaneously. Instead, it needs active interventions from the therapist. This can reflect the presence of two different attachment related action systems. One would be for attachment seeking; the other would be the caregiving system. Adults with dismissing attachment who were parentified as children can often provide adequate caregiving while remaining impaired in their capacities for meeting their own attachment needs.

The second situation is a client without any positive attachment relationship, past or present. In this case, there is no positive network to link with. So the therapist needs to adopt a more active attitude, and do a lot of psychoeducation. In these cases, the therapeutic relationship is much more important, becoming in itself a way of introducing positive information into the client´s nervous system about the possibility of having safer relations. Here, we generally see severe impairments in the self-care system (see chapter 6).

In the first situation, with some positive, stable adult caregiving experiences, we may be able to redirect the caregiving capacity back toward the self as a foundation for restoring a healthy self-care pattern. In the second situation, we need to construct an entirely new foundation as the basis for an adequate self-care pattern. In both cases, attachment tendencies may be blocked by avoidance phobias regarding attachment. Early developmental deficits also have negative effects on information processing (Leeds, 2009).

Which of these explanations should we choose? We believe this can only be answered with research. But clinically, we will focus on repairing as much as possible, for example, processing the phobia of attachment and working on healthy self-care patterns, as we will explain in chapter 6.

Summary

Our proposal is to expand the AIP model and give an extended framework for cases of severe traumatization. The role of I-DSI as distinct elements different from E-DSI (traumatic memories) should be remarked, because for many therapists only working on E-DSI is considered "EMDR." To just work on E-DSI implies a misinterpretation of what a memory is, and what dysfunctionally stored information may represent. A wide range of intrapsychic phenomena can be overwhelming, and disrupt the adaptive information processing system in some ways that are similar to the effects of extrapsychic traumatizing events and in some ways that are different. A number of alternative EMDR procedures are based on this concept, which has been in need of theoretical development. For EMDR therapist, this clarification is not just of theoretical interest. It has a practical importance in structuring therapy interventions that can safely dismantle dysfunctional dissociative personality structures or uncover protective layers.

Many psychological defenses (I-DSI) are colored with positive affect, not negative post-traumatic disturbance, and therefore appropriate treatment, with full use of the AIP model, will involve targeting the positive affect. Resolution of the I-DSI can then occur, resulting in increased mental level, and movement toward adaptive resolution and integration of previously separate personality elements of parts. The crucial aspect is not the positive or negative quality of an emotion, but the characteristic of being "dysfunctional."

When we target interoceptive DSI (phobias, defenses, etc.), we are using the same mechanism that we use when we are reprocessing a traumatic memory. We are doing EMDR when we are processing the urge to drink or a car accident. By processing the urge to drink, we are preparing the client for further trauma work, but overall, we are planning each intervention from the same theoretical model.

In this broader definition of AIP, interoceptive experiences associated with disorganized attachment would be clearly included, but our reflections about dismissing attachment related experiences need further discussion. Some of these attachment situations are not associated to overwhelming emotions but with deactivation processes, and probably do not block the AIP system in the same way as disorganizing attachment related experiences or discrete attachment-related traumatic memories. We need to understand which elements are common and which are divergent between the process of unblocking AIP when working with a traumatic memory, and when working with EMDR on the attachment system itself. The degree to which they are divergent phenomena needs to be discussed in order to develop a comprehensive theoretical model that can explain how and why these elements function differently in clinical observations.

Chapter 4
The Dissociative Language

Dolores Mosquera, Anabel Gonzalez, & Natalia Seijo

Knowledge about dissociation cannot be reduced to a simple collection of protocols and procedures. In order to deal with severely traumatized clients, we need to learn a completely different language. If we do not understand their language, we might miss out on relevant information for therapy. Furthermore, we will have difficulties establishing effective communication with the client, which will hinder the establishment of a therapeutic alliance.

If we fail to pick up on pertinent information, we might not know when to proceed with an intervention, when to interrupt it, or how much can the client tolerate. The therapist must become attuned to the individual who was unable to learn emotional regulation and modulation during development. Difficulties, misattunements, and lack of insight provide important information about the client´s history. The therapeutic setting is a privileged space in which the person can become aware of these issues and identify what is needed to make changes.

Dissociation can be very subtle and oftentimes, the most relevant communication takes the form of "indirect" information: the untold. For a severely traumatized person, words do not mean the same as for someone who grew up in a supportive environment. This is one of the many reasons we need to learn "to speak the dissociative language" before we learn the procedures, in order to translate it to direct communication and help the client learn how to do this.

Indirect signs of structural dissociation include:

a) Inconsistent or contradictory information.
b) Talking about non-relevant issues or switching topics when we are asking about relevant aspects.
c) Lack of emotional resonance, such as talking about trauma without any signs of disturbance.
d) Difficulties in recognizing emotions, sensations, or feelings.
e) A façade of apparent normality, the "apparently normal processing."
f) Somatic symptoms as sensations, body posture, movements, etc.

g) Lack of insight regarding the trauma. Referring to body parts or the body in general in the third person, as if they were not integrated with the head, "My head said…" "The body feels this sensation…"

h) Frequent "not-me" expressions, "I can´t understand why I did, thought, felt…"

Identifying and understanding these signals is crucial for EMDR therapists.

Why is it Important to Understand the Dissociative Language?

Traumatized people have learned alternative means of communication: ways that were safer for them in the there and then but that are causing problems in the here and now. In therapy, they need to participate in the decision-making and, in order to do so, they need to learn new ways of communicating.

Therapists may be misled by the "apparent" communication and, hence, unaware of parallel communication, thereby proceeding with interventions that can be counterproductive for the client. For instance, targeting the worst memory because the client is saying "I want to work with this," and not realizing that the client has stopped noticing her body until she totally disconnects and has a dissociative reaction.

People who cannot notice their needs or recognize their sensations, who are unaware of their trauma, or who are strongly phobic of traumatic memories have difficulties identifying what is okay with them and what is not. This must be kept in mind. Many EMDR therapists have had the experience of detecting dissociative features for the first time during phases 4 to 7. As we commented before, clients can lack contact with emotions related to the target (two feet in the present), relive the memory as if it were happening right now (two feet in the past), or experience a large variety of blockages during the processing, as somatic symptoms, intrusive thoughts, auditory hallucinations, etc.

The best way to prevent these situations is to detect subtle manifestations during phase I and understand dissociative communication throughout the therapeutic process.

The following is an example of indirect communication:

> Client: I feel it here.
>
> Therapist: Can we go on for a bit?
>
> C: Yes (nodding her head).
>
> BLS.
>
> T: What do you get now?
>
> C: Well, now I don´t know what the hell I did or why, but I made this (touching her stomach) go inside, so I got lost.

T: It´s okay, go back to the memory.

C (shrugs her shoulders): I know... It´s like shrinking... of course...

The therapist goes back to the target, trying to maintain the reprocessing focused.

T: If you go back to the incident, what do you get now?

C: A sweating sensation and trembling.

Her body is more tense than usual.

T: Do you think it´s a good idea to go on?

C: Yes.

T: Okay, go with that.

BLS.

C: Oh...

Client covers her eyes and face with her hand.

T: What do you get?

C: The beak (bird) and the crow... this (crow) is a different story, a different battle...

T: Okay, we have two choices, we can go with that (the crow) if you think you can, or we can go back to the memory.

C: As usual, I want to get to the core... I want to go with the crow.

She puts her hand behind her neck making a little girl´s face.

T: What do you think is best? This is not about what you always do; it´s about doing what is best for you.

C: I think I should go with the crow (making gestures with her face). I don´t know if I told you about this... I had a nightmare repeatedly where I gave birth to a crow and the sensation of the beak on my hand switched to the vagina. That´s the reason this came now.

T: Check if you notice any resistance inside... this would be an important signal.

C: No, I really don´t (but makes a gesture).

T: You don´t...

C: No, but this doesn´t mean that two hours later, when I get home, I won´t need to take more medication... But I can´t foresee this...

T: No, you can´t, but you can close your eyes and do an inner scan, you can check and see if it´s okay to do this, if it´s a good time.

C (closes eyes): My inside doesn´t know or doesn´t answer...

T: Do you notice any alarm signs?

The therapist was working on identifying alarm signals in previous sessions.

C: No.

T: Okay, so let´s go with that, with what you got before.

C: Okay.

BLS. Client seems to have difficulties following the fingers.

T: What do you get?

C: I got blocked by a word "partorishe, partorishe," which means "to give birth."

T: And is this word something that came from inside?

C: Yes, because I´ve never heard it before and never in the imperative.

T: Okay, check inside again. See if this is a signal; check and see if this means that it´s not a good time.

C: Okay.

Client touches her throat, as if she´s having a hard time swallowing; she shakes her head.

It´s a good time, I´m just a little afraid of falling asleep... But that would be okay wouldn´t it? You can wake me up right?

T: Why are you afraid of falling asleep?

C (points to her genitals): Because I am going into some type of oneiric state...

T: So, that might mean that this not the right time, do you realize this?

C: Oh! Okay!

T: This is what your psychiatrist referred to.

She laughs and her body seem to loosen up.

C: Okay, I get it! So if I fall asleep and this turned into a nightmare, it wouldn´t fit with the protocol...

T: That´s right... That would not be good for you or your inner system.

C: I am groggy... (She touches her forehead and rubs her eyes.)

T: So, this is telling us that it´s not a good time, it´s saying "no."

C: Nods.

Her body is completely relaxed now.

T: ...and I think we should listen to your inner system.

C: So (realization), I can´t come to our sessions feeling so tired... because I tend to go into these states.

T: Notice how important this is...

In the following sections we will describe the dissociative language along the 8 phases of the EMDR protocol.

Dissociative Language and Phase 1

Dissociative communication is complex. Different dissociative parts may feel differently about therapy, so we should keep this in mind during our first contact with the client. Some parts might want to "tell" and get help, and others may not. This can happen for different reasons: some parts may be afraid, others may think they "have to keep the secret," etc. Even during the evaluation and history-taking phase, different EPs may become activated. The EMDR therapist must be careful during this phase, since severely traumatized clients are often unable to give us a list of their "top ten" traumatic events. In some cases, this is due to amnesia, but in others, they have a very hard time deciding "which are the worst ones." Sometimes they have the "top hundred" and just thinking about them is overwhelming.

Case example:

A 45-year old man has made a list of "general" top ten events. The first one was when he was 2 years old; it was his birthday, and his mother had bought him a cake. The man remembered that he had been hungry - his parents repeatedly forgot to feed him - so he had taken a piece of the cake with his hand. His father kicked him in the stomach and he had to be hospitalized. In this case, the worst part was his father´s face, just before kicking him (his hateful, out-of-control face). This session went well and we were able to follow the standard protocol. Next, we proposed to target a memory related to the frequent beatings from his father. When we tried to select a memory that could represent those moments, he became blocked. When he finally found a memory that was worse than all the others, he got stuck in the "worst part" and said, "This is really hard. I can´t pick a ´worst´ part... My mother (often) went to work and left us tied to a chair for hours. If she came back before him (father), we would get yelled at because we wet ourselves, and when he got home he would beat us. But if she didn´t get home before he did, he would untie us and beat us, saying: ´You must have done something bad to be tied up.´ So just waiting there was horrible, not knowing what would happen was terrible, not knowing who would beat us was atrocious, and then the beating itself was horrendous. How can you ask me to pick?" He describes his experience with EMDR reprocessing like a computer blocked by the opening of countless windows. In the previous example, the client is capable of communicating many things, but as we have already mentioned, the "untold" can be highly relevant in some of the more amnesic or phobic trauma cases. Amnesic gaps are usually related to the most traumatizing events.

During therapy sessions, silences can be very significant. As Janet pointed out years ago (1935), trauma-based disorders are illnesses of non-realization, and those aspects that the client minimizes or denies should be carefully observed. The concept of negative dissociative symptoms (Van der

Hart, Nijenhuis & Steele, 2005), such as the absence of character traits in the ANP, can provide information about the characteristics of unknown EPs. For instance, in some cases, a lack of assertiveness may be telling us about an enraged EP that contains the worst traumatic experiences.

Dissociative Language and Phase 2

The "Safe" Place: Translating "Stabilization" and "Safety"

It is frequent that the safe place installation presents problems in severely traumatized clients. In EMDR, the safe place installation is a basic stabilization technique. It helps develop safety and serenity, a goal for many clients. But for survivors of early trauma, the word "safe" can be a trigger in itself. A dissociative client might experience severe disturbance just trying to do this "simple" task. In many cases the client may say, "I don´t feel comfortable doing this," or "I can´t think of a safe place."

As we commented in the introduction (Chapter 1), for certain clients, this "stabilization" technique can turn into a complicated picture.

Resource Installation

Resource installation is a very useful intervention, but sometimes the translation of the word "resource" into dissociative language is very different from its meaning in English. Installing resources is considered a strengthening technique. The goal is to empower the client and its efficacy has been proven (Korn & Leeds, 2002). However, sometimes, difficulties related to the system of dissociative parts can emerge.

In one case, while installing resources, the client (from the ANP) appears to feel comfortable with the exercise. Then intrusions from the EP(s) appeared as auditory hallucinations saying, "What the fuck are you doing?" So, in this case, in dissociative language, there is a contradictory double meaning. On the one hand, the apparently normal part of the personality (ANP) says, "I agree with the exercise, it will be okay for me." But for the emotional part of the personality (EP), the meaning is very different, "You are allied with my enemy (ANP) against me. Any friend of my enemy is my enemy."

The meaning of the word "positive" can be reversed as well in early trauma and neglect. Some clients find it hard to feel good about positive emotions (Leeds, 2006), and classic RDI can be distressful for them.

Relational Aspects

Some communication can only be understood from a relational stance, and the relational situation between client and therapist can only be understood from the early attachment and trauma history (of both client and therapist). The therapist must become a secure attachment figure, a figure that many clients have never had. We will delve deeper into this topic in Chapter 10.

Phases 3-7 and Structural Dissociation

When not to Process

Phase 3 will give us relevant information regarding the possibility of doing trauma work. A specific aspect of this stage is to know when NOT to process traumatic memories. The stop signal is critical; however, this is not as straightforward as it might seem. We can ask clients if they are doing okay and are willing to proceed with trauma work, and we can ask them to give us a "stop signal" if they need to stop. But, is it possible for severely traumatized people to do so? Many clients will not give us the stop signal for various reasons such as the following:

a) They do not remain emotionally connected during the reprocessing; therefore, they are unaware of their discomfort.

b) They are so overwhelmed by their powerful emotions that they are unable to think of what to do or to express anything at that time.

c) They might not know their boundaries, especially in cases where they have been repeatedly violated.

d) Saying "stop" is not the same for an assertive individual than for someone who feels incapable of saying "no" to other people's requests, no matter how unpleasant the requests are.

e) They may try to please the therapist by doing "what they think the therapist expects," showing a submissive response to trauma reprocessing that reproduces the submissive response to early trauma.

f) Severely traumatized individuals often do not express their discomfort directly; we must, therefore, check for indirect communication.

When to Process

The opposite situation is also relevant: when to process trauma. The insistence on having a cautious attitude has led to many therapists waiting for years to reprocess traumatic memories (Leeds, 2006). Some clients, even severely dissociative ones, can benefit from EMDR trauma reprocessing very early in therapy. Sometimes by doing this, we are actually stabilizing the client faster and safer than with a long preparation phase without introducing BLS.

We believe that this is a false dilemma, based on an all-or-nothing perspective regarding EMDR trauma reprocessing. One of this book's main goals is to overcome this all-or-nothing perspective. If we use modified procedures, reprocessing can be introduced gradually: initially with an aim toward stabilization and, subsequently, toward reprocessing traumatic memories. Nonetheless, this gradual approach requires a good knowledge of dissociative language, because the process must be carefully titrated with each client.

Phase 8

An apparently "bad session" with frequent looping and no changes in the SUD level may be interpreted by therapists as a sign of "poor reprocessing" or as a signal that EMDR is not appropriate for the client at this point in time, or that it is simply not appropriate at all. But what happens if in phase 8 the client says that he is feeling better and reports that the self-harming behavior dramatically decreased after this session? This is giving us important information: EMDR can help this client at this stage of the therapy.

Phase 8 is a very good guide for structuring further interventions and to orient therapy sessions.

The following is a good example: A severely traumatized, borderline client comes to session very disturbed because she has remembered details about an incident of sexual abuse by her uncle. She has gained over 10 pounds in less than a week and cannot sleep for more than 2 hours straight, "I am exhausted and I can't stop eating; I feel disgusting." With a float back exercise, we targeted the first time she had this sensation (she was forced to perform oral sex on her uncle when she was 7). The session appeared to be terrible; the client felt overwhelmed, and we stopped with an incomplete session. Following this session, the client stopped overeating and was able to sleep normally.

Characteristics of Dissociative Language

Dissociative language has specific characteristics that differ from normal communication. It is indirect, polysemous, and inner-focused. Expression tends to be extreme and alternate with opposing tendencies that can be overt or very subtle. Many meaningful messages are hidden behind silences and the untold. Others may be expressed through the body rather than verbally. The main characteristics of dissociative language will be described in this section.

Specificities about dissociative language:

1. Indirect communication: A family where things can be expressed openly is less likely to generate severe traumatization.
2. The importance of "the untold" (non-realization).
3. A world of opposites: Traumatic environment is ambivalent and contradictory.
4. Polysemous: Multiple meanings, because different dissociative parts understand and express differently, in line with different action systems.
5. Inner communication: A lot of communication in the inner world may contrast with difficulties in communication with the outside world.

6. The body is key in dissociative language and learning to read it is one of the most important lessons for the therapist working with trauma.

1. Indirect Communication

Imagine a family where you can openly express your needs and desires. You are heard and understood, and within appropriate boundaries, your needs are met. Your parents have identified your needs in advance and helped you do the same. You are confident and can express disagreement and say no to others.

This is not the usual picture in clients with structural dissociation. Direct communication is usually non-existent during their childhood. Manipulative attitudes, double binds, denial of the child's needs, repression of emotional expression, secrets... This is the communication style that they have learned and continue to use in the present. It is difficult for them to differentiate their early traumatic environment from their present reality; they interpret the here-and-now relationships through a "trauma code" based on the there-and-then.

Hence, severely traumatized clients tend to communicate indirectly. Their symptoms tell us what they cannot say openly and this can sometimes be misunderstood as a voluntary attempt to manipulate or get attention from the therapist. But this attitude is usually far from being premeditated and intentional. Clients cannot speak a language that they have never learned.

2. The Relevance of "The Untold" (Non-Realization)

Non-realization is a key aspect in severe traumatization. Let's take a look at some examples:

Case 1

A client with a DDNOS diagnosis tends to rationalize when she shows somatic symptoms that resemble sexual abuse. Due to other issues, a reasonable hypothesis is that she has been an incest victim, but the client systematically rejects this possibility. Denial and minimization often tell us about the abuse. The first clue was an auditory hallucination that told her, "When will you fucking realize that he raped you?" The second one happened while she was doing an automatic writing exercise and "suddenly" she wrote the word "pederast." The client shares her surprise about this issue with the therapist, "Why did I write this word? Such a stupid thing..." She gave a rational explanation to the therapist and changed the subject. The third and final clue was that her sister told her that she had been sexually abused by their father and that she (the client) had probably also been abused. The client reacted by minimizing and denying her sister's comments, "I don't know why she says those things... how absurd!" The client's reaction is a clear expression of a strong phobia toward the traumatic memory in the ANP. It is probably informing us of a touchstone memory regarding a sexual abuse committed by her father.

Case 2

A client does not want to work on a memory but she says she does, trying to please the therapist. During trauma reprocessing, she becomes overwhelmed and cannot feel her body, but she does not tell the therapist what is happening. The therapist asks her if she is okay to continue and she says "yes." Suddenly she says "she is feeling much better," SUD 0, VOC 7. That night the client is hospitalized for a suicide attempt.

Case 3

A man comes to therapy to work on recent events that are bothering him. During history taking, he minimizes a dramatic childhood and insists that he is "over it." He complains about his present relationship, but remarks that everything was fine during his first fifteen years of life. However, he cannot describe any situation from that period of time; he expresses discomfort with the history-taking, and tells the therapist to stop asking irrelevant questions. The client agrees to work with present situations, but becomes blocked in different ways stating that "EMDR doesn´t work."

The previous cases illustrate the difficulties we may encounter if we are not aware of structural dissociation and dissociative language. All these situations give us more information than the verbal content. As we commented before, many clients cannot tell us about the "top ten" traumatic memories. When this happens, we should detect the "underground" trauma guided by the negative dissociative symptoms, like amnesia and lack of emotional resonance with traumatic events that are highly relevant.

3. A World of Opposites: Traumatic Environment is Ambivalent and Contradictory

All communication involves its opposite. If we do not bear this in mind, we may make many mistakes. For instance, the ANP may express a strong desire to "know the truth" about her history while also presenting extended amnesia. This amnesia is telling us that there are many aspects of the history that she cannot face at this point in time. We need to respond to the whole client, not just the ANP´s curiosity. We must not forget the EP´s fear of disclosure.

The same can occur when we suggest trauma reprocessing to the client. If we are not experienced in dissociative language, an apparently "very normal" part of the personality may present as being very open to working on the worst part of the traumatic memory. However, this "worst" memory may actually be just the tip of the iceberg and if the client is not be able to tolerate EMDR reprocessing, she will become blocked or decompensate after the session, as we saw in Case 2.

As a general rule, each extreme reaction has its polarized opposite. Non-realization in the ANP implies that some EP is stuck in trauma. An ANP who is very interested in knowing about the past usually counterbalances with an EP who wants to keep secrets, who is ashamed, or afraid of disclosing. Extreme vulnerability generally has its counterpart in an enraged EP. If a client shows us one face, we should be prepared for the opposite one.

The decision to do therapy itself is often ambivalent; there is a mixture of feelings and thoughts. On one hand, the client wants desperately to get better, to trust the therapist; but on the other, she is afraid of change and a normal life. She is phobic to trauma and has learned from a very early age that people who should be caring can actually be harmful. The reactions toward therapy and the therapist alternate between idealization and disdain, trust and distrust, excitement and desperation. These reactions tell us about relevant parts of the client's history and will be described in depth when we discuss relationship problems in Chapter 10.

4. Polysemous: Multiple Meanings

Different dissociative parts understand and express things differently due to different action systems. The opposite tendencies that we described in the previous paragraph are usually represented by different dissociative parts. Emotional parts of the personality are rooted in different action systems, which are usually manifested through defensive reactions. One part may be stuck in a submissive response while another may be enraged, representing a fight response. The first part is extremely compliant and will agree with everything the therapist proposes. The second part may be triggered by the therapist's proximity because attachment is experienced as dangerous (early attachment figures were dangerous). This part can manifest internally, as an auditory hallucination or an intrusive thought; or externally, as an outburst of rage against the therapist because of some apparently irrelevant detail.

The client does not have the integrative capacity to understand that both tendencies were normal adaptations to the contradictory early environment. An attuned therapist who accepts both tendencies is a good model to help the client understand the ambivalence and learn to accept both sides of the coin (see more about ambivalence in Chapter 11).

Therapy should include the entire system of dissociative parts, particularly those that the client rejects or disowns. All parts represent a positive function, even when they are acting or reacting in dysfunctional ways; but the client generally needs help to understand this. These parts might be evident from the very beginning of therapy, albeit in some cases, they become clearer only in further stages. As we will comment in different chapters of this book, oftentimes, the parts that resemble features from abusive figures will tend to appear once we get closer to working with traumatic memories.

5. Inner Communication

Much of the communication in the inner world may contrast with difficulties in communication with the outside world. People with dissociative disorders spend a lot of mental energy on interactions between different dissociative parts, struggles over power and control, and mental conflict. The therapy cannot minimize or ignore the relevance of this internal experience, otherwise we run the risk of being unaware of the most relevant issues in the client's experience and of being "blind" to essential issues in the therapeutic process.

A good way to understand the dissociative language is to explore inner communication and what happens inside (see picture below) when we ask or propose something to the client. Understanding the inner world is very meaningful, and the work in the first phase of therapy should focus on this task. At the same time, we should help the client to orient towards the "outside world." Inner communication in structural dissociation is not usually effective and resembles pathological communicative interactions that were present in the original traumatic scenery. An important goal of therapy is to diminish the inner conflict and facilitate better adaptation to current situations and present relationships.

The client must help to identify and understand how and why different dissociative parts get activated consecutively or simultaneously when facing an external event, and how each part meets a necessary function on the outside.

Orientation toward the outside world should be combined with exploratory work from the early stages of therapy. If we do not pay attention to this, we may get lost in the client's dissociative system and chaos.

6. The Body is a Key Element in Dissociative Language

The body has its own language: pain, physical symptoms, physical posture, gestures, or micromovements, even immobility. These words tell us about trauma and about which part or action system is activated at any given time. Without a supportive attachment figure, many experiences have "no words" and remain at an implicit level.

However, not only body expression provides us with relevant information. We should notice "what" is happening, "when" it happens, and what happened before that. Sudden fatigue during an EMDR reprocessing session may be telling us "I can't go on," or expressing the control of a hostile-protector part which does not want to approach traumatic memories.

Continuous exploration of the inner experience is essential in order to minimize difficulties. Body changes are points for investigation. It is useful to ask, "What is happening inside?"

Interventions

There is no one specific protocol to guide us in understanding dissociative language and becoming a good "translator." We should attune to the client, keep the client's history in mind, and trust our clinical judgment and our capacity for continuous learning.

To access the internal system, we must begin using the client's language and gradually introducing elements of direct communication. Metaphors can be useful, since they allow us to introduce elements adapted to each person. Symbolic elements can also facilitate communication. We can use intermediating objects: puppets, drawings, or figures, among others.

The client (and the dissociative parts) needs to understand the advantage of direct communication (psychoeducational interventions, "translation," etc). It is helpful for the therapist to translate symptoms into explicit messages frequently, encouraging the client's acceptance of personal needs and desires, and allowing for a more effective relationship with the environment.

We can say, for example, "You told me that you want to know about your past. When a person cannot remember things that happened, there are usually good reasons for not remembering. Some part of you may object to disclosing (secrets, fear of negative consequences). Perhaps you could find it hard to deal with these issues. So, we need to find a balance between both tendencies, undertake the process carefully, reach an agreement, and use appropriate timing. We cannot keep going unless every part of your mind is willing and able to do so."

EMDR procedures with these clients should combine flexibility and order. On one hand, clients should not be forced, because this happened far too often during their childhood. We must remain extremely respectful, ask for permission, and adapt procedures to the client's possibilities in each specific comment. What is possible for the client is always the best. On the other hand, interventions should have the structure that the inner chaos of the client's mind cannot achieve on its own.

How to use EMDR with Clients who are Unaware of Trauma

Non-realization represents the phobia of traumatic memories in the ANP and of the dissociative parts that contain them.

Different procedures can be used to overcome this situation, but as previously mentioned, non-realization should always be understood as relevant communication. By translating the untold, we are improving realization in the here and now. We can translate the client's behaviors, silences, changes of subject, symptoms, etc, into direct communication.

The client should participate in the process of understanding the underlying meanings. We can also respond to the "untold" as if it were direct communication. For example, a client changes the subject when we ask about trauma. Translating this "untold" information, we understand that approaching trauma is too hard. We can try to translate it in this way, "I understand that it is very difficult for you to approach these issues (translating to direct language). I don't want to force you to go there. I know you will be able to do so when the time is right. We won't go there until you are ready and until the most remote part of you agrees with this." This last bit of information often changes the client's avoidance into greater willingness to approach traumatic issues. We are also communicating very relevant information at an indirect level, "Your boundaries will never be forced here. There are new relationship norms based on deep respect and care. Change is possible."

Finally, with each intervention, we explain the advantage of direct communication, "I can try to imagine what is happening, but I cannot read your mind and I can make mistakes. It would be clearer if you told me, 'It's very difficult for me to talk about this.' Be sure that I will respect everything you say to me."

We can talk around the untold. Using a progressive, respectful style, we can decide not to talk about the issue, but instead talk about the aftermath. We explicitly say, "We won't talk about the abuse, but would it be alright if we talk about why this is so difficult for you?"

Or we can talk from afar. When the client is not even ready for the previous intervention, we can introduce healthy information regarding a never-told issue. For example, saying, "We won't fight your amnesia. I'm sure that you have good reasons for not remembering, but I know that whatever happened then was not your fault, because a child is never to blame. Adults are the ones who should take care of children."

When the client is showing an extreme reaction (or an extreme lack of reaction), we can comment on the other extreme. For instance, a client expresses her inability to be assertive in many situations. We can talk to her about how the rage contained in a hostile EP will be useful (when collaboration increases) to say "no" and to fight for her needs. These types of messages will help the ANP understand that a collaborative attitude toward the system can benefit all parts.

When we are talking with the client we can "talk through" the untold (Braun, 1984; Kluft, 1982) using a "double message." We are talking with the ANP, but sending messages to the entire system.

We must never lose sight of the fact that the client is not just the ANP, but also the entire system. We need to keep in mind how our messages and behaviors might be understood by other parts. In Chapter 13, we will explain some procedures that can be used in the meeting place to achieve more direct communication with dissociative parts. Even with these kinds of procedures, some parts - the more rejected ones - may remain separated for a long time, and we need to have some kind of indirect communication with them. When the ANP and the known EPs lack perpetrator characteristics, we can assume the existence of parts containing these features that sometimes imitate perpetrators. We can talk about these characteristics, searching for their adaptive function. Being able to accept that "I may have traits from my parent, but this doesn't mean that I am like them or that I will hurt other people as they did," is a necessary step in therapy.

For an effective therapeutic relationship to be established, we need access to inner communication. When we cannot access the system - or part of it - we can use what we call the "inner scan" (Gonzalez, 2008; Mosquera, Gonzalez & Seijo, 2010). This is always useful for checking the existence of unknown elements. We ask the client to focus on the inside world and notice the most remote signal of anything, be it emotions, images, thoughts, or physical sensations (this last one is very relevant). The client should take some time, it is important not to accept quick answers. Any feedback or observable sign is relevant and should be translated into direct communication. For instance, an uncomfortable sensation can be a "no." We must check these signals with the client so he can learn to do the same.

In dissociative clients, sometimes the body "speaks" clearer than words. Remember that somatic elements are not just sensations, but also body posture and movement tendencies (action tendencies). We can translate somatic elements into direct language, for example, by exploring when they happened: Clients may be disturbed by the intensity of a somatic symptom, but "what happened before" can be more relevant. From these elements, we can ask clients "to go back in time" to the first time when they felt this. If they are not prepared to get in touch with the trauma, we can ask, "How old do you think this sensation might be?" When they have difficulties placing the somatic element in time, we can ask them to visualize past images of themselves at different ages from birth to present time and to notice when any sensation appears or increases. Another possibility is to search for the dissociative part connected to the sensation, "Go to the meeting place and observe which parts are activated when you are noticing this."

Our language is also very relevant. Communication from the therapist includes more than words. Clients sometimes understand our behavior (or the absence of it) from their traumatic connections. Because of this, the therapist's attitude can be a powerful interweave. What we are doing (the procedure) is relevant, but the timing (when) and how we are doing it may be even more important. Our own neuronal networks may get activated when working with severely traumatized people, more than with other clients. Supervision and personal therapy are crucial for working with these clients if we want to survive as therapists for many years.

Chapter 5
Enhancing High Order Mental Functions: Beyond Resource Installation

Anabel Gonzalez, Dolores Mosquera, & Andrew M. Leeds

One of the basic principles of EMDR therapy is helping the client to reproduce natural adaptive information processing, which has become blocked or impaired as a consequence of adverse and traumatic life experiences (Shapiro, 2001, p. 32). When reprocessing a memory for a single traumatic experience in a person with a reasonably healthy previous life history, dysfunctionally stored information will generally link spontaneously with adaptive information contained in other memory networks. This is what we expect with standard EMDR procedures, but this natural process of spontaneous adaptive linking is severely impaired when there is structural dissociation.

With secondary and tertiary structural dissociation, the dysfunctional information about adverse and traumatic life experiences is stored in memory networks that are separated and divided by "brick walls," such as rigid dissociative defenses. These walls protect the ANP from the memories and emotional aspects related to adverse and traumatic life experiences. In secondary and tertiary structural dissociation, dysfunctional stored information (DSI) is contained in different emotional parts of the personality. In cases of tertiary structural dissociation, these parts have a high degree of first person perspective and mental autonomy, which leads to the need for specific and sometimes complex procedures. One of the key aspects we must be aware of is the need to establish means of communicating with these emotional parts of the personality. Without specific interventions to establish communication, we will not have access to all the DSI and we (therapist and client) are likely to encounter many difficulties during and after reprocessing. The linking with adaptive information usually does not happen spontaneously because defensive barriers between dissociative parts are strong, the capacity for dual attention is limited, or there is a lack of adaptive information.

Resource Installation

Resource installation was proposed (Korn & Leeds, 2002; Leeds, 1995, 1997) as an effective stabilization intervention for complex posttraumatic stress disorder and has become internationally adopted as an intervention for skills building in a range of clinical cases and in performance enhancement interventions.

The use of bilateral stimulation (BLS) for enhancing positive elements was described first by Daniels (unpublished), who proposed a procedure for combining an image of a safe place with bilateral eye movement to increase feelings of calmness and to address paradoxical anxiety responses to traditional structured relaxation training. Other EMDR therapists reported clinical benefits enhancing functional elements with BLS (Greenwald, 1993a, 1993b; Martinez, 1991; Wildwind, 1992). Leeds was the first to refer to this type of intervention as resource development and installation (RDI; 1995) and to develop a general, standardized script. Leeds (1997) incorporated aspects of several ego-strengthening techniques in the hypnotic tradition (Brown & Fromm, 1986; Erickson, Rossi, & Rossi, 1976; Frederick & McNeal, 1999) and described RDI as compatible with Linehan´s (1993a, 1993b) dialectical behavior therapy (DBT). See Leeds (2009) for a review of the use of resources in EMDR and other trauma informed psychotherapy. In 2001, Shapiro incorporated the standardized model of RDI described by Korn & Leeds (2002) in the second edition of her text.

From the perspective of the AIP model, RDI focuses on enhancing connections within and between functional "memory networks" (Leeds & Shapiro, 2000; Shapiro, 1995). The inclusion of BLS in the procedure appears to lead to spontaneous, calm, positive feelings within an initially selected memory and in many individuals to richer, emotionally vivid associations to other functional (adaptive) memory networks. New functional associations bring additional ego-strengthening material into consciousness. Client reports of these changes during RDI and case report data (Korn & Leeds, 2002; Leeds, 2009) lead to the widely-held view that this process reinforces the client´s ability to access affective, cognitive, and behavioral coping skills linked to these functional memory networks when the client is later confronted by stress-related stimuli. The potential for decreased vividness of positive imagery with BLS has been reported (Engelhard, Van Uijen, & Van den Hout, 2010). While increasing vividness of imagery is not the primary aim of RDI, such responses can be effectively addressed in the standardized RDI procedure.

In the original RDI procedure, clients are asked to think about a particularly challenging situation in their current life, imagining being able to face a traumatic memory or cope with any particular current life situation. Clients are asked to think about the qualities, resources, or strengths they would need to face the situation and what they would they like to do, feel, and believe about themselves when facing that situation. Then the therapist guides the client to search for images of experiences of: mastery (situations in which the client experienced the desired quality), relational resources (positive role models and supportive figures), and symbolic resources. Each selected resource is accessed and strengthened with guided imagery and then linked with BLS to verbal or sensory cues. Then the therapist guides the client to rehearse, making use of several resources in a likely future situation, to verify the client's sense of possessing adequate resources to cope effectively with their triggers.

But two concerns have emerged from this useful and widely-used intervention. One is the recognition that in spite of identifying and working on positive elements, this intervention can lead to minimal or even destabilizing responses (Leeds, 2001). This is due to lack of tolerance and rigid defenses for some positive affects or to initially hidden (structurally dissociated) negative associations to selected "resources." Possible problems with safe place and resource installation procedures have been described in chapter 4. The second concern described by Shapiro (2004) and Leeds (2006) involves the misuse or overuse of resource installation, unnecessarily delaying standard EMDR memory reprocessing, sometimes for months or years, or inappropriately avoiding it all together. Some clinicians may inappropriately overuse or turn toward RDI because of: their own limited tolerance for confronting the client's traumatic memories; limited knowledge and skills for titrating and managing EMDR reprocessing of highly emotionally charged traumatic memories in clients with structural dissociation or borderline personality disorder; a professional bias toward always helping clients to feel "good;" or vague fears of the client being "unstable" or not being able to "complete" a reprocessing session.

Resource development and installation is a relevant contribution, but the preparation phase in severely traumatized client should not be limited to RDI, as we will describe in this chapter.

EMDR and Higher Order Mental Functions

The general philosophy of EMDR is to stimulate the natural capacity of our brain, of human mind-body, to self-heal. We introduce additional interventions, such as interweaves and resource installation, only when reprocessing does not occur spontaneously and fluently. Resource development and installation provides a way to develop and to reinforce functional memory networks and self-capacities. However, there are a number of higher order mental functions (that we will describe in this chapter) that are foundational to the ability to form the kind of functional memory networks enhanced during some RDI procedures. During EMDR reprocessing, interweaves can be offered to further support the tendency to connect with functional memory networks, which we see happening spontaneously in the reprocessing of single incident trauma. In clients where these functional memory networks are underdeveloped or when the client has difficulty connecting with them, we attempt to stimulate adaptive information processing with specific procedures. But in severe traumatization and neglect, more fundamental aspects of mental functioning are underdeveloped. We will globally describe these as higher order mental functions.

We will describe how we can promote the development of higher order mental functions with EMDR in the early and middle stages of therapy. Then, in the later stages of the therapy, after these higher order mental functions and sufficient resources and self-capacities have been developed, we can offer trauma reprocessing to clients with severe traumatization and structural dissociation, in a way that resembles, as close as possible, the efficient and spontaneous reprocessing we typically see in cases of single incident trauma.

Higher Order Mental Functions

Higher order mental functioning is impaired in people who have grown up in neglectful and traumatizing environments and who present with attachment disturbances. These aspects can evolve when an effective therapy process develops.

This client explains accurately her experience, "What do I think? My mind was never really with me, you know? I couldn´t think about anything, I just felt different things which they (two dissociative parts) made me feel and I had no choice at all. Now (after two years of therapy), I can realize that all these sensations are only memories, and I can be here at the same time." Using modified EMDR protocols in which the processing of dysfunctional information was systematically interweaved with psychoeducational and supportive interventions, these achievements seemed to be enhanced.

Literature from severe traumatization, which describes neurodevelopment and disorders related to early adverse experiences like those that lead to borderline personality disorders (Fonagy et al., 2002; Kernberg, 1993), help us understand which mental processes are underdeveloped or impaired in these clients, and therefore, which is the healthy direction that we should follow. Many theories (Linehan 1993, regarding mindfulness; Teasdale: metacognitive insight, 1999; Van der Hart et al., 2006: high order mental actions; Bateman & Fonagy: mentalization, 2004; Ogden, Minton, & Pain: mindfulness, 2006) are coming together in giving more relevance to high-order mental processes. EMDR can use general scientific knowledge to improve and strengthen procedures. As Shapiro (2001, p 6) remarks, "The real strength of EMDR is found in its integrated approach to treatment. The wisdom of all the psychology orientations is needed to make sure that no one is left behind. The goal of EMDR is to achieve the most profound and comprehensive treatment effects possible in the shortest period of time, while maintaining client stability within a balanced system."

In standard EMDR procedures, we make sure the process follows what we know the brain can do naturally (innate self-healing). But in severe traumatization, we should make sure that a healthy process occurs. In standard reprocessing, we intervene when things do not go as expected, introducing short cognitive interweaves to return to "the path," and we reinforce resources (adaptive coping responses and healthy information) to potentiate the tendency to connect with adaptive memory networks.

In severe neglect and traumatization, when there is a positive evolution during reprocessing, changes may be more subtle and complex - increasing mental efficiency, differentiation, personification, realization about past history, etc. - than in pure cases of "simple" PTSD. However, but with careful attention, we can still observe and be confident about the innate tendency to heal. In order for this evolution of high order mental capacities to happen, we may need to address more subtle and foundational aspects of clients´ intrapsychic experiences than can be achieved by simply reinforcing positive memory networks through resource development and installation procedures

(Korn and Leeds, 2002). In part, this can be understood as due to the relative paucity in survivors of severe neglect and abuse of positive memory networks that could be reinforced. But more importantly, it also reflects the absence of an adequate development of the foundational metacognitive capabilities, which are needed to successfully engage in emotional information processing. How can we do this with EMDR?

Reflexive, metacognitive processes and a reflexive capacity should be potentiated (Teasdale, 1999). Higher order mental actions can replace lower and substitute mental actions (Van der Hart, Nijenhuis, & Steele, 2006). The capacity to mentalize others´ and one´s own behaviors and mental processes should take the place of primitive ways of thinking (Fonagy et al., 2002). Differentiation between the self and the others should be established (Kernberg, 1993). To recover the sense of ownership regarding one´s self, one´s mental contents, one´s personal history is what Van der Hart et al. (2006) call personification. Differentiation between past, present, and future and the ability to be in the here and now (presentification) need to be developed in order to proceed with EMDR trauma reprocessing. That issue underlines not only the TSDP concept of presentification, but is included in mindfulness training, which authors such as Linehan (1993a) point to as a key aspect for the treatment of borderlines, and which is the basis for sensorimotor psychotherapy of trauma disorders (Ogden, Minton, & Pain, 2006). Being able to differentiate themselves from others is crucial in these cases; there are specific psychoeducational interventions to support developing this understanding for clients who tend to "need others" to feel better (Mosquera, 2004). PA clients who need others to regulate themselves will have many difficulties following the standard EMDR PTSD procedure because they are used to turning toward others and have not learned self-soothing skills. In many cases, the client is unable to link positive information because what is "positive" for them is a learned defense that has to be worked through.

When we use EMDR procedures with complex trauma, the process can be blocked or get stuck at many points, and the therapist´s interventions will be needed. As part of the progressive approach, we propose the idea of working with interweaves to enhance high order mental actions and the use of BLS for reprocessing and installation of healthy information. We can see an example where the introduction of small fragments of reprocessing introduced significant changes in the evolution of the case, toward the emergence of higher order mental actions:

A 40 year old DID client was attending therapy on a weekly basis. During 5 months of work on enhancing inner communication and cooperation between the system of parts, BLS was initially used only for resource installation. In one of the sessions, we introduced BLS to reprocess the dissociative phobia in the ANP toward the EP. In the subsequent session, she described how she became assertive for the first time with her abusive partner:

> Client: As a way to let him know, "If you don´t respect me when I am telling you something about my son, that is so important to me… If you don´t respect me, and tell all these bad words, and you go crazy… Then, see you later, the conversation is over…" but without being rude…

I am not conscious about this but I am aware that it came out without me wanting to, "Okay, see you later…"

I felt so bad during the night! The voices were saying, "Kill him, kill him, kill him!!!" But just look at my reaction: Instead of getting scared and being frozen (reflex reaction), I spoke with the voices (increase in reflective, metacognitive capacity), "Wow, look at this!" I was feeling afraid, a sensation in my body (mindfulness)… I don´t know how, but I allowed myself to ask them, "You (to the voices) know what, you must be really mad…" But are you noticing how much I have changed? I said, "Thanks for being there and telling me all these things, because for the first time I have realized that I have misinterpreted what you were saying. I was blaming you, thinking it was about P (her son) and this was only my interpretation. This was about J (her partner), this is my rage (personification). The rage I never allow myself to feel during the conversation, now you are forcing me to face this situation that I never wanted to face. For this reason the voices emerge (realization)." It´s a desperate way to say: "Come on, girl! For fifty years you have been pretending not to notice when they mistreated you. They have humiliated you. You have been damaged in all the possible ways," because few human beings have suffered the humiliations that I have… And there I was, saying, "Nothing is happening! How happy I am!"

Therapist: So actually the voices were not telling you to kill P (her son). They were only saying "Kill him."

C: It was yesterday was when I realized they never said, "Kill P." But I know that there is an important detail in all this issue…

T: Ask this part about it.

While the ANP is focusing on inner communication we do a short set of BLS (tapping).

C: I can remember another thing I had asked him: When I had been feeling like this for the first time. Then I was able to realize the situation that was happening with J (her partner), but then my mother came up. Maybe lately I was more with my father´s theme and didn´t allow myself to understand that actually this attitude was always my mother´s. She was so intrusive! She came into my room at any time, she touched our feet with her hand and, after this, she put her hand into our mouth saying, "Are they clean?" You know, I think that this reaction that I am having, feeling so bad due to J´s call, to that lack of respect, is connected with this part. It´s like I don´t really deserve to be respected. This rage, because this man is who he is… But if all these things are summed with past issues, the reaction will be much more intense (presentification).

(After another set of BLS) Now I am realizing that I was very angry with him, but what is happening now is only an echo of the past. But look, how unconscious! It was entirely unconscious, I was completely unconscious about my rage, how to move forward then?

T: You have allowed yourself to fully feel your rage.

C: Oh, yes. This was the first time I have allowed myself to feel this. And I believe it was absolutely relieving: Such internal satisfaction, such happiness! I believe that for the first time the voices said, "Hallelujah! Finally you realized, pay attention to us!" (More integrative capacity).

T: We are working with EMDR precisely because these things are so unconscious. After the last session, you could understand many of these things, but you couldn't change them.

C: Yes, these are incredible changes. And with P (her son) I think that the guilt has disappeared. Until now it was there, for twelve years. Such high tension every day in the morning! Now I am not so concerned with his education, his feeding... And I think it's really good because at last I can sit peacefully with my son for dinner, I can shout at him when it's needed. I feel more linked to him, I am accepting him entirely as he is. This will be the authentic happiness for him and for myself.

So, all these high order mental functions are aspects that we can, and in many cases will need to, enhance in the client prior to offering reprocessing of adverse and traumatic memories with the standard EMDR procedure. We could hypothesize that, in the same way that positive memory networks tend to link to dysfunctionally stored information when we unblock the innate brain processing system, these high order mental function can develop when we unblock dysfunctionally stored information. In this client, we observed that realization and reflexive capacity appeared after the introduction of EMDR specific procedures, and this happened spontaneously. Probably all the previous work could be integrated with the BLS, even when these interventions did not show until this moment relevant clinical changes.

But in other clients with a lower level of mental functioning, as with cognitive interweaves in standard trauma procedures, it may be beneficial to use active interventions to promote development of these higher order mental functions, which different theories and research on disorders based on severe traumatization are showing us.

A Developmental Perspective

A child who grows up in a neglectful and abusive environment, cannot develop certain capacities, which form through interaction with an attuned, balanced, and coherent caregiver (Siegel & Hartzell, 2004). The caregiver who is able to give form and meaning to the young child's affective and intentional states, through facial and vocal mirroring, and playful interactions, provides the child with representations that will form the very core of his developing sense of selfhood (Bateman & Fonagy, 2004). The child who has not experienced the caregiver's integrative mirroring of his affective states cannot create representations of them, and may later struggle to differentiate reality from fantasy, and physical from psychic reality. The neglected self will be not fully representational or reflective.

Those self-capacities that were not developed early in life can be acquired through the therapeutic process. Developmental processes are not based on a single issue. A child grows in a caring relationship, where different elements should be present. A core aspect of the therapeutic process in severely traumatized people is to repair after-effects of developmental disruptions and rehabilitate the personality.

What can we learn thinking from a developmental perspective? When we are working with a highly functioning adult, the minimum intervention from the EMDR therapist will be needed. We just observe how the client´s AIP system does the work and our intervention will be only the minimum necessary to redirect the process if it diverts out of the way or becomes stalled.

But with a person who has not achieved a high level of functioning, our interventions must explicitly incorporate more of the elements from an early safe attachment. We must actively help the client to develop undeveloped functions by reprocessing dysfunctionally stored information which is blocking his system. We must keep in mind that, in such cases, to remain out of the way, as we should do in the standard EMDR protocol for trauma memories, can be a reenactment of early neglectful relationships that actually triggers more disturbance. So, in such cases, our interventions should not be the minimum possible; instead we should give the client the precise amount of intervention that she or he needs from the therapist.

On the other hand, just as in a secure attachment, we should not do everything for the client. We must potentiate the survivor´s autonomy and capacity for making choices. In the words of Judith Herman (1997), "The core experiences of psychological trauma are disempowerment and disconnection from others. Recovery, therefore, is based upon the empowerment of the survivor and the creation of new connections. Recovery can take place only within the context of relationships; it cannot occur in isolation.... The first principle of recovery is the empowerment of the survivor. She must be the author and arbiter of her own recovery. Many benevolent and well-intentioned attempts to assist the survivor founder because this fundamental principle of empowerment is not observed. No intervention that takes power away from the survivor can possibly foster her recovery, no matter how much it appears to be in her immediate best interests."

Thinking from a developmental perspective gives us an equilibrated and integrative view that we will take into account as we describe, in this chapter, different capacities that need to be enhanced in the work with severely traumatized people. This developmental perspective fits very well with EMDR theory, which understands the present problems of the client as consequence of early experiences.

A Progressive Approach from Installation to Processing: the Constant Interweaving

EMDR can offer much more in the treatment of severely traumatized people than just resource installation and standard reprocessing of traumatizing memories. We believe in a progressive approach, where adaptive elements can be interweaved with reprocessing of a wide variety of dysfunctional elements - not only traumatic memories - in a dynamic way.

At the beginning of the therapy, more emphasis should be given to introducing adaptive, functional elements. We propose that small fragments of reprocessing can be introduced to unblock stuck points (see chapter 9), to relieve part of a dysfunctional (defensive) emotion, to reduce phobias for other parts of the personality, or to diminish a disturbing sensation. We hypothesize that the effects of parasympathetic activation (Elofsson et al., 2008) help to relieve such dysfunctional elements, reinforce adaptive elements, and increase healthy neural connections.

Throughout the therapeutic process, we can introduce information that the system lacks or with which it cannot connect. We can use psychoeducational interweaves to enhance these therapeutic interventions, using a reprocessing procedure and not be restricted to using interweaves only within the standard EMDR procedure for trauma memory resolution work.

So, we consider the therapeutic process as a dynamic procedure where, understanding the principles of the AIP and TSDP models and the effects of bilateral stimulation to decrease dysfunctional activation and increasing neural connections, therapist and client can decide in each moment of each session, what amount of intervention with BLS can be done. This dynamic process of enhancing high order mental processes combined with installation of healthy information and reprocessing of dysfunctional elements is what we have called *the constant interweaving*, and it is one of the elements of the progressive approach that we are proposing in this book.

When we are working on severe traumatization, the content of our interventions is not always the most critical aspect. Rather, it is how they are done, their timing, the nonverbal communication, and the degree of attunement with the client.

Higher Order Mental Processes that Need to be Developed

We will describe in the next section a series of higher order mental processes that need to be developed and possible interventions to enhance them. These processes are: mentalization, mindfulness, "meta" processes, differentiation, synthesis, and realization. One foundational element we use to promote these higher order mental processes is working through the *adult self*. Working through the *adult self* emphasizes the "here-and-now" aspect of the client´s present circumstances and the intrinsic autonomy of the client. Survivors of severe early neglect and abuse often struggle with what present as childlike, emotional parts of their personality with insufficient development of many of their higher order mental processes. These include: present orientation in time and space; realization of current physical safety; capacity to trust their sensory perceptions; and ability to differentiate when their emotional responses are appropriate to current circumstances and when they represent a reactivation of dysfunctional affects from their traumatic past. Some clinicians believe it is necessary to address the problems expressed in developmentally young emotional parts of the personality by forging alliances with these young parts and encouraging a dependency between these young emotional parts of the personality and the clinician. However, we view this approach as intrinsically regressive and prone to increasing the client's difficulties in developing higher order mental functions.

Mentalization

In phase 3 of the standard EMDR protocol, we elicit negative and positive self-statements, but patientclients with insufficiently developed higher order mental processes may need to address foundational mental processes before moving to phase 3. For people who suffered early disorganized attachment and childhood trauma, with an underdeveloped capacity for mentalization, a thought is not just a thought, a mental action, but in many cases, it is experienced with a high degree of reality.

Bateman & Fonagy (2004) defined two primitive modes of awareness of mental states:

A. One equates the internal with the external: What exists in the mind must exist in the external world, and what exists out there must invariably also exists in the mind. They call this first mode **psychic equivalence**. From this perspective, the client's imagination about the world is experienced as absolutely real. So, when a client is feeling guilty during an EMDR processing about having a fantasy of aggression toward an abusive caregiver, a useful interweave could be, "A fantasy is just a fantasy, imagination cannot damage anybody." This apparently obvious phrase often surprises these clients, since they have never thought about this view as a possible option.

B. Another primitive mode is the **pretend mode**. Their own mental state is decoupled from external or physical reality, with no recognition that this internal state is connected to events in the outside world. The dissociative client can be lost in the inside, and one of the risks for the therapist is to be trapped in the fascination of this inner world. A specific interweave to relate changes in the internal world with outside situations could be asking, "What part of you gets activated when you think about this situation with your partner?" To explore "what happened before," an intrapsychic event or external situations that might be related to changes in the inner system of parts, is very relevant. Clients are sometimes so afraid of their mental actions, that they cannot realize what the external triggers for these changes are (not without help).

In clients with an extremely low mentalization capacity, we often need to work on these aspects before using standard EMDR reprocessing procedures. For example, in chapter 13, we explained that in the meeting place we use the screen strategy as a way to separate the outside world from the inside one. Some clients place people from the outside world inside the meeting room.

Another option is using drawings, as in this case: when we ask the client to draw different parts of herself, she draws only two figures representing herself and her partner.

When we told her, "He is not inside you, he is not part of you," she began to cry. We can give messages such as, "Your partner is very important, but he is not a part of you. Draw a circle representing yourself. Place him out of this circle and notice how he is really on the outside." We can install this new perspective or the awareness about boundaries between the outside and the inner world, or we can reprocess a dysfunctional emotion in one dissociative part that gets activated in front of the partner. For example, when memories of her abusive father are triggered and associated with this partner. As we will explain in chapter 8 about dissociative phobias, we generally do not reprocess the early memory itself in the first stages of the therapy, but instead reprocess the peripheral emotion: that is, the consequence of that experience. This reprocessing work focused on the relationship between current triggers and internal states supports the development of essential capacities for mentalization. These essential capacities for mentalization are needed to improve the client's day-to-day functioning and should be in place before directly confronting memories of early relational trauma to lessen the risk of decompensation responses to reprocessing.

Mindfulness

A stable observer stance is a key part of the EMDR approach (Corrigan, 2002, 2004; Shapiro, 2001). Bishop et al (2007) described a two component model of mindfulness: The first component involves the self-regulation of attention, so that it is maintained on immediate experience and the conscious awareness of one's current thoughts, feelings, and surroundings, which can result in metacognitive skills for controlling concentration. The second component is the orientation to the here and now experience, which is seen with curiosity, openness, acceptance, and thinking in alternative categories (developing decision-making).

Linehan (1993b) described mindfulness skills as core skills in DBT for borderline personality disorder. The sensorimotor approach to trauma therapy from Ogden, Minton, & Pain (2006) has mindfulness as a basic element. Acceptance and commitment therapy (Hayes, Wilson, & Strosahl, 1999) works from the related concept of "radical acceptance," which can be very difficult for severely traumatized clients. A way of learning to do this is for the client to observe this radical acceptance from the therapist.

This component of EMDR (Shapiro, 2001) is especially relevant in severe traumatization, where the mindless emoting mode described by Teasdale (1999) (clients immersed and identified with their affective reactions with little self-awareness, internal exploration, and reflection) perfectly describes the activation of a dissociative emotional part. Corrigan (2002) proposed that EMDR procedures bilaterally activate the anterior cingulate to decrease states of dissociation and increase "the attentional state of concentration mindfulness in which affect is well regulated," but this process seems to be impaired in severely traumatized people.

With more disturbed clients, we can first do mindfulness exercises and interweave bilateral stimulation both to develop foundational capacities for mindfulness and to reprocess dysfunctional elements in the here-and-now, to further work on processing, interweaving mindful questions. With these clients, we can add linkages to here-and-now sensory information by adding, "Where do you notice that sensation right now?" to the question, "What are you aware of now?"

One of the key aspects of "mindful" interventions is reducing judgmental thinking. We observe this frequently when applying EMDR reprocessing with cases of severe traumatization. When we use EMDR procedures with complex trauma, the process can be blocked or get stuck at many points and the therapist's interventions will be needed.

Case example

A client is referred by an EMDR therapist who believed it was too difficult to do EMDR with her. The client tended to judge everything that she thought, felt, and said. With EMDR reprocessing, the judging got even worse. She not only judged herself, she also judged her spontaneous associations (interfering with the natural reprocessing). This self-judging is similar to the ways her family judged her when she was a child. In this session, the client is working with a memory of her grandfather yelling at her that we selected with an affect bridge from a current concern. To acknowledge this and to work with it during the sessions allowed the client to reprocess and get some realization regarding her idealized grandfather.

> Therapist: What is coming?
>
> Client: Stupid things, nothing important.
>
> T: It is important to stop judging, to allow this to flow... (We had talked about this on previous sessions).
>
> C (nods): Okay.
>
> T: You are doing very well. Go with what you were getting.
>
> BLS.

T: What is coming?

C: Nothing.

T: Okay, go back to the memory, to the memory we were working on today (Client nods) what do you get now?

C: I don´t know, it´s... I don´t know...

Client seems to have difficulties to verbalize what is coming. Since there are many defenses, we measure the level of disturbance, to see if she is less disturbed.

T: From 0 to 10, what level of disturbance do you notice now, when you think about that event?

C: Well... it´s not a 9 anymore.

T: How much would it be now?

C: It´s not a nice memory. Can it be without numbers?

T: Well, do you still notice disturbance?

C: Can I talk and not give numbers?

The client has a lot of difficulties to say no or to set boundaries, so in this case, it is positive, we want to reinforce her assertiveness.

T: Of course

C: Okay (relieved). It´s not a good memory... Phew! (Silence)... and... that´s it.

She tries to verbalize what is coming, but a defense comes up because she is judging what is coming.

T: Okay... "It´s not a good memory..." What do you notice in your body?

C: No, it´s done... I don´t notice anything...

We give her time.

C: I think worse things have happened to me, and... I think that´s silly.

T: Okay, go with that.

We try to allow the natural processing to take place, but the client keeps judging everything that comes: her feelings, what is coming, the memory...

T: What do you get now?

C: Bah! It´s a silly memory... It shouldn´t bother me... and I don´t understand it... my grandfather who was the one who treated me less badly... my grandfather was the one who never did anything... He is only guilty of keeping quiet... he never beat me... So, why would something he did come to my mind?

The client is trying to hold on to the attachment figure that was "less harmful."

C: ... when he never did anything... she (grandmother) was the one who did.

T: If you think about it...

C (interrupts): I'm very surprised by this.

Psychoeducational interweave:

T: Well, we began with a memory that was connected to other situations where your grandfather did not hurt you directly, but you heard or witnessed, how he fought with your father.

C: Yes, that's true.

T: So, it makes sense, it's not silly... (Client nods)... It's important that you try not to place words such as "silly" or "stupid" in things that are important...

C: Yes but... He never... to me... I always thought about him as a... excuse me... as a weakling... Bah! Always apologizing!

T: Yes, you don't need to do this here.

C: Let's see... my grandfather... How can I put this? My grandmother would say, "I saw a donkey flying," and he would say, "If grandma says that happened, it did..." He never came up to me and said, "You are stupid," he never did that... And he would treat me "fine," but if my grandmother said whatever... it was sacred... So when my grandmother would say, "This girl is stupid," he would say, "This girl is stupid..." But when she wasn't around, he would treat me fine... So I never felt the things I felt towards her because it wasn't his idea ever... it was always her's... He simply saw how my grandmother insulted me and did all these nasty things and he would just sit there, watch TV, and not do anything...

Psychoeducation:

T: Notice the chain "She's stupid" – "She's stupid" – "I'm stupid."

C: Right, but he never did anything, that's why I always thought of him as a weakling.

T: Okay, so keeping in mind what you just said, go back to the memory. What do you get now? Without judging...

C: I tend to judge a lot, right?

T: Well, that's what I'm here for, to remind you.

C (smiles): Okay... why do I do that?

T: Because you learned to do that...

C: To judge constantly...

T: What would they say to you constantly?

C: That I was stupid.

T: Nods.

C: So, I shouldn´t judge so much, right?

T: Ideally no.

C: And I spend my life judging everything.

T: Yes, and you do it with yourself...

C: Nods.

T: Think about that memory, knowing the information we just talked about...

C: Phew, okay.

T: Think about that memory, don´t judge anything that comes... What do you get?

C: I can´t help thinking that he was a weakling.

T: Go with that.

BLS.

T: What is coming?

C: That he wasn´t a weakling (looking down)... I´m very messed up (realization)...

T: You are not messed up, and that is a judgment... Look at me (client looks)... Go with what was coming...

BLS.

T: What is coming?

C (sad): That he did that because he felt like it.

T: Notice that.

C: He was overwhelmed with my father (drug addict) and he took it out on me...

T: Go with that.

BLS.

T: What is coming now?

C: That I didn´t have to know how to multiply.

This was the target, her grandfather yelling at her because she did not know how to multiply.

T: Go with that.

BLS.

T: And now?

The client is connecting now. She has tears in her eyes.

T: What is coming?

C: I was afraid of him.

T: Concentrate on that.

More reality... She tries to justify him again.

C: But... It was in that moment... There were times... It doesn´t mean I was afraid of him all my childhood.

T (with a very calm tone): Okay... I don´t need you to clarify these aspects to me, we can talk about it later... (Client nods)... Just allow whatever comes, to come... I promise I won´t judge anything, I´m only going to listen, and help you to go on with the process.

C: I´m sorry.

T: We will comment afterwards, you don´t have to apologize, it´s okay.

C: Okay.

T: Think about what was coming.

BLS.

Client is clearly processing, with tears in her eyes.

T (without stopping BLS): Very good...

T: What is coming?

C: Anxiety.

T: Notice that.

At the end of this session the client places the responsibility on the adults, "They were overwhelmed with their situation," "I was just a little girl," "There was nothing wrong with me, I wasn´t stupid," "I was a brave child."

In this session, the clinician worked patiently with the client´s tendency to judge everything she thought, including the associations that emerged during reprocessing. The clinician offered repeated encouragement to simply be "mindful" of what was emerging and to "just notice" body sensations. These interventions allowed the client to achieve significant reductions in her defensive tendency to pre-judge her mental contents.

The timing and nature of these interventions focused on addressing the client´s limited capacity for emotional self-regulation. In this session, she was able to achieve some realization regarding her longstanding defensive idealization of her grandfather. This work on the grandfather might have been potentially destabilizing were it not for the client having current positive attachments with her husband and her aunt. Knowing this was an important factor in the clinician´s decision-making process for this session.

"Meta" Interventions

Many different theories remark the importance of "meta" processes and their underdevelopment in psychiatric disorders. Depending on the theory, they use different terms or pay attention to different aspects. For example, mentalization emphasizes the relevance of being aware of what we are experiencing, which implies a "meta" perspective (Bateman & Fonagy, 2004). Without establishing a relationship with early experiences, cognitive theory (Teasdale, 1999) arrives to a similar point when it gives more importance to metacognitive insight (experiencing thoughts simply as events in the mind, rather than as direct readouts on reality) than to metacognitive knowledge (knowing that thoughts are not necessarily always accurate). Cognitive analytic theory for personality disorders (Ryle & Kerr, 2002) states that metaprocedures are disturbed or underdeveloped, and different patterns of reciprocal roles remain disconnected so the self-reflective capacity gets interrupted by these changes between (dissociated) states. Van der Hart and colleagues (2006) point out high order (reflective) mental actions versus low order (reflex) mental actions. Psychoeducational interventions (Mosquera, 2004) allow the client to understand what is prior to impulsive reactions and that leads to reflective actions. Putnam (1997) explains the developmental process of the child as an evolution from discrete behavioral states toward more flexibility and complexity, emerging a meta-consciousness (reflective consciousness) that unifies, modulates, and regulates them.

Neurophysiological studies have related prefrontal cortex with higher cognitive functions (Crick, 1994). Llinas (2001) proposes that consciousness results from recurrent thalamo-cortical resonance. Different brain structures have been related to conscious awareness, including the superior tectum coliculum, different cortex inputs, thalamus, anterior cingulate gyrus, cerebellum, etc. Being a developed, global, and integrative capacity, higher conscious functions are probably related to the conjoint, simultaneous, and interrelated activation of different brain systems (Strehler, 1991).

Early attachment disturbances have been correlated with lower development in frontal areas (Schore, 2005). Having in mind that to relate "meta" capacities just with prefrontal cortex is too simplistic, as we commented in the previous paragraph, we can consider that to rehabilitate prefrontal functions is one goal for working with early traumatization. This brain region has been implicated in planning complex cognitive behaviors, decision making, and executive functions (Yang & Raine, 2009; Miller, Freedman, & Wallis, 2002). This means that executive functions relate to abilities to differentiate among conflicting thoughts, determine good and bad, better and best, same and different, future consequences of current activities, working toward a defined goal, prediction of outcomes, expectation based on actions, and social "control" (the ability to suppress urges that, if not suppressed, could lead to socially-unacceptable outcomes).

So, conducting each procedure from the beginning stages of the therapy with this "meta" style, we are contributing to the development of higher order mental processes. When clients participate in the step-by-step decision making, when we help them to observe their mental states, when we plan an intervention reflectively having in mind different possible results… we are enhancing these "meta" procedures.

One clinical example of "meta" interventions is the development of the capacity to experience different emotional reactions toward the same situation, at the same time. The work through the *adult self* is itself a metacognitive procedure. We are helping the client to develop a comprehensive perspective, observing from the adult all the inner experience, often composed of contradictory, ambivalent, and always complex phenomena.

Let´s see an example of a DDNOS diagnosis, exploring the inner system´s reaction to a problem in current romantic relationship:

Therapist: Go to the meeting room and check what part is more activated with these issues and which one would be more urgent or interesting to work with today.

Client: I think this (submissive) part is manifesting herself. The child (angry) part is more holding back.

T: Do both parts understand that they are aspects of the same thing?

C: Is this a question for them?

T: Yes.

C: Yes (client nods).

T: Well… we will do an exercise that is a little bit different… Hold both parts´ hand, and explain to them that as an adult, you can accept both aspects, knowing they are contradictory things, but both are consequences of the same situation (a disorganized attachment pattern in childhood). To be in front of a contradictory person, provokes contradictory reactions. It´s a logical response when confronted with such a contradictory father.

C nods.

T: One part was the best way to cope with one aspect of your father (attachment action system). The other one was the best way to cope with the opposite (aggressive) reaction in your father (defense-fight action system). And both aspects were needed for survival… And as an adult, you can hold both hands and understand both things.

C nods repeatedly.

T: Feel that, this new capacity for understanding and integration. Feel their hands in your hands, and when you are noticing that, open your eyes.

Short set of eye movements.

T: How do the girls look now?

C: They are stronger and happier.

Differentiation

We need to differentiate elements: Outside and inside, me and others, parts which imitate the abusers and abusive figures themselves, and past and present. We can find descriptions of these phenomena in the work of Kernberg (1993) and Van der Hart et al. (2006). Kernberg writes about two developmental tasks. The first one is the **psychic clarification of self and other**. Until this task can be accomplished, one cannot develop a dependable sense of the self as separate and distinct, because one cannot make a distinction between one´s own experience and the experience of others, between one´s own mind and the mind of another. This concept is, as we have commented, very close to that of mentalization (Bateman & Fonagy, 2004).

Only when the developmental task of differentiation is accomplished, can we work on **overcoming splitting**, the second developmental task. The child needs to see objects as whole (good and bad) and the self as loving and hating at the same time.

Differentiation between the self and the others affect different elements. One of the aspects that is difficult to differentiate for traumatized people, are core negative beliefs. In some cases, such negative beliefs are very strong and difficult to change, and may be generated by the internalization of phrases repeatedly expressed by early abusive figures (Mosquera, 2009).

Anna Salter (2003) explains, regarding sexual abuse, how the perpetrator and victim "agree" on the cognitions. For example, "She is a whore - I am a whore." Salter described how non-sadistic pedophiles first offer "attention" and show "affection" before starting sexual stimulation and inducing sexual pleasure. Then these pedophiles use the evidence of the victim´s sexual arousal to claim, "This proves you wanted it. I was only doing this because this is what you wanted." For the pedophile, their cognitive distortion of reality reduces their own guilt. It then induces self-blaming cognitions in the victim such as "It´s my fault," "I am disgusting."

Separately, we see a different path to pathogenic beliefs in children of mothers with narcissistic personality disorder. These mothers overly control their children´s activities, behaviors, and attitudes, often making highly demeaning remarks when their children fail to match the mother´s goals or standards, "You are ungrateful. Everything I do for you. You are such a disappointment to me. You´ll never amount to anything." When the child eventually tries to differentiate and form alliances in the world with others, the mother acts as if she has been attacked and attacks the worth of the child, his friends, and romantic partner. Reprocessing such memories generally yields significant shifts, only when the clinician makes well-timed and repeated interweaves over a number of sessions to support a differentiated, adult perspective.

This would be what Van der Hart calls "malignant kernel statements" (Van der Hart, Solomon, & Gonzalez, 2010). Specific techniques can be used to facilitate this change in beliefs, changing from externally based beliefs toward an identity based on personal evaluations (Mosquera, 2004).

Presentification and Personification: Realization

Another related, but higher level integrative mental action is realization, that is, the capacity of becoming consciously aware of the implications and meaning of our personal experiences. Based on the work of Janet (1935), these concepts have been developed as aspects of the process of integration in the Theory of Structural Dissociation of the Personality (Van der Hart, Nijenhuis, & Steele, 2006). Personification (Janet, 1903) involves integrating the synthesis of an experience with an explicit, personal sense of ownership, "That happened to me, and I think and feel thus and so about it." In contrast, "not me" experiences are characteristic of dissociative presentations and can be observed as ego-dystonic symptoms experienced as intrusions by the apparently normal part of the personality (ANP). The recognition of a dissociative part as a part of the self, can be facilitated with the processing of dissociative phobias, which we will explain on chapter 8. By first reprocessing dissociative defenses (Knipe, 2008), we can make it easier for the client to make contact with and then to realize an otherwise disavowed emotion. Without explicitly defining it, Knipe (2010) uses in clinical cases what we could call a "realization interweave." He asks the client, "What can you understand now?" or, "What do you realize now?" actively activating high order mental functions. With these questions, Knipe stimulates reflexive thinking, meaning, and realization, which are frequent spontaneous consequences of EMDR reprocessing, enhancing the effect.

Presentification (Janet, 1928) is the mental action of being firmly grounded in the present and integrating one´s personified past, present, and future. It manifests in acting in the present in an adaptive, mindful manner. Typically, emotional parts of the personality (EP) lack presentification, living instead in the time-frame of traumatic memory. Working on here-and-now reality orientation with emotional parts should be the primary aim of the first interventions that we do. The CIPOS method from Knipe (2008) is a progressive intervention that interweaves reality orientation and gradually increases contact with traumatic memories as the client is able to handle it.

The Adult Self

We propose to work with dissociative clients through the *adult self*. Our concept of the adult self has parallels with the *healthy adult mode* from schema therapy (Young, Kloska, & Weishaar, 2003). This mode is the healthy, adult part of the self that serves an "executive" function relative to the other modes. The healthy adult helps to meet the child´s emotional needs, and this idea will be related to the work on self-care patterns that we will develop in chapter 6. Young, Kloska, & Weishaar state that severely disturbed clients usually have a weaker healthy adult mode. The therapist should model or help to create this mode. For these authors, this mode met the functions of a good parent.

Our concept of the *adult self* is not equivalent to what the theory of structural dissociation of the personality defines as the apparently normal part (ANP) of the personality. This ANP lacks relevant personality characteristics which we want to enhance in the client. The adult self is the integrated, healthy, well-functioning self, the future integrated adult self (Korn and Leeds, 2002). The *adult self* is an emergent set of self-capacities, which are not yet developed in any one part of the personality, including the ANP. Related concepts are the true self (Winnicot, 1960), the psychic center of the self (Wolstein, 1987), the ideas of Kohut (1991) about the destiny of the self or the central program, or the implicit procedimental description of emotional states (Fonagy et al., 2002). By working through the *adult self*, we are enhancing metacognitive processes, self-reflection, and many other functions that we will further describe.

We proceed from the implicit understanding that the future self is already present, as a seed. We do not need to explain this in detail to the client, but we will gradually introduce this understanding at different times in therapy. As a good enough parent, we are confident in the client´s possibilities of improving, and do not become "infected" by the client´s experiences of helplessness and insecurity.

We do not choose a single part of the system for this function; we are looking beyond any one part of the personality. In our view, it does not matter if different ANPs perform this role at different times or in different sessions, or if the ANP is not confident about its capacity to guide the process or to take care of others. Some parts or the entire system may feel insecure about the possibilities of change - the phobia of change is a usual dissociative phobia - but we will remain calmly confident about the client´s possibilities.

In many approaches to working with dissociative parts, as ego states therapy (Forgash, 2007, Paulsen, 2009) or the theory of structural dissociation of the personality, this *adult self* is not contemplated. When these approaches propose a meeting place, the ANP is present inside that place as another "part." In these other approaches, a specific part can play a mediator role, but the development of an integrated self would be developed as a consequence of the integrative process. It is not a specific element from which to work from the beginning but a consequence of the therapeutic process. In our conceptualization, to work from the *adult self* is a key principle from the beginning. We consider it essential to have this perspective always in mind as we work with dissociative parts. This means that, for example, in the meeting place, the ANP is not proposed in to be part of the meeting room, but instead we use it as a mediator to communicate with other parts. In our approach it is the ANP, as adult self, which will implement all actions regarding the internal system, borrowing and finally integrating different aspects from other parts.

The Adult Self as a Way to Repair Attachment

By working through the *adult self*, we are developing a new self-capacity: a new attachment pattern. The therapeutic relationship is frequently an emotionally corrective experience. Attachment disturbances are the norm in secondary and tertiary structural dissociation. The "good enough therapist" must be attentive to these problems, dealing with attachment difficulties, but being cautious at the same time of fostering in the client the necessary autonomy and empowerment.

In offering secure attachment, the good enough parent can see (with mindsight) not only the present child, but also the woman or the man that the child may be when he becomes an adult. A good enough parent does not project his frustrated wishes or needs on the child. This parent can see the authentic potential, possibilities, and particular character features of the child (even minimal traces of it), and is confident in the child's possibilities. The parent also has realistic expectations about what the child can do at any specific time, and asks him to do things at the level of capacity and responsibility that is appropriate for each stage of development. The child learns to be self-confident, responsible, and autonomous because he sees himself through the parent's eyes.

When a client lacks good enough parents he will grow up with many learned difficulties and deficiencies. In these cases, as we said, the therapeutic relationship may work as an emotionally corrective experience. The therapist treats the client knowing how he can be in the future. This confident view of the client's possibilities is implicit in our concept of *adult self*.

Empowering the Client

Another aspect, which can potentiate working from the *adult self*, is to give the client back his power. The idea is to "return the power others have taken from them," a key aspect in the therapy of survivors (Herman, 1992). Clients who have been traumatized frequently have a sense of being powerless. Many learned that fighting made things worse and seldom had the experience of being in control (power). Working from the framework of the *adult self*, we consistently place the power, the capacity of decision, of self-soothing and self-care in the client. The therapist is only a facilitator. We support the adult self in managing daily living, taking care of himself and communicating internally in order to gain collaboration, power, and integration with emotional parts of the personality.

By working through the *adult self*, we help the client to be in control (real control). The client learns to be attentive to his needs, including the internal needs of emotional parts. In our framework it is the adult self who, with our support and guidance, is leading the therapy; all interventions are implemented by the *adult self*. The client's autonomy is consistently reinforced. We do not talk directly with the parts, but instead we show the *adult self* how to talk and communicate with the parts. We help the adult self learn how to understand what they need, how they feel, how to take care of them. Through this work, the *adult self* achieves relevance and autonomy. In this way, clients develop their capacities for self-care and self-soothing, and become capable of using these capacities outside the consultation. The therapist places himself from the beginning as peripheral, lowering the risk of excessive dependency from the client.

Working on Healthy Self-Care Patterns

As we will discuss in chapter 6, clients who grow up in a neglectful or abusive environment have not internalized a healthy self-care pattern (Chu, 1998; Ryle, 2002). Very traumatized people did not learn to take care of themselves because, as children, nobody taught them to do this. In many cases, the adults who were supposed to take care of the child mistreated him or failed to provide adequate care. Many learned that having needs was bad, having needs was selfish and was not permitted. Others learned how to punish themselves instead of learning how to care for themselves. They continue to look at themselves through the neglecting attachment figure´s eyes or the abuser´s eyes (Mosquera & Gonzalez, 2011).

Through consistently working with the *adult self*, we model a new way for clients to look at themselves. We foster their capacities to understand their needs, and to develop empathy and true communication with dissociative parts. These issues are in our opinion extremely important, and we will dedicate a complete chapter to working on self-care patterns.

Reinforcing Integration

As a part of the natural process of integration, an integrated self gradually develops and appears. We can see this evolution graphically through clinical work in the case of a DID client, with a complex inner system, where EMDR reprocessing focused on memories from each dissociative part was introduced very early in the therapy.

Case example

Susan was a severely disturbed DID client with a comorbid psychotic disorder secondary to cannabis and cocaine abuse. Her level of functioning in daily life was very poor, with difficulties in basic self-care, frequent engagement in abusive relationships, frequent self-harming behaviors, and drug abuse.

Although she did not meet the necessary conditions for trauma work (no ego strength, incapable of any emotional self-regulation, no supportive relationships, suicidal ideation, substance abuse, low general functioning), she tolerated standard EMDR processing of early traumatic memories in combination with self-care interventions, and most of her improvement was based on this work and a strong therapeutic alliance.

She kept a diary, in which she described her evolution and changes. She illustrates the development of the *adult self* with a series of drawings.

In the first drawings that she did about the internal system, an ANP was absent. She could only describe a chaotic tug of war between an activation of parts that was constantly shifting. There was no metaconciousness level that could unify or reflect on these shifting self-states. There are only undefined parts in the internal system.

The presentation is similar to the disaggregated thoughts seen in schizophrenic disorder. The client's notes at that stage were associations without apparent sense. She wrote something like, "The ball jumps and turns, the-ba-all-jum-ps-from-o-ne-hand-to-the-o-ther," as if there were a ball in her mind that was constantly jumping from one dissociative part to another. When we asked her about the adult woman, she said she did not know where she was, that she did not exist.

On the next drawing, elements that represent communication with the external world appeared. Parts are more defined.

The client was more coherent, and she began to relate to others in the external world, but in a very limited way. She writes, "With all these people in my head, it's normal that I cannot have personal relationships or that these relationships are so complicated for me." These social interactions were not supportive and sometimes abusive, presenting a pattern of approach and avoidance. In the drawing of some parts, we can see more childhood details, different emotions, reflecting that she seemed more aware of her internal states.

Only from this moment, could we start working with the inner system, and exploring different memories from different states. Previously, due to the global lack of mental efficiency, they were very blurred and not accessible. But the most useful intervention was standard EMDR trauma reprocessing, based on specific memories of one part, or shared memories. During the reprocessing, different parts became activated in a fluent (fluid and adaptive) way. Only in some sessions, when strong phobias between parts appeared, were specific interventions needed.

This orientation toward the external element is a very important aspect that appears as therapy evolves, which we can enhance from the first stages of the therapy.

After some months of treatment, including reprocessing of traumatic memories with EMDR, a core *adult self* began to appear, and this *adult self* remained present even during the shifting between different mental states (dissociative parts). This *adult self* was the start of a metaconsciousness from where she could reflect on what was happening, both in the inside and in the external world.

On the next drawing, we can see that she continued to evolve. She was more focused, she established continuity of consciousness all the time, and experienced other dissociative parts as intrusions. She writes in her diary, "Me and my other selves. Now my SELF is big... the biggest. And it´s in the center. My SELF has the rudder most of the time. There are still many impulses, states that are not me. They are my other selves."

She began to love herself, to understand (metacognitive) her mental changes and her experiences more completely. The work with self-care patterns was important in this achievement. She looked at her past with a sense of temporal and personal perspective. She achieved more personification and presentification.

In the next session, she drew her face for the first time. She is forming an integrated identity. Her sense of a chaotic inner experienced has diminished. The evolution of the drawings parallels the improvement in clinical symptoms and her daily life functioning. She no longer engaged in or maintained abusive relationships. She learned to protect herself and to take care of herself. The therapy with this client still continues, more focused now on daily life aspects, interpersonal relationships, and personality features. But now we are working with a much more integrated person.

A central principal of the EMDR approach is to help the client´s brain to learn to do what it can innately do. In clients who fail to develop this core adult self spontaneously, we can help them to develop it. We may propose to the client to imagine this "central point" where all the tendencies would be equilibrated, to imagine a "middle point" between polarized tendencies, or when he is able to do it, to locate this core anywhere in his body. Even when it is much too soon to look for integration, we can introduce this perspective of the adult self, and eventually to strengthen it with BLS. In this way, we are enhancing the foundation for a healthy development of an *adult self*.

Summary

Specific interventions to enhance higher order mental functions are key aspect of recovery in survivors of early neglect and chronic and severe traumatization. We do not consider this development as a separate process to be done only before the use of EMDR reprocessing on early adverse and traumatic memories. Instead, we approach enhancing higher order mental functions as a central goal and key element of the EMDR approach to therapy, which that can be interwoven with many alternate forms of installation and reprocessing such as *the constant interweave*.

From the *progressive approach* that we propose in this book, this enhancing of high order mental functions, the reinforcing of healthy information, and the reprocessing of dysfunctional elements are all aspects which can potentiate each other when they are combined in a dynamic way. In order for the therapist to do this, he must have a good therapeutic plan, which contemplates the specific characteristics, resources, and self-capacities of each client, having clear goals and carefully structuring the therapeutic process at all times.

Chapter 6
Introducing Healthy Patterns of Self-Care

Anabel Gonzalez, Dolores Mosquera, Jim Knipe, & Andrew M. Leeds

Positive Self-care can be thought of as having three distinct elements: 1) an attitude or state of mind of valuing and loving the self – an attitude that motivates the individual to take good care of the self, 2) an absence of self-defeating actions, and 3) specific actions that provide benefit, growth, or value to the individual Of these elements, the attitude of positive self-care seems intuitively to be primary: An attitude of positive self-care provides the motivation for the other two elements.

Knipe (2008) described the *loving eyes procedure*, where the adult looks at the child as he was in the past, without judgment, with acceptance and unconditional love. If the client is able to do this, a stronger feeling of inner connection and self-acceptance results. More often, with highly traumatized clients, this connection with the traumatized childhood self is difficult, and the client´s obstacles to self-love thereby become more evident. When this occurs, identified obstacles can be processed with BLS.

The clinical experience of using this procedure has shown us powerful and interesting effects and therapeutic possibilities. For example, a client, who still periodically attempted suicide after two years of very slow and limited improvement, experienced an impressive change after this intervention. Another client, who was focused on the thought of killing herself for over 3 years, started to put in practice some positive actions that were previously unsuccessfully in therapy. A severely unstable DID client began to improve daily life function after working with a modified loving eyes protocol with an emotional part.

Different modifications from this initial proposal from Knipe have been developed (Gonzalez, Seijo, & Mosquera, 2009). The main idea is that children internalize early experiences with their caregivers: They see themselves the way they have been seen by valued adults. The way they have been treated shapes their understanding of what self-care is. The work on self-care patterns is proposed as one of the initial interventions, because it prepares the client to adopt a positive stance in the therapeutic process.

Early neglect and trauma severely disturb the ways in which people take care of themselves. Clients who grow up in a neglectful or abusive environment have not internalized a self-care pattern (Chu, 1998; Ryle & Kerr, 2002). Highly traumatized people did not learn self-care because, as children, nobody taught them either the behaviors or the attitudes of valuing and caring for themselves. In many cases, the adults who were supposed to take care of the child mistreated him or failed to provide adequate care. Many learned that needing was bad, needing was selfish and was not permitted. Through their caregivers' poor modeling, others even learned how to punish themselves instead of learning how to care for themselves. Frequently, they continue to look at themselves through their neglecting attachment figure's eyes or the abuser's eyes.

When necessary mirroring, healthy modeling, and validation of experience from caretakers are lacking or absent, the consequences are different from those of active maltreatment, but both neglect and abuse affect the person's self-image and attitude toward self-care. Following the work of Schore (2003), Knipe (2008) has hypothesized that caretakers of young children validate and consolidate the child's experience as they observe that experience with "loving eyes." This nurturing connection (which happens to varying degrees in different families) is an essential element in the child's learning of self-nurturing skills, basic trust in others, and basic valuing of self. In contrast, a lack of sufficient nurturing by caretakers can disrupt healthy development in several ways.

If a child's inner experience – particularly the child's emotions – are not acknowledged by a caretaker, or even are punished by that caretaker, the child will learn to imitate and internalize the negative attitudes of the adult. An internalized negative concept of self may conflict, within the child, with needs to value the self, leading to chronic feelings of insecurity, especially in the presence of other people. This could be viewed from the perspective of insecure attachment leading to forming an inadequate sense of self-reliance, autonomy, and efficacy (Weinfield, Sroufe, Egleland, & Carlson, 1999, p 76-77) or from the perspective of structural dissociation as the deactivation and disorganization of action systems for self-care (Van der Hart, Nijenhuis, & Steele, 2006, p 55).

Self-care originates in the nurturing actions of others, which then are imitated and internalized as care-taking and nurturance towards the self. Nurturance affect has been identified by Panksepp (1998) as a core affect in mammals, and this affect seems to be activated through the early nurturance of others. If on the other hand, caretakers are neglectful, abusive, or disinterested, the child may internalize these attitudes towards their own inner experience, particularly those inner experiences that do not receive external validation.

The idea of focusing on improving self-care is related to the reorganization of the attachment system. Insecure attachment patterns originated in neglect and mistreatment by adults during childhood, and are now reproduced in the client's pattern of not taking adequate care of self. For this purpose, we need to develop a reflective stance, a meta-cognitive position. Schwartz (1995, 2002) has hypothesized that this *observer self* is intrinsic in all people, and lies dormant even in highly traumatized people. This concept overlaps significantly with what Francine Shapiro (2001) has described as a "natural, physically-based information processing system of the brain, that moves disturbing life experience to adaptive resolution." Regardless of the theoretical context, we can say that there is an observer self, which has the capacity to think, feel, and empathize with an experiencing self. This compassionate self is not entirely present in the apparently normal part of the personality, which often will not wish to connect with a childhood abused self. The *adult self* (as we will understand it) is the future integrated "new, healthy self" who can now learn to take care of the self adequately.

A secure attachment is both realistic and optimistic. The good enough parent can see the mistakes that the child makes, correcting them in a positive style, without minimization or denial For example, when facing the child's negative school results due to lack of effort, the parent will say, "I know you can do it better, and you will feel good when you do it." This parent has mindsight, knows what problems underlie the child's behavior, proposes alternatives, and encourages the child to follow them. This healthy style of parenting promotes autonomy, responsibility, and constructive self-criticism. When this child becomes an adult, he will be able to do things on his own, will be responsible, and will learn from mistakes.

Children need adult validation of all of their experiences, in order to learn to compassionately accept, learn from, and integrate all experience in order to expand their sense of self. This ability, to compassionately accept all elements of one's own experience, is related to other aspects of mental health: That of self-compassion, which is also strongly related to healthy functioning in interpersonal relationships (Neff et al., 2007).

Children also need other things from parents, like guidance, rules, and even negative consequences for undesirable behavior. But guidance, rules, and consequences are compatible with loving validation when the parent delivers those consequences for the benefit of the child, not out of uncontrolled anger at the child or out of the parent's self-centered focus on their own needs. If the parent punishes or ignores the child's feelings, thoughts, or behaviors in a way that is selfish and not nurturing, the child must internalize the adult caretaker's response, even at the expense of the child's needs, in order to maintain the essential connection with the caretaker. This can split the child's sense of self into "a made-up part of me that is acceptable" and "a hidden part of me that is not acceptable."

When such a child grows up and appears in a therapist's office, that person may lack a positive self-care attitude, due to over-identification with the punishing, dismissive, or ignoring attitudes of their caretakers. Especially in such cases, the acceptance of the therapist is crucial in modeling for the client a different attitude of client acceptability; but in some cases, therapist acceptance is only the beginning. There is an old joke, "I would never belong to a club that would accept me as a member." Some clients have a similar dilemma with regard to their therapist, "My therapist must not be that good. He thinks I'm okay." The influence of these phenomena in the development of the therapeutic process, and the problems that they can provoke, are evident. These obstacles to self-care, self-acceptance, and self-love should be addressed, and positive aspects of the client's self concept should be strengthened, in order to establish a collaborative work between client and therapist.

A good caregiver guides a child with total and unconditional acceptance. As a general rule, children need to have their inner experience witnessed and validated by a caring adult. This is especially true for unpleasant experiences. For example, when the child´s fears are recognized by a parent and responded to with compassion, the child develops the ability to recognize their own fears and to respond to his fears with compassion. This, in turn, makes more likely an effective response by the child to the source of the fear. Children who grow up in conditions of neglect tend to be impaired in their self-concept and their self-care for several reasons. For example, the child is seen as "good" and valuable only to the extent that the child is quiet, does not ask for much, and does not show needs or feelings. This child is likely to learn that he is not valuable or worthy. If the child also endures an overt act of abuse, that act is likely to be far more damaging. The client who feels she is "cursed" may regard a new traumatic event as "more of the same" or "what I deserve." When adults are not paying attention, the child will not be able to make sense of the trauma through interaction and acceptance by caretakers. Before clients can successfully resolve memories for traumatic acts of commission, they often first need to have or to develop certain self-capacities including self-acceptance and self-love.

The *loving eyes procedure* can serve as both a diagnostic tool and a way of repairing these missing self-capacities. We ask the adult self to look at the traumatized child - the child that he was in the past - without judgment, with unconditional love and acceptance. The difficulties that the client experiences doing this task, (e.g., the wish to not look at the child, or the trauma the child is in, or feelings of rejection or disgust on the part of the adult toward the child; or the child part not wanting to be seen by the adult part) tell us about early attachment problems. When these difficulties are managed, the *loving eyes procedure* can strengthen the person´s awareness of their own value, which in turn can lead to a greater interest in self-care. Therapy often builds on the part of self that already has some degree of positive self-care. Most clients come to therapy because of a part of their personality that really does want to have a better life. But often there are other parts also, that are self-destructive, self-hating, stuck in despair, and inaction, or stuck in indifference to the welfare of the self. These self-defeating elements of personality may have originated in misguided attempts at self-care (for example, in TSDP language, substitute actions: Van der Hart, Nijenjuis, & Steele, 2006), thereby reproducing old patterns from the early traumatic environment. With each new interaction between the adult self (see chapter 5 about high order mental functions) and each dissociative part, we have an opportunity to model a healthy caregiving attitude. With the guidance of the therapist, the adult self learns to realize the needs in each part and the healthy possibilities that even the most rejected part in the system has, helping them (as a good enough parent would) to give their best. This work is complex, because human beings and human problems are complex. We will develop related aspects in chapters 5 and 8 about high order mental functions and dissociative phobias.

Self-caring is a central aspect of effective, comprehensive therapy. Without an adequate self-care pattern, the client may be in our office for other purposes: to investigate, to seek justice, or to self-harm. In some cases they can tell us they come to do therapy, but say they cannot let go of their rage because they think it would be like forgiving the damage, and the abuser "wins," and thus there is a reason for not becoming better. Or they may feel driven to discover what happened during a period of time for which they cannot remember anything, as if the purpose of therapy is to uncover old memories, not to get better at living a satisfying life. Sometimes this investigation is overwhelming to their current stability and self-care: They have learned to think that their suffering is not important. They may feel driven to search for old memories that validate their suffering rather than see themselves as intrinsically defective or just "crazy."

Projective identification can occur in a way that is not detected by either client or therapist. The client´s automatic behavior may emotionally induce the therapist (sometimes through subliminal communication) to become frustrated or enraged, which can lead to hostile countertransference reactions from the therapist to the client (or vice-versa) that resemble and re-enact early relationship patterns (see chapter 10 about relational problems). We propose using the work on healthy self-care patterns as a part of the stabilization phase, in order to develop a "therapeutic stance" from the client. This is often a necessary step before other therapeutic interventions can be successfully used.

Case example

A 30 year old woman who has been chronically depressed for over 10 years is referred for a consultation. She feels bad for not being able to follow her previous therapist suggestions. Her therapist had told her different reasons why she should take care of herself and constantly insisted in her being more active in her care. Giving advice to clients, like this, is usually not helpful unless the client has an attitude of self-care. The client frequently attempted suicide because she thought she was a "lost case" and felt useless and depleted constantly. In her last suicide attempt, she injected insulin and when her family casually found her. It was a careful planned attempt where nobody was supposed to come home that weekend, she was almost unconscious and could not move. She received a beating, was kicked while lying on the floor and was told she was a selfish bitch. This client could not "feel bad," whenever she did, she was insulted and yelled at; but she could not feel good either, because she never received adequate care or loving attention from her parents. The father was an alcoholic who used to beat them, and she was the only one in the family that would stand up to him, frequently to protect her mother and siblings.

While trying to do RDI, we realized there was no positive sensation or feeling we could work on. Just the idea of thinking about her resources triggered self-devaluation. She could not find any positive issue and this made her feel defective and frustrated. So a "positive" task was used by the client to self-criticize. These are the type of situations that can emerge when self-care patterns are "inverted." So, we switched to a self-care intervention. We proposed the adult self to look at the child selecting a picture that she had "stolen" from her mother because she thought it was cute, "I don´t have many pictures of my childhood, maybe 4 or 5, I keep one that I stole from my mother, I was a cute baby." Although the client thought she did not have resources to take care of her, or to take care of her little inner child, the therapist knew she had resources to take care of other: her niece and nephew who loved her dearly.

So keeping in mind the client's capacities, we helped the client's adult self client to imagine taking care of the child she was. After an initial hesitation, she was very capable of imagining how she would nurture and support that little girl, with very little intervention from the therapist, who just guided the work reminding her about moments of efficacy and how well she cared for her niece and nephew.

Following this intervention the client's inner child felt safe, cared for, and seen. The adult self felt relief and was proud of her response. This gave her hope and led her to think, "I can learn to take care of myself." In the next session, the client said she felt much better and explained how she had begun to take care of herself in different ways, including limit setting. The change was impressive, the physical stance was tougher, and the attitude toward others had become more assertive, managing adequately interpersonal boundaries. These aspects had been explained previously (psychoeducation) to the client and although she could rationally understand the importance and logic of this information, she could not put them in practice until we worked on self-care patterns with BLS. After this single session on self-care, the client has not attempted suicide or tried to self-harm. Two years have passed so far.

The *loving eyes procedure* can be used both as a way to assess barriers to self-acceptance, and as a way to repair a lack of self-acceptance. When this method is being used, significant time and attention is devoted in the therapy to identifying and resolving the obstacles for the adult self to be able to see the child self with loving eyes.

We can think of these obstacles, whatever they may be, as psychological defenses, or, within a different theoretical context, dissociative phobias or substitute actions as explained in the theory of structural dissociation of the personality (Van der Hart et al., 2006). For example, an adult client might experience rejection or disgust toward an image of the child self. When this occurs, the disgust of the adult self is an overdetermined defensive response, which satisfies a defensive need to distance from the child's emotional pain, while still forming a connection with the child. Or, in terms of the theory of structural dissociation of the personality, this rejection or disgust can be understood as an expression of a phobia of a dissociative part. Other clients may say they have no emotion connected with looking at the child's image, but may have access to emotion when focusing on somatic sensations. Our main goal, in describing the procedures in this chapter is to present ways of removing defensive obstacles to self-acceptance, of actively enhancing self-acceptance and self-love, and in this way facilitating the clients' self-care.

Frequently, clients learn to look at themselves in a new way through the therapist's eyes. This is especially important for clients who are initially unable to see their own traumatized child parts in a compassionate way. The therapist can act as a model and as a safe attachment figure. In severely neglected and traumatized people, the therapist may be the first person to look at them with unconditional love and without judgment. Through the therapeutic relationship itself and by using specific techniques and interventions, we can guide the client to internalizing their capacities for adequate self-care. By doing this, we are introducing and developing a key concept for installation: a *self-care pattern* (Gonzalez, Seijo, & Mosquera, 2009).

The restoring of healthy self-care patterns can be woven into many interventions. For example, we can work with this approach from the meeting room (see chapter 13). Each time the adult self interacts with a dissociative part in the meeting place, we ask the adult self, "Look at the part and see what he needs, what do you the adult know that would help this child?" We teach the adult self how to recognize different necessities in different parts of their personality, how to care for other parts of their personality, how to help different parts to communicate, establish dialogue, find mutual acceptance, and resolve the fears and conflicts that initially existed. We help the adult self to establish a respectful relation with all parts of the personality where the needs of each part are respected; the adult self is leading the process with our modeling. By doing this, we facilitate the internalization of this healthy self-care pattern as we return the power to the client, increase his autonomy and decrease the risk of dependency from the client towards the therapist.

The Concept of a Healthy Self-Care Pattern

We believe adult self-care patterns tend to reflect and reproduce an internalization of the early patterns of caregiving between caregiver and child. Therefore, we define a healthy self-care attitude as the ways in which the adult self (the observer, *reflective self*) relates with compassion and acceptance for the *experiencing self*.

This concept is related to the self-compassion concept (Neff, Rude, & Kirkpatrick, 2007) and self acceptance (Shepard, 1979). In a broad sense, it is also related to self-valuation and self-esteem.

Elements of a Healthy Self-Care Pattern

To Look at Oneself with "The Best Possible Eyes"

This aspect can be summarized in this statement: to be one´s own best friend, with all the empathy, affection, and loyalty that the phrase implies. The person should treat himself the same way as he would treat the person they love the most. Some survivors of neglect offer more consistent mindsight and care to their own child or children, or other people, than to themselves. We can use their capacity to offer mindsight and care to a child or a loved one, even a loved pet, as a resource toward self-care. These "good eyes" are related to what Marsha Linehan (1993a) calls "radical self-acceptance," a sense of being loyal to one´s self no matter what. The radical acceptance and the observer stance in the acceptance and commitment therapy (Hayes, Strosahl, & Wilson, 1999) and the nonjudgmental view of mindfulness approaches (Bishop et al., 2004) are part of many psychotherapeutic approaches, as in recent years CBT (Segal, Williams, & Teasdale, 2002) and EMDR itself (Shapiro, 2001).

To Look at Oneself with "Realistic Eyes"

Healthy self-acceptance and self-care is different from pathological narcissism, which is typically an unrealistic self-image that defends against early trauma, neglect, and lack of adequate mirroring. Healthy self-care is founded on capacities to be: realistic (about past, present and future), to be empathetic and respectful towards others, and to gracefully acknowledge faults and errors. When people can truly accept themselves unconditionally, they love and accept themselves as fallible individuals who do not need to be perfect.

To Recognize and Validate One´s Own Needs

That means to be aware of our needs, based on the most basic sensations. Survivors of severe neglect have grown up without the ability to recognize or to differentiate basic sensations underlying their needs. A child who grows up with her basic emotional and physical needs ignored or shamed, lacks a clear discrimination between different sensations and needs, and as an adult, may only feel an undefined discomfort, that she cannot identify as a specific need that could or should be meet. Clients need to learn how to identify their sensations and emotions, to learn how to pay attention to them, and to consider them relevant and important. By being able to do this, they can develop the attitude that they have the right to meet their needs and to search for whatever is needed in order to do it.

To Protect Ourselves Adequately: Setting and Understanding the Need for Boundaries

When caregivers failed to recognize the client´s boundaries and/or failed to model healthy boundaries, clients may not just feel guilt about an impulse to assert boundaries, but may actually lack any internal model or recognition of where their boundaries need to be. Psychoeducation and the development of healthy models for personal boundaries need to be introduced and reinforced overtime. These interventions can lead to acceptance of the belief, "I am easily able to say ´no´ when I feel ´no,´ with complete respect for both myself and the other person."

To Achieve Equilibrium between Our Needs and the Needs of Others

Survivors of neglect often struggle with "black and white," "all or nothing" thinking, because healthy ways to balance conflicting needs were not modeled in their childhood. Clients, who not detect or give importance to their needs, may focus on meeting other´s needs. This can oscillate to the opposite extreme, when some of their needs guide their behavior without reflection or control (for example, binging). In this opposite extreme, some clients adopt a narcissistic stance, considering it their right to claim for immediate satisfaction of all of their requirements. The introspective or reflective stance intrinsic in the concept of self-care prevents impulsive acting on the needs of one part of the personality without considering the impulse from the perspective of the reflective capacity of the adult self and the impact on the whole self and others. An impulsive tendency of searching for needs influences our decisions. An adult decision-making is not driven by needs, the same way than a loving caretaker guides the child decision-making, teaching the child to recognize and respect other's needs, with reciprocity. This type of reciprocity is part of a satisfactory life.

Exploring Self-Care Patterns

The Self-Care Patterns Scale (SCPS) is a self-rated instrument of 55 items that was initially designed by Gonzalez and Mosquera (Gonzalez, Seijo, & Mosquera, 2009) and is being re-designed in this chapter. The client is asked to circle the percentage (from 0 to 100%) that fits best with the way they take care of themselves in different aspects of life: physical health; basic needs, such as eating and sleeping; healthy boundaries and balance in relationships; self-destructive behaviors; and positive statements about oneself. These questions are related to the usual pattern of the person's functioning, and not just to depressive states, low mental level, or any specific pathology.

This SCPS is still under analysis, but may already be useful for clinical purposes. As we have commented, different aspects of self-care are explored:

Physical Self-Care

Physical health and basic self-care activities (regular sleep, eating, exercise, and hygiene) are frequently impaired in severely traumatized people (Forgash, 2009, 2010). The following items of the Self-Care Patterns Scale explore this area:

- I get enough sleep to fit my needs.
- I try to have appropriate eating habits and eat healthy food.
- I exercise on a regular basis.
- A visit to the physician or the dentist is my last option.
- I have regular checkups (medical checkups).
- I go for a walk on a regular basis.
- I try to have a good aspect.
- I take care of my personal hygiene, even when I feel unhappy.

These problems may be not evident at all. The superficial and apparent "normality" of the client often does not allow us to be aware of these aspects, unless we specifically explore them with clinical sensitivity (Shedler, Mayman, & Manis, 1993).

Let's see an example. A DID client had a good professional performance as a teacher. She was a clever woman and, in some aspects, she could give amazing descriptions of her problems, and could maintain an excellent level of general functioning, in spite of her severe dissociative features.

Because of this, the therapist was not aware of her difficulties in very basic activities until several months had passed in the therapy. It then emerged that she never cleaned her house, and had some type of Diogenes syndrome. Exploring this problem, the therapist found out that she actually did not know how to clean, what products she could use, and so on. Her mother had never explained these basic things to her, because the mother was not a neat woman, and the client was absolutely focused on her studies while trying to isolate from her adverse environment. Her difficulties in relationships made it impossible for her to exchange this type of basic information with other people.

Some clients with histories of early and "complex trauma" show an evident deterioration. Others, like this client, maintain a façade of "apparent" normality that is superficially convincing. She cleaned the living room with damp tissues and did not realize how strange this was. The other rooms were in absolute chaos. On some occasion, she had tolerated an abusive partner because, among many other different reasons, he helped her to maintain "order" in the environment. When she finally broke up with him, the situation deteriorated dramatically. She suffered infectious diseases probably generated by noxious agents in a house where the garbage piled up. This information came up in therapy because the client was going to receive a visit from her mother, from whom she always tried to hide her problems. The therapist was shocked, since she could never have imagined that a "well-functioning" client (ANP) could have these types of difficulties.

The psychoeducational work with severely neglected and traumatized people often needs to include very basic knowledge on daily life activities. The reason for this client's behavior was not uniquely lack of information, but it was one of the related factors. Such clients may also need work to shift their motivation when the motivation of the ANP has been just to appear normal to the world. The goal of successful therapy would be to help the client experience the satisfaction and enjoyment of a clean house, regardless of whether anyone else notices.

Recognizing and Responding to Their Own Needs

Little babies do not know about needs: they only feel them. The caregiver is the one who names the child's needs, and by doing this, the infant learns to recognize them. The adult is the one who says, "You are just tired and need to take a rest," when the baby is crying from tiredness. By this interactive process, children learn to identify, recognize, value, and develop patterns of responding to their needs.

When the caregiver is not attentive, cannot attune with the children, or is not able to recognize the child's needs, this process can become distorted or impaired. Sometimes neglect develops with some needs but not others. For example, the caregiver may be focused on attending to material needs, but ignoring emotional ones. Other times, there are some specific needs that are denied. For example, the need for emotional expression and discharge may be repressed by the mother, by saying things like, "You are always complaining about everything," or "You are not really sad, you shouldn't be sad because of this insignificant problem" (invalidation). The mother may be avoiding her own sadness or is unable to regulate in her child an emotion that she cannot identify or regulate in herself.

Sometimes, the need might have been recognized but the satisfaction of it was impaired. When the child is used to satisfying the adult´s needs, it does not matter what the child needs, he will never search for it. Children learn they do not deserve to have their needs met. Many learn they do not deserve anything. As an example, a sexually abused girl tended to focus on her father´s needs because he always acted in order to get his needs met and just ignored hers. The mother was a submissive and depressed woman, victim herself of an abusive childhood environment. The mother could not model a psychic ability she lacked. The girl tended to be preoccupied with the mother´s needs, who often looked extremely vulnerable and hurt. Nobody was aware of what the girl needed or felt. She learned to do the same.

A malignant form of neglect with verbal abuse occurs when the mother suffers from a narcissistic personality disorder. In these families, the child sees the mother as highly attuned only to the fulfillment of her own needs and persistently experiences maternal invalidation of the child´s feelings and needs. The juxtaposition of the mother´s exaggerated sense of entitlement and the denial of the child´s feelings, needs, and aspirations, creates a complex layering of disconnection from self, highly distorted and negative self-perceptions, and a compulsive and defensive substitution of excessive care-giving for self-care. These are the items in the Self-Care Patterns Scale related to this issue:

- If I need something I can ask for it.
- I think that my "obligations" (what I have to do) are more important, than my wishes (what I would like to do).
- I usually consider other people needs come before mine.
- I can put my needs before other people´s needs if it is necessary.
- I tend to abide by my obligations and meet other people´s needs.
- I know how to take care of myself in an adequate way.
- I worry about other people´s needs just as much as I worry about mine.

A Realistic View of the Self

It is important not only to look at oneself with the best eyes. We also need to be realistic, to recognize our mistakes and imperfections, and consider the other´s needs as something relevant. A good enough parent feels an unconditional love toward the child, but also helps her or him to become a good human being and to adapt adequately to the environment.

This narcissistic, nonrealistic vision of the self can be a result of too much attention or lack of attention from the parents (Mosquera, 2008). Some parents treat their children as if they were at a superior level regarding others, only seeing grandiose possibilities for them. These parents frequently have narcissistic traits or try to "compensate" their own sense of unworthiness, or of not being good enough or important, through the child. They can seem "perfect" parents that "apparently" support the child, but they are truly relating to a "constructed and idealized" child. This child is not really being looked at with unconditional love; in reality this child is not even being "seen" (Mosquera & Gonzalez, 2011).

An exaggerated desire for "greatness" can be a way to build a sense of worth in the absence of parental praise or reinforcement (Stone, 1993). The sense of being special that he shows others is compensatory and actually covers an internal lack of self-worth. Sometimes guilt is so unbearable, that the person falls in the opposite extreme: the total absence of adequate responsibility and self-criticism. From the structural dissociation lenses, we can see both, narcissistic and vulnerable parts. The narcissistic aspect may be the "shell" of a helpless part, or the mask of the apparent normality of the ANP.

The capacity of looking at oneself with realistic eyes can be reflected in the following items:

- People should always be there when I need them.
- I don´t understand why other people don´t recognize how much I am worth.
- There are very few people who can be at my level.
- If I take care of others, they should do the same, and recognize and value me.
- I take care of others much better than other people.
- I always feel treated unfairly and I don´t understand why.
- I get angry or upset when people don´t respond to my needs immediately.
- People who are close to me have the obligation to take care of my needs.

Self-Harming Behaviors

Self-harming behaviors are present in 82% of dissociative disorders (Ebrinc et al., 2008). Clients who self-harm have higher scores on scales of dissociation and early trauma. Between 61-72% of clients with dissociative disorders attempt suicide and 1-2,1% commit suicide (Coons & Milstein, 1990; Putnam et al., 1986). In addition, 65% of clients with disorders of extreme stress have self-destructive behaviors (Van der Kolk et al., 2005) and over 65% have suicide concerns or attempts.

Childhood sexual and physical abuse correlates in an independent way with suicide and self-harming behavior in different mental disorders (Ystgaar et al., 2004). In clients with DESNOS or a severe dissociative disorder, the risk of suicide attempts should not be minimized (Coons & Milstein, 1990). Self-harming behaviors and suicide attempts can be considered extreme inversions of a healthy self-care pattern.

These clients frequently hide or minimize these behaviors, and even when detected, many therapists inaccurately associate these features with an attention seeking attitude. The same client we have commented on before presented many scars on her arms and abdomen caused by self-cutting, but she usually covered them with her clothes. When a therapist asked her about them, she minimized their importance and changed the subject.

Therapists may misunderstand these attitudes, attributing self-injury to attention seeking attitudes, and thereby inadvertently worsening this harming cycle, as we will describe on chapter 10 about relational problems. A more extreme expression of an "inverted self-care pattern" is found in some people who think of suicidal behavior as a way of "taking care of themselves," by seeking an escape from unrelenting misery, "In my worst moment, I treat myself in the worst way." In less extreme cases, the impulse for self-injury may reflect a reaction against the self: Because they are suffering or depressed, they blame themselves for feeling badly. It is as if their anger, an emotion which is often not accepted by survivors of abuse - they suffered the consequence of extreme and uncontrolled rage from the abuser - cannot be expressed, so they turn it against the self.

This inverted self-care pattern can also express an attempt to kill off some hated part of the self. Sometimes there is a mixture between this tendency and a desperate attempt of getting other people to take care of them, because they believe they do not have any resources at all for doing this. Both suicidal and non-suicidal self-injurious impulses are a good example of substitute actions (Van der Hart, Nijenhuis, & Steele, 2006), an extremely ineffective action to achieve the desired result.

Several items of the Self-care Patterns Scale explore this area with different kinds of self-regulation behaviors and interpersonal issues:

- I interact with people who don´t care for me and mistreat me.
- I stand situations or relationships which are harmful for me (for too long).
- I do things that I know are bad for me.
- Sometimes I behave in a self-destructive way.
- Sometimes I act in a self-destructive way because I deserve it.
- I have used alcohol or drugs to "feel better."
- Sometimes I use medication to sleep and try not to think.
- When I feel bad, I get angry with myself for feeling like that, and I am always blaming myself.
- When I feel bad, I try to cheer up and do things that make me feel better.

Tolerating and Assimilating Interpersonal Positive Affect and Recognition

Survivors of early neglect and abuse often were insufficiently exposed to early maternal play and maternal infant dialogue (Dutra et al., 2009), as well as normal caregiver recognition in childhood of the positive aspects of their inner lives (Mindsight: Siegel, 1999). As adults, they therefore may find normal experiences of positive social recognition anxiety producing. As a result, they may fail to even notice such interactions (covert failure to perceive), or while noticing them, they may develop a variety of overt (behavioral) and covert (mental actions) defenses against assimilating these experiences. Other survivors may have been explicitly verbally and/or physically abused by one or more caregivers for expressing pride, excitement, or personal interests. This could be because their specific interests or activities were in conflict with the preferences of a narcissistic caregiver. It could also be because the caregiver was generally intolerant of such expressions of positive emotional states related to their own impaired self-image or narcissistic defenses. Here are items from the SCPS reflecting capacities to tolerate and assimilate interpersonal positive affect:

- Others regularly give me compliments, appreciation, and positive recognition.
- I change the subject, make a joke, or verbally reject the compliments, appreciation, and praise others offer me.
- When others give me praise, appreciation, or compliments, I suspect they are trying to trick, use, or manipulate me.
- I get good feelings about myself when others give me praise, compliments, and appreciation.
- The good feelings about myself that I get from others when they give me appreciation, praise, and compliments stay with me and help me feel good about myself when I am coping with difficult situations.

Engaging in Activities or Relationships that are Positive for Oneself

Even when individuals experience good feelings with recognition and appreciation, or in direct relation with these aspects, severely disturbed people are not used to dedicating time to pleasant activities or actions oriented to their wellbeing. They are not used to thinking of things that can bring on positive emotions or sensations. They often think that they do not deserve to be good or to enjoy live. Many are trapped by shame and guilt and are convinced they only deserve bad things. In their early environment, enjoying life was not a common feature, so they did not learn this basic aspect of life. In many cases, their enjoyment of life was punished or criticized. Basic aspects as play were seen as selfish behaviors by the parents, for example, "You only think about playing when there are so many things to do in the house, you are so selfish."

Often they cannot relax and just not do anything. They tend to fill their time with never-ending activities, but these activities are not necessary pleasant or useful. They tend to have difficulties being by themselves and not doing anything, thinking in terms of "this is wasted time." One consequence of this pattern is that the client becomes exhausted without ever "recharging batteries."

Some of the items that take these aspects into account are:

- I spend part of my time occupied in activities that are pleasant and fun.
- I spend time with my friends.
- I usually dedicate some time to myself.

Being Able to Ask for Help and Accept it

Trauma survivors are frequently people who had to survive on their own. Primary caregivers were not attentive and were not there when the client needed it. Some people in the family of origin were abusive, and a non-abusive parent was usually victimized by the abuser, sometimes presenting a depressive state. Frequently there was nobody to turn to for help. Sometimes, when the client asked for help, he was blamed, distrusted, or punished by the non-abusive parent. So they adapted to not ask for help. They learned that asking for help is not useful and sometimes even makes things worse. They associate asking for help as a sign of weakness. Some have a very hard time asking for help because they have learned that this "bothers others."

At other times, distrusting is a relevant factor in this pattern. Severely traumatized people have many difficulties in relationships. Their early adverse experiences and attachment disturbances have taught them that "people are evil" and they "can´t trust anybody." To seek help is understood as an expression of weakness, and people could take the opportunity to damage them. They remain fixated in their memories of adverse experiences in relationships, where people betrayed their trust by abusing or asking for inappropriate things. Some suffered in help-seeking situations with other people, due to their perceptual errors in failing to recognize and respond to danger signals, leading to a tendency for re-traumatization.

There are two items in the Self-care Patterns Scale that are related to this aspect:

- There are people that I can talk to about my problems.
- When I feel unhappy, I can ask for help and let other people take care of me.

Hypertrophic Caregiver Role

The common natural phenomena in human beings are two adults taking care of their child. But frequently things do not turn out that way. One of the adults ignores or hurts the baby and, at the same time, ignores or damages the other parent. The child tends to strongly attach to the non-abusive parent and the reciprocal role procedure (Ryle & Kerr, 2002) is usually inverted: The child takes care of the victimized, vulnerable, or depressed parent. Sometimes, in a home where no adult enacts a caregiver role, children need to take care of each other or one of them takes care of their siblings. This out-of-place caregiver role gives the person a sense of control and mastery often absent in other early life situations, which makes it a preferential, reinforced action system. These people tend to take care of others while minimizing or completely denying their own necessities and desires.

The need to please others in order to avoid damage from them is another mechanism underlying this pattern. Although this could serve as a protective mechanism when the client was a child, in adulthood it becomes pathological.

Several items in the scale are related to this lack of equilibrium between caring for oneself and others:

- I am always taking care of other people, but nobody takes care of me.
- I accept and take care myself.
- I treat myself the same way I treat other people.
- Sometimes I think that people only turn to me when they need something.

- There is a balance between what I give and what I receive

Adequate Boundaries and Limits

Boundaries of an abused child are frequently violated systematically, both at a bodily and an emotional level. Nobody effectively protects the child, and he does not learn self-protection. In the client´s early environment, to say "no" was not only impossible, but also dangerous. A submissive (Herman, 1992; Ogden, Minton, & Pain, 2002) response was often the only available surviving mechanism, becoming chronic with time (learned helplessness).

These clients often experience themselves as extremely vulnerable and weak. The proactive action systems of fight/flight (Van der Hart, Nihenhuis, & Steele, 2005) had to be blocked in the interest of survival Furthermore, the fight action system is mediated by the rage, and this emotion is usually associated in the client´s mind with the abuser´s figure. The ability to say "no" needs an adequate and proportionate anger for performing it. But the anger and rage are partially or totally dissociated in survivors of abuse, and in more dissociative clients, are associated only with persecutory parts which generally direct the anger internally. The apparently normal part of the personality (Van der Hart, Nihenhuis, & Steele, 2005) often presents – as a negative dissociative symptom – a lack of assertiveness that has as it reverse an extreme rage, which may appear in the inner world or as uncontrolled outbursts on the outside.

Clients may have difficulties with being aware of their personal limits. They have survived such adverse circumstances that they fail to realize they cannot cope with everything all the time. They tend to take care of other people´s problems, to bear too much, to persist too much… until some circumstances stop them. "I am strong" is a compensatory belief which helps them to feel protected from further damage and to des-identify from the victimized-weak parent. But, as a compensatory belief, it is rigid and does not allow flexible, alternative coping mechanisms when the "I" who can "deal with everything" fails. The following items in the self-care scale are related to this aspect:

- I am able to know when to slow down my pace and take a break.
- When somebody asks me to do something I know is wrong, I am able to say no without a doubt.
- I let other people approach me with inappropriate manners.
- It´s hard for me to say no, even when I have to do things I dislike.
- It´s hard for me to defend my rights
- I am easily influenced by other people´s opinion, even when I know I am right.
- I am a worthy person and feel that I should be treated the same way that I treat others.

Interventions

Psychoeducational Interventions

Survivors of early neglect and trauma often lack positive memory networks containing adaptive information. When they do have relevant positive memory networks, they have difficulty accessing them when dysfunctional memory networks are triggered. Frequently, the therapist needs to introduce adequate information about what children need for healthy development to learn emotional self-management: to be deserving of good self-care, to form positive models of receiving support from others while having clear boundaries, and to develop balance in their interpersonal relationships. This explicit information should be coherent with modeling of all these aspects in the therapeutic relationships.

The Self-Care Patterns Scale provides a structured instrument to reflect on "How am I taking care of myself" and "How my present problems are related to my self-care." Even clients who cannot tolerate directly confronting their traumatic past, usually show no distress when they score the SCPS. In some cases, we can try to search for and reprocess the early memories that are feeding the present pattern of impaired self-care. But when doing this is not appropriate in the beginning of therapy, we can help the client realize that he can learn to take care of himself differently in the here and now, no matter how badly he was cared for others during his childhood.

Many clients with dysfunctional early attachment have difficulties on one hand, realizing what was inadequate regarding their primary caregivers and, on the other hand, saying bad things about them. When we are talking about a victimized or idealized parent, they may perceive such disclosures as a betrayal toward their family. The therapist should help these clients to understand that thinking and speaking about what hurt them is not a judgment about those people, but a way to improve themselves, and this cannot provoke any damage. Time needed for doing this process differs from one client to another, and the therapist should be attentive to the client´s timing.

The Self-Care Patterns Scale is a useful tool to help clients realize their difficulties in these aspects. More than as a psychometric instrument to obtain a percentage, we think it is useful for clinical purposes, to help clients to be aware of how they are functioning in this area. This instrument can be used from the first sessions, and is not so difficult as approaching early traumatic memories. But even with people who are not prepared for talking about their difficult past, we can explain how some adverse early experiences influence the way we take care of ourselves. This way, we introduce an interesting reformulation of the client´s problem, "The problem is not me, it is something that I learned, that everybody would learn in the same circumstances." A healthy self-care pattern is something I could not learn during my childhood, but I can learn now. This will be a good goal for therapy.

Working with the Inner Child

The work with the inner child has been proposed by different therapeutic approaches (Missildine, 1963; Watkins & Watkins, 1997; Whitfield, 1987). In the EMDR approach, Jim Knipe has proposed the *"loving eyes" procedure* (2008, pp 184-188). In this procedure, Knipe proposes to ask the client to look at the child without judgment, just observing the child, from the perspective of the safety of the therapist´s office.

This instruction, to "just look at that child, and see what you see," combined with bilateral stimulation, typically results in a lessening of the phobia in the ANP (the adult) toward the EP (the child). The client notices (from the adult) the experience of the child who is in an overwhelming and traumatizing situation, and in the process, the dysfunctional memories of the child part are witnessed, validated, and shifted into resolution (narrative memory). The dissociative separation then, between the ANP and the EP, is lessened or eliminated, resulting in what the structuralists call "synthesis" and Shapiro calls "adaptive resolution." We propose to introduce more elements in this procedure, working from the same structure. As the adult continues to "see" the child, more information will emerge regarding what the child needed at that time. When this child represents an EP with a high first person perspective (mental autonomy), the adult self can have a complex interaction and dialogue with this child, who may have information, unknown to the adult, about trauma events, or may act in ways that may surprise or cause dislike in the adult. Even when the child has low or no mental autonomy, this dialogue is possible, but the way in which this process develops can give us information about structural dissociation and early attachment.

Case example

> Therapist: When you look at this child´s eyes, what do you see?
>
> Client: I can´t really see the child, her back is turned.
>
> T: And what do you feel when you see her that way?
>
> C: I don´t like it.
>
> T: And where do you feel it in your body?
>
> C: I feel an uncomfortable sensation on my stomach.
>
> T: Focus on that sensation (BLS). What is coming?
>
> C: The sensation decreases.
>
> T: And how do you see the child now?
>
> C: I can see her face, but I can´t see her eyes, she is looking down.
>
> T: Can you understand why it is so difficult for her to look at your eyes?
>
> C: No, I can´t.
>
> T: Okay, just think about that (BLS). What is coming?

C: She seems ashamed.

T: Go with that (BLS). What is coming?

C: She seems to be calmer.

T: Fine. And how do you feel?

C: I feel I am unable to take care of her.

T (knowing that the client can perform a caregiver role with her niece): How do you take care of your niece?

C: That´s a different issue.

T: Just think about how you do it with your niece (BLS). What is coming?

C: I can understand how she feels, other people can´t.

T: Go with that (BLS).

C: My niece likes to be with me.

T: Now try to look at that child inside you with the same eyes that you look at your nice (BLS).

C: I don´t know how to take care of her.

T: She doesn´t need that you know everything. Children don´t need perfect parents, they just need to be important and special for somebody. Even when you didn´t feel this in your childhood, to look at this child in a new way, the way you look at your niece, can repair this… Maybe she only needs that you see her and tell her that you are learning to take care of her. This is true, you are learning, aren´t you?

C: I don´t know.

T: I know you have learned some things (giving examples from the client´s history and progress in therapy).

C (feeling recognized by the therapist): Yes, I did.

T: So just tell her that you are learning to take care of her (BLS).

C: Okay.

T: How do you think about it?

C: I think I could.

T: And how does she look?

C: She seems to be better.

T: Could be this a good point to stop?

C: I think so.

T: And what about the child?

C: She says it´s okay.

T: Fine. We will continue working on this.

We can propose different interactions between the adult and the child:

1. "Seeing."
2. "Seeing feelings."
3. Eliciting a response from the child to the adult, "What if that child could hear what you are saying right now?" "What would she say to you?"
4. The adult identifying the child needs, considering them important, and searching for ways to meet them.
5. The adult responding to the child´s self-referencing negative cognitions.
6. Psychoeducational interweaves of safe attachment aspects.
7. Dialogue between adult and child.
8. A caregiving interaction from the adult to the child.
9. Asking the child to "look out the eyes" into the therapist´s office.
10. Joining with the loving adult: "The child is here in my heart now."
11. Contact and caring through somatic sensations.

When the EP has enough first person perspective to dialogue with the adult, the therapist should modulate this communication. Phobic reactions from the adult can be processed with bilateral stimulation, in a similar way as in Knipe´s procedure. If an ANP is phobic of an EP, the dominant affect is likely to be the ANP´s urge to avoid thinking of the EP, and this urge can be targeted with bilateral stimulation (Knipe, in Luber, 2009). But this work goes beyond the processing of the avoidance; we introduce during processing relevant information about self-care, which will be linked at this point by BLS. The adult should understand what the child needed at the time of the trauma. This question is in itself a change of perspective, very relevant when nobody was attentive to the child´s needs during those years.

When a child is very little, it is the responsibility of the good enough caregiver to notice and name the real needs of the child and to try meeting them. Through the attuned responses of the caregiver, the child learns to recognize his sensations and emotions and the needs they are expressing. The client needs to reactivate this process, to re-learn it from the first steps, with the help, the information, and the modeling of the therapist. It does not matter how old the inner child is, we always should ask for permission and explain each step we are doing, showing a deep respect. In neglectful and traumatizing environments, children are often ignored or treated as objects for meeting adult´s needs. Their boundaries are violated and they are treated as a person with few or no basic needs and rights. All these aspects should be kept in mind and guide not just the specific procedure, but the style and the language that we use, caring not only about what we are saying, but about how the client and each dissociative part can be understanding our words. We should have in mind that the child part might initially be afraid of the adult part and the therapist, because of previous negative experiences with adults.

Some clients are easily able to care for others, but have great difficulty in caring for themselves. These clients may express hatred for the self or disinterest in their own welfare, in a way that appears odd or highly irrational Therapists may be tempted to get into a strange debate with such clients, where the therapist is presenting evidence of the client´s adequacy and "okayness," while the client is arguing and pointing out examples of how they have failed, or how they were unworthy. This is an example of projective identification, where the therapist is verbalizing the positive half of the debate that actually is within the client.

Cognitions and affect of shame often serve a defensive function. Experientially, for a child in an abusive or neglectful environment, to think, "I am a bad child with good parents," may be factually incorrect, but nevertheless may feel better to the child than the truth of the situation, "I am a good and innocent child in a situation where I am being neglected or abused by the only people available to take care of me." That thought is too frightening for most children to hold even briefly, although the affect of that reality may linger with the child, or the child-grown-up, as an affect of helplessness, abandonment, or despair that lingers in the background.

In Tomkins´ affect theory (1962), primary shame affect is triggered whenever there is mismatch between needed responses from a caregiver and actual responses. Infants and children instinctively reach out with their eyes, their voices, and their arms to express their attachment needs to their caregivers. Children with neglectful and abusive caregivers recurrently experience primary shame when expressing their most basic needs. These states of shame induce downcast head and eyes and mental confusion. As language and self-concept emerge, their self-concept is associated with these recurrent states of shame leading to self-concepts of unworthiness and defectiveness and avoidance of expressing basic attachment needs. The self-statements that emerge from these recurrent experiences of shame affect may serve a defensive function.

Another reason that shame is so often observed in abused children may have to do with learned helplessness (Seligman & Maier, 1967) and the dorsal vagal pattern of parasympathetic activation (Porges, 2008), that can occur as a result of situations of recurring, inescapable pain, immobility, or imminent death. And, sadly, children are often explicitly shamed and blamed by parents for situations that actually were caused by the parents. For all these reasons, shame – both as a core identity and as a dominant affect – is often observed in people who experienced severe abuse and neglect as children.

Adult clients who come to therapy with this dynamic often benefit by a twofold approach: First, it can be helpful for the client to reach a cognitive understanding of the defensive function of their shame feelings – that it was a way to keep hope and a positive image of caretakers during childhood. And then, it is often useful to target, using EMDR, key images of neglect or abuse, with the focus on the physical sensations of shame affect – the shutdown feeling, the sense of being intrinsically "bad," the lowered head (Knipe, 2009).

The client often has caring capacities that can be expressed toward others, but cannot turn these capacities toward the self. Sometimes by introducing short fragments of BLS in the procedure, the system spontaneously evolves toward a healthy self-care pattern, connecting the caregiving networks with the neglected self-care networks. But more commonly, the therapist will need to direct the intervention toward this synthesis.

A frequent situation is that clients become locked into a negative view of themselves, when they regard themselves in the same way as their own early caregivers did. In this situation, it can be useful to ask clients if they are looking through their own eyes, the same eyes through which they look at other people around them. When a pathologic idealization of the caregiver is present, careful psychoeducational interventions should be interweaved in the procedure. Then, we ask clients how they would look at the same situation if they were looking at the person they love most in the world in that situation. We help clients to connect with their caregiver role, asking questions and promoting talking about it and connecting with that role. When they are doing this, we then ask clients to just change the image and look at their inner child this way. Once the client is doing this, we introduce BLS.

The goal of the procedure is that the adult can look at the child with unconditional love and acceptance, with loving eyes. The adult should be able to say to the child, "I will (learn to) take care of you a different way than they did." A useful interweave from the therapist is, "Would you know how to take care of this child?" "Would you do a better job than they did?"

The steady eye contact from adult to child is very important, because it increases true connection. Without eye contact, the adult can be rationalizing, but eye contact activates emotional aspects of the attachment system. Focusing on the somatic sensation in the adult part is also important. Emotions can be interpretations, and the body sensations can be divergent. We always choose the somatic element: The body does not lie.

The exercise can end when both parts agree to an imaginary demonstration of love, like a hug, holding hands, or something like that. Sometimes more disturbing elements come in, and we can reprocess these with BLS. When child and adult can experience some kind of physical connection, we reinforce it with BLS. We can propose the client to hold himself and imagine that he is holding the baby. Or he can notice where in the body he is feeling the child inside and then put his hand on this place and feel the contact, reinforcing it with BLS.

When a self-care pattern is successfully installed, we can propose homework to reinforce and integrate this experience into daily life. The client can repeat the exercise at home, and take care of the child, talk to her before sleep, or notice contact with the child during activities that she could "enjoy like a child," now that she is not stuck in the past. We can prepare this homework during the session, identifying which activities or aspects of daily life this child could enjoy (or learn to enjoy), reinforcing the sensation with BLS, and then prescribing it as homework. Understanding the basics of the work with this procedure, we can be creative adapting this to the client's situation and timing. This procedure is a useful early intervention, which facilitates further therapeutic work.

Working with Parts and Self-Care

Different parts should learn to take care of each other. This is part of the process of increasing cooperation in the dissociative system. Every time that we make contact with a dissociative part, for the adult self, it is an opportunity for modeling and enhancing a healthy self-care pattern. The adult part should learn to notice and understand the needs underlying each part, to realize that all these needs can find an adaptive expression. We work to develop a more integrative capacity, which can allow a new equilibrium between all those elements.

The therapist should be attentive to interactions between different parts and should encourage changing competitive, fearful, and antagonistic attitudes toward an understanding of the other part´s needs. We foster the perspective of looking at other parts as resources, not enemies. One part can take care of another, and this can be a powerful stabilization ability.

We can interweave psychoeducational bits into this process. Severely traumatized people do not have the necessary adaptive information about what is and is not adequate in relationships. For example, when the adult self is looking at a very little child part, he should learn to figure out what needs this part has. The experience when he was a child could be that the child might be attentive to the adult´s needs, denying his own needs. Modeling a new relationship between the adult self and the childlike part, we introduce relevant healthy information.

We can say, "Sometimes adults are so overwhelmed with their own problems that cannot look at their children. In these situations, children usually tend to meet the adult´s needs in order to maintain some type of attachment, but this creates many problems. It´s as if you give meat to a two-month-old baby. He is not prepared for this. It is not the time for this… When you learn to take care of others before adequately being cared for, very early, you don´t learn to take care of yourself or to feel comfortable focusing on your own needs. It´s like now, in your life. You often pay more attention to taking care of others, than you do to taking care of yourself."

We connect the past experience with the inner pattern of relationship. BLS can be introduced to reinforce new patterns or moments of realization, or to process any element which is blocking the "change of paradigm" toward valuing self-care.

Increased compassion between inner parts tends to expand to outside relationships (Neff, et al., 2007). But we can enhance this and "turn it toward the outside" by helping the client understand how changing this pattern of self-care will influence his interactions with people in current life.

Self-Care as a Form of Emotional Self-Regulation

Frequently these clients have problems tolerating different emotions. Sometimes they are overwhelmed by intense emotions, other times they reject any specific emotion. For example, they cannot tolerate shame, and this can alter the global emotional management. Or they cannot tolerate anger, because early experiences related to rage involve hurting: Because "my abusive enraged parent harmed me," it somehow implies that rage is "always damaging."

The reaction toward the emotion can be understood as a dissociative phobia of trauma-derived mental actions (Van der Hart et al., 2006) and can be reprocessed with specific procedures (Knipe, 2009; Leeds, 2006; Gonzalez, Mosquera, & Seijo, 2010). In chapter 8, we will discuss the reprocessing of dissociative phobias, which can be understood as a variant of defense processing. Van der Hart would process intense anger with his method of bringing parts together and creating realization through "sharing" of experience and mutual cognitive understanding. This procedure of guided synthesis shares many elements with EMDR trauma reprocessing protocols (chapter 12 about trauma processing).

The Caring for the Baby Procedure

As we mentioned before, from the self-care perspective, the client can learn to see his emotions as expressions of needs, which should be understood and met, instead of as enemies. A way to change this pattern is the "caring for the baby procedure" that, besides being a mindful exercise, introduces a pattern of adequate caregiving.

We use the caring for the baby procedure with a client while he is experiencing a disturbing emotion:

1. We check that focusing on a little baby evokes caring tendencies. If the client has a negative experience with babies (e.g., abortion, loss of their own children), we can change the baby image for a pet or use a symbolic representation of the emotion.

2. With some clients, it is useful to symbolize the emotion in order to get perspective and imagine the emotion as something that we are observing. This symbolization can benefit both clients who tend to "immerse" into the emotion and those who experience difficulties to connect with it. To introduce this symbolic aspect we can say, "Imagine a sculpture of this emotion: what color, size, texture, temperature... does this emotion have?" Another option is to draw the emotion or use any intermediary object to represent it, like a stuffed animal or a doll.

3. Looking at the symbolic representation of the emotion or directly noticing it when it is possible, we embody the emotion, saying, "Notice where you feel that emotion in your body."

4. We change from the pure emotion to the baby figure, "Imagine that in this place there is a little baby, or directly notice it."

5. When a baby evokes negative associations, we use the same suggestion with a pet, or we ask the client to place the paper with the drawing of the emotion, or the stuffed animal or doll, on the body, where the emotion is located.

6. When we have a wound, we instinctively put our hand on it. When we see a baby who has suffered an injury, to caress the injured area is a usual ritual between mothers and little

children. In this stage, we promote this caring gesture associated with the somatic sensation, "Now put your hand on this place, and take care of this baby who is feeling so badly."

Often, clients who are rejecting an emotion place their hands on the somatic area associated with the emotion, but the gesture is not of caring, it seems more like if they wanted to rip the emotion out. When we observe this, we can introduce "mindful" information, "Some people fight against their emotions, but it only makes emotions get worse. To fight with our emotions is like fighting against ourselves: we cannot win... it´s important to try to let the emotion be there, and just try to take care of it."

We model this interaction because clients often do not have good regulatory capacities with others. We will say this as if we were talking about general examples, "To regulate a little baby we need a lot of patience, you know... Sometimes it helps to speak to them in a low voice, very softly... Sometimes they only need to feel we are there, being present and attentive to whatever they are feeling. It doesn´t matter how badly they feel... Sometimes they feel our warmth, our breath, and slowly they become more and more regulated... At some moments, you might become worried because he is not yet feeling better, but you are client. You take a breath and remember that he will be better with time, and that for the baby it is very important to feel that the adult is there, present; that he is comforting him. With time, this experience will help him to learn to comfort himself..."

When a client is able to perform an adequate caregiver role with other children or other people, it can be useful to help the client to stand in this role so he can learn to turn it toward himself, "Sometimes it is a difficult and long process to regulate a baby, especially when he is crying a lot, and he is suffering... It´s difficult, but you know that by being there, he won´t feel alone while is experiencing that, this is the most important thing... You don´t become desperate when he doesn´t become immediately calm, because you know that you are doing the best for him."

The most important aspect of this intervention is not the content of the verbal message, but the non-verbal way of doing it. We model putting our hand on the same place (on our own body) where the client is noticing the emotion, and we use a slow, peaceful tone of voice. When the client experiences frustration, desperation or impatience in the face of his emotion, we show how to regulate it with trust in the client´s capacities, serenity, and patience. But we always talk about this in an indirect way, as if we were speaking about how adults care for babies in general.

For example, when we see that the client is becoming upset because the emotion does not immediately decrease, and we say, "Sometimes it takes time. We can feel desperate, but we remember that emotions always change, that a baby won´t be crying forever... Because of this we think: This is difficult, but I know that it will change, I know that me being here and remaining calm is helping the baby..."

Depending on the client, we may choose to introduce or not to introduce BLS in this process. Some clients experience a direct relaxation response with BLS, which can help the regulatory process. Others experience a more intense sensation, which can be counterproductive. So, from previous clinical experiences with the client, we will decide whether to use BLS or not. As a general rule, we can start without BLS and progressively use it to install the developing regulatory ability, and finally use it during the entire process to reinforce achievements. But this general rule should be adapted to each particular case.

Positive Affect Tolerance

Leeds (2006) has proposed a modified EMDR protocol for Positive Affect Tolerance and Integration (PAT). His approach begins with psychoeducation on the importance of shared interpersonal positive affect. Next, clients learn and practice a 3-step behavioral exercise in the office. When they return, they are asked to report on their observations of their ability to practice this exercise in their daily lives. Then moments of interpersonal positive affect and connection, which trigger a mixture of positive affect and defensive anxiety, are selected and reprocessed with the PAT procedural steps. This process is repeated until clients demonstrate a growing and stable capacity to tolerate and assimilate experiences of interpersonal connection with shared positive affect into their self-capacities and self-image.

Survivors of pervasive emotional neglect, with little or no regular exposure to early shared positive affect and caregiver mindsight, may benefit from working "in the present" with the PAT protocol, which can help them learn to gradually tolerate and assimilate shared positive affect into their self-concept and their interpersonal schemas. Alternately, survivors of early abuse may recall recurrent childhood experiences of being "punished" - with verbal or physical abuse - for showing positive affects of pride, excitement, or joy. Their defenses against experiencing or showing these positive affects may need to be addressed with standard EMDR reprocessing on these early childhood memories.

Installing the Equilibrium

Sometimes the problem is not a single emotion but the change between emotional states and the difficulty in tolerating the coexistence of different, and sometimes contradictory, emotions toward an issue. The client grew up in an often contradictory and chaotic environment, where separating these extreme reactions was one of the few available ways to adapt to that situation (separating the rage against the abuser from the powerlessness and the need of attachment). But now he no longer needs to do this. We explain that ways of coping that were useful in the "there and then" can be a problem in the "here and now." In the present he can learn "a different way of experiencing things."

This capacity can be trained with the adult self, looking at his different aspects, reactions, or emotions. It is useful to draw a future picture of how it would be to experience this mixture of emotions. The sense of rejection toward each emotional aspect or reaction can be reprocessed one at a time. When all these separate reactions are held in a less defensive manner, a "global look" encompassing them all can be installed. This can lead to an experience of "equilibrium" and the capacity to reflect in the face of a mixture of emotions.

Including Memories of Dysfunctional Self-Care Patterns in the Therapeutic Plan

Memories of early dysfunctional patterns of self-care from childhood should be reprocessed with EMDR as soon as the client's readiness and stability allow EMDR memory reprocessing. Some clients, even with relevant structural dissociation, tolerate the reprocessing of memories with standard procedures or with minor modifications. For others, it can be overwhelming. When the client can realize how these memories are related to present dysfunctional self-care patterns, they may agree to reprocess them.

The decision about when to proceed with trauma work should be based on both a collaborative discussion between client and therapist and the therapist's clinical judgment. When the client can tolerate this intervention, it is important not to delay it. When we realize the client cannot tolerate direct reprocessing of early disturbing memories, or when we have doubts about it, the previous procedures can be a way to progressively approach confronting these early memories while monitoring the client's responses.

As these memories are resolved, other issues may emerge that impinge on achieving consistent self-care, which can lead to selecting other interventions. Unless we explore working on the origins of impaired self-care, clients can become focused on trying to get from the therapist all that they never received from primary caregivers; or, without being aware of it, they may blame the therapist for their suffering. Clients seek psychotherapy for diverse reasons and present various symptoms. When we introduce work on self-care patterns early, we can define therapy as caring while holding the client responsible for learning to improve their self-care. By introducing specific strategies and skills to enhance self-care, we define the therapeutic process as a way of changing the impact of early experiences of neglect and abuse on the clients' capacities for self-care.

Case-description

A client38-year-old woman who suffered severe emotional abuse and neglect in childhood passed from an extremely authoritarian father, head of a religious sect, to an authoritarian partner, also part of the same sect. She had never had an independent life until her partner abandoned her. So, she had no resources to be autonomous. Her self-esteem and self-reliance were extremely low. After three sessions of working on resources and some limited self-care interventions, testing the effects of short sets of BLS, we tried to reprocess a difficult moment with an emotionally abusive new partner, who was not allowing her to make adaptive changes in daily life.

She said things like, "I am always questioning myself." During reprocessing, she said she was calm, but when the therapist asked her (because her nonverbal language did not seem calm at all), "Do you really feel calm, or are you forcing yourself to be calm?" she said, "I am forcing myself." After some minutes of apparent improvement, she looks tired and said:

> Client: I am trying to control it (the emotion) but, as I am following your fingers, there is that voice in the back of my head questioning myself.

Therapist: Focus on that voice. How old does it seem?

C (after thinking for a while): You are making me think … I recognize that she is the one who is questioning me.

T: How old does she seem?

C: Seven.

T: If you look at her eyes, without judgment, just observing, what do you see?

C: She is very responsible.

T: She needed to become very responsible, is this right? (Client nods) What do you think she needs?

C (reflectively): Love.

T: Just notice that.

BLS (installing).

T: Take a breath… what is coming?

C: A little bit of sadness.

T: It must have been hard, to be so responsible being so little.

When we see that the client is reflectively thinking about this we do a short set of BLS.

T: Take a breath… How does she look now?

C: She is lost; she is searching for an exit.

The adult self has told us before what the EP needs: love. So, we can sense what would be the exit.

T: Can you hold her and tell her that you know that she had to become very responsible since she was very little, but that things can begin to be different now, and that you are there to take care of her?

C (nodding while the therapist was asking the question): Yes.

BLS.

T (during BLS): Let her notice, by holding her, that you are there….

T (after BLS): Take a breath… What is coming? What do you notice?

C: I am tired, but I want to fight… but…

The client seems to be connecting with memories from the past, but at this moment, we did not think focusing on traumatic material was a good idea. Directly addressing early experiences was seen as important, but the therapist, reflecting on the intensely depressive state of the client and the ongoing traumatization she was still experiencing, asked the client if she thought she could tolerate going into those memories. She had previously said, "I don´t know. It was very hard." So, in spite of her present statements indicating that she wants to overcome those memories, the therapist decided to do a balanced intervention.

T: There are many things from the past that we can start to work on, but we will do it little by little... How does the girl look?

C: I recognize her, I see her.

T: How do you think she feels?

C: After hearing all these things?

T: Yes.

C: She is holding my hand, getting closer to me.

BLS (reinforcing connection).

T: Take a breath... What is coming now?

C: Calm, a little bit of calm.

T: Can she notice it also?

C: Yes.

BLS (reinforcing a co-consciousness issue).

T: What is coming now?

C: She wants to overcome all these issues.

T: Tell her that we will work on these sensations. Today we have begun this work, now she is aware that she is not alone, that you are there. Can she notice that you are there?

The emotional part and the adult self seem to be more ready for trauma work. But two issues were relevant in the decision not to commence it at that time. The first one was to guarantee enough time to adequately deal with trauma work, because the time of the session was close to its end. The second one was to maintain the focus of the session. We should balance a flexible stance with the need to maintain a certain degree of coherence and structure in our interventions. Working around a specific focus (self-care in this case) allows us to identify more clearly the effects of each intervention.

C: Yes.

T: Notice it both, you and her.

BLS.

T: Take a breath.

C: I realize she needs help.

T: Can you notice her with you? Client nods. Where can you notice her in your body?

C (placing her hands on both sides of her trunk): Over here.

T (mirroring the client´s gesture): Let her notice that you are there, (during BLS) that you will take care of her.

T: Take a breath... What do you notice?

C: She doesn´t let go of me.

T: And how do you feel?

C: Fine. I want to have the capacity for doing this (take care of her).

T (promoting the adult self): You know you have it, you are very good at taking care of others.

C (nodding): I have a lot of capacity to care for others, but none for me.

T: It´s about learning to use it with yourself. You have this capacity, it´s very developed... Let her know this.

This can be understood as a two-step interweave (Leeds, 2009). Step one, accesses adult self-capacities toward others. Step two, expresses the possibility to redirect this capacity toward self.

BLS.

C (after a deep breath): I am thinking about what I will say to her... I am holding her, and she feels better... I feel better.

When the emerging *adult self* was concerned about saying the adequate words to the little one, the voice appeared again, with different characteristics than before (less hard and rigid, she was feeling better), reminding the ANP, "I am here." The child EP was changing from a perfectionist style, which she had to learn due to her authoritarian father, to a childlike style, more adequate for the age that this part represented. The function of this part in the system could be reformulated from an internal censor to an expression of basic needs that needed to be attended. This emotional part agreed to remind the ANP that "taking care of ourselves is important" whenever she is focused on other people´s needs and ignoring her own.

After three months of therapy (twice a month sessions), the client described many changes:

She had accepted her new situation regarding her ex-husband, "I know I don´t belong to him. I have the divorce documents. I have signed them, and I experienced a feeling of freedom... I remember what you told me in therapy, about realizing I deserve good things." She visited her children and was a supportive adult to them (previously she was extremely depressed and they had decided to live with their father because they did not feel she could take care of them), "I told them they shouldn´t be concerned about the situation between their father and me. We are the ones who should solve all these things. I always loved them. It doesn´t matter they decided to live with their father. I am not judging them because of this. To have this talk with them was wonderful, and to recover the relationship with them."

She was also able to visit her parents and look at them from a very different perspective: "My father was very old, very ill. I didn't visit them for over ten years. It was very hard for me to see him that way. I helped him to walk, to go to the bathroom. To see him depending on me... I felt like a bad person for a while, because although I didn't want to see him that way, it made me feel safe. He can't hurt me anymore. His insults are over... At that moment, when he needed my hands, I felt how he never made me feel... I felt valuable, as if all my 38 years of life were concentrated in that day. It was like a turning point for me, as if saying: 'Now is my turn, dad. Now is my turn to live, finally!' I couldn't really live, even being far away from him. He was always in my mind, because he taught me to live in a wrong way. From my early childhood, I was living for others. I did everything for my siblings, for others, never for me... I suffered, I suffered a lot, but it was because he put this in my mind, his voice was always in my mind..."

"That's what I learned from the last two sessions. I thought, 'Why does she ask me about my childhood, if I suffered a lot with my ex-husband, I was always thinking about it...' but finally I understood. My desire is to be able to let go of all this stuff, to become distant of all those memories."

After this realization, the client was ready for standard EMDR trauma reprocessing. She was managing better in her daily life. Her current couple relationship was evolving to a more healthy and supportive style. She was better managing interpersonal boundaries and helping her partner to make changes. She was taking her medication regularly and making good practical decisions.

The time for trauma processing is not just when the client says, "I want to do it." We need to use our clinical judgment to provide a healthy foundation for self-care and self-love. In this way, our progressive model works gradually and prepares the client for the steps that come later.

Summary

This work on self-care patterns can be considered as a preparatory work, but it is also a way to repair attachment disruptions, to overcome defenses and dissociative phobias, to increase high order mental functions, and to develop an integrative capacity. These aspects will be described in the following chapters.

The Self-Care Patterns Scale can be used to clinically evaluate dysfunctional self-care patterns, to reformulate the client's problems, and to shift attention toward needed areas of psychoeducation. The work with the inner child, using as its foundation the *loving eyes procedure*, will guide many self-care interventions. Some of these proposed self-care interventions can help to increase emotional regulation, as the *caring for the baby procedure*, the "installation of the equilibrium," or the *positive affect tolerance protocol*. The self-care perspective can be introduced in the work with dissociative parts or in more structured interventions, such as the meeting place. When the client is ready to work on specific memories, we can extend the gains in self-care by reprocessing specific experiences related to the origin of defective self-care patters.

Ultimately, work on patterns of self-care is much more than the use specific procedures. It is a fundamental aspect of the progressive approach, which can be present in each intervention that we perform throughout the therapeutic process.

Chapter 7
Working Toward Integration:
Co-Consciousness and Connection

Anabel Gonzalez, Sandra Baita, & Dolores Mosquera

Most of the psychotherapeutic proposals for dissociation consider integration as a goal. It is also the focus of the third phase in the phase-oriented treatment (Van der Hart et al., 2006; Kluft, 1993; Putnam, 1989; Chu et al., 2011). This goal is shared by both EMDR and the theory of structural dissociation of the personality (Van der Hart, Nijenhuis, & Solomon, 2010). However, integration is not only a goal, but also a process that evolves during the entire therapeutic journey.

What does integration mean? Steele (2009) reflects about the multiple meanings of the word "integration." According to the author, the constant synthesis of perceptual elements, thoughts, feelings, intentions, and awareness of action with a sense of time gives us the experience called "now." Integrative actions provide us with a seemingly unified "me" across different times and settings (Cleeremans, 2003; Siegel, 1999; Stern, 1985). In other words, our self or personality is not the active agent of integration, but is rather its result (Loevinger, 1976; Metzinger, 2003; Van der Hart et al., 2006). Thus, integration is a dynamic state of being that is in constant flux, yet stably constant. In words of Kathy Steele (2009): "Integration is not something we achieve, but occurs in moments of fully being and doing. Integration is not something the self does, but what the self is in the present." It is our mental model of who we experience ourselves to be (Metzinger, 2003).

In this chapter, we want to delve into some procedures that can promote integration from the very early stages of therapy. We will focus on the development of co-consciousness and describe different techniques that can promote the sharing of experiences among dissociative parts. We must keep in mind that the work with severely traumatized clients is not a step-by-step method in which integration is the last phase after trauma processing. Hence, these procedures should be adapted to each stage of the therapeutic process. We agree with the theory of structural dissociation of the personality, where integration is described as a dynamic process that goes from basic synthesis to realization and starts from the early stages of therapy.

Co-Consciousness

Co-consciousness is one of the first stages of the integrative process. In regards to DID, it has been defined as "a state of awareness in which one personality is able to directly experience the thoughts, feelings, and actions (and perceptions) of another alter" (Morton Prince, 1906; Kluft, 1984). This is developed throughout the therapy process: Some ego states begin to share their conscious contents with other ego states. This sharing of consciousness is called co-consciousness.

From the ego-state theory perspective, Phillips & Frederick (1995) outline that "in the ego-state continuum, ego states are normally separated from one another by something that can be thought of like a semipermeable membrane. At one end of the continuum is the situation of extreme separateness; at the other, certain variations of the normal human personality. The key word in understanding ego-state pathology is separateness." They propose different stages in this pathway toward integration: recognition, development of communication, development of empathy, cooperative ventures, sharing of interiority, co-consciousness, and continuing co-consciousness. This is related to the process of overcoming the phobia of dissociative parts of the personality (see chapter 8).

Knowing that integration is a main goal of the therapy, we can try to enhance it from the very first stage of the therapeutic process. In this chapter, we will explain techniques that promote co-consciousness between dissociative parts. It is important to keep in mind that these procedures should be carried out carefully, because premature contact between previously dissociated neural networks could be destabilizing. A progressive process, beginning with well-tolerated interventions, can be safer for the client.

Co-Consciousness in EMDR Therapy

According to Shapiro (2001, pp. 31), three different mechanisms seem to be responsible for the activation and facilitation of processing: (1) deconditioning caused by a relaxation response, (2) a shift in brain state, enhancing the activation and strengthening of weak associations, and (3) the client's dual attention: the simultaneous attendance to present stimuli and past trauma. The relevance of dual attention as an active ingredient of EMDR therapy has been shown by the research of Lee, Taylor, & Drummond (2006).

However, the fact that dual attention is relevant to EMDR therapy does not clarify which underlying mechanism is in place. According to Lee, Taylor, & Drummond (2006): "When dual attention is present both in phase 3 and during the desensitization phase 4, EMDR results are better." Clients with structural dissociation easily lose dual attention. They can either stay with two feet in the past, reliving trauma and acting as an EP, or completely disconnected from the memory, with two feet on the present, acting as an ANP. According to the conclusions of Lee, Taylor, & Drummond (2006), we could hypothesize that clients with structural dissociation of the personality might have more difficulties engaging in dual attention, and as a consequence of this, the standard procedure might not work as efficiently and spontaneously as it does in clients without structural dissociation.

The CIPOS method (Knipe, 2008) shows us that when we help the client maintain dual attention, by titrating the exposure to traumatic material while pendulating this exposure with present safety, EMDR works better. This does not imply that without dual attention EMDR processing does not work at all. Dual attention or co-consciousness would not be a natural consequence of EMDR processing, but a needed condition for implementing it effectively. In clients with structural dissociation, we need to reinforce this aspect.

Difficulties with dual attention are also related to the deficit in high order mental functions described in chapter 5. The global brain activity is what allows a "meta" perspective, which is necessary for integration.

Co-Consciousness Facilitating Techniques

When structural dissociation is present, dissociative parts are partially separated. Co-conscious work attempts to make the barriers more permeable, by enhancing connections between these disconnected neuro-networks. Two aspects should be kept in mind. The first one is that separateness between emotional parts and their neuro-networks is never complete. The second one is that this division increases in the face of traumatic issues or situations related to attachment, where dissociative phobias become stronger, but it is not so rigid for other stimuli not related to traumatic content.

As we commented before, we should proceed with caution, since a premature connection between parts that were separated by traumatizing experiences can generate unbalance. In order to titrate this intervention and make the process safer for the client, we may start by enhancing experiences of connection, away from traumatic issues. This work may increase communication and collaboration among the internal system, facilitating further trauma work (see chapter 12). When partial co-consciousness is already present in the system, these interventions may strength it and shorten the process toward integration. Co-consciousness techniques can also be used to enhance the therapeutic process in clients whose amnesic barriers are strong. In these cases, barriers should be carefully weakened, making sure not to overwhelm the client´s capacities for emotional regulation and avoiding premature contact with traumatic contents.

Some authors have proposed interventions, such as the hypnotic facilitated co-consciousness (Caul, 1978) for dissociative disorders. This author proposed that co-consciousness could be facilitated by placing the client in a trance, directly addressing the targeted alters, and instructing them to blot out all issues and distractions except this process. The therapist then suggests that some alters (dissociative parts) will be able to see and hear everything that any of them can see or hear. The therapist can suggest that, during times of minimal stress, they continue to maintain this co-conscious state. Caul warns that this procedure does not always have a predictable positive outcome and might result in increased anxiety due to the loss of amnesic barriers among alters. He concludes, however, that when it is used at the stage in which therapy is approaching the resolution of multiplicity, this technique can result in significant benefits for the client.

Co-consciousness is also present as an inherent part of other techniques. One example is *talking through* (Braun, 1984; Kluft, 1982). When we say to the client, "All the parts in your mind can hear what we are saying," we are promoting co-consciousness between mental states. The dissociative table technique (Fraser, 1991, 2003) is another useful tool that promotes co-consciousness, because different parts are sharing the same imaginary place (an EMDR procedure proposal for the meeting place will be described in chapter 13). Enhancement of collaboration and cooperation between parts includes co-consciousness, but it is not specifically oriented toward it.

The therapist is often the first co-conscious experience for dissociative parts, but this can be possible only if the therapist displays the exact same behavior in front of an ANP, a dependent part, or a hostile one. When the therapist has a good alliance with child parts and most collaborative parts, but cannot do the same with more hostile parts or abuser´s introjects, different dissociative parts will have a very different experience of a therapist who is kind to some parts but defensive or critical toward others.

The EMDR standard protocol (Shapiro, 1995) implies co-conscious work or dual attention "between safety, present orientation, and a sense of mastery, on one hand, and traumatic relieving on the other. If an individual can simultaneously activate the traumatic memory while maintaining an orientation to the safety of the present, and then engage in bilateral, right-left sensory stimulation, adaptive processing of that memory material is greatly facilitated."

In structural dissociation, the activation of a traumatic memory while maintaining orientation to the here-and-now suggests that the emotional part and the apparently normal part should be co-conscious during the processing. As stated above in this chapter, co-consciousness is not an easy task to achieve in these clients.

In order to enhance co-consciousness in a way that is safe for the client, we can take advantage of the characteristic of fragmentation between different dissociative parts. Inter-identity memory transfer is different for traumatic and for neutral stimulus (Kong et al., 2008). It means that neutral stimulus can be shared by different parts, being isolation more significant for traumatic issues. We propose that the sharing of neutral stimuli can be a well-tolerated exercise, and from this point on, we can progressively increase the complexity, being the co-consciousness of traumatic elements the most difficult issue. This is a gradual and controlled exposure to the sharing of information and increases the tolerance of the avoided, rejected, or feared parts.

Development of high order mental functions (Chapter 5) should be parallel to co-consciousness work. When the client has reflective capacity, he can "think about what is happening," therefore remaining present while both parts are activated. This in turn, will allow him to manage different reactions and tolerate more intensive work on co-consciousness. It is important to assess the level of action tendencies in each part, since it helps the clinician design the best interventions to increase internal awareness, empathy, and collaboration between parts. This is especially true in those cases with a child EP, where the clinician might consider the use of interventions with drawings, toys, or puppets, which involve lower action tendencies.

Experiencing Neutral Stimuli in the External World Together

This is probably the best-tolerated co-consciousness exercise and has additional advantages. In this procedure, the therapist proposes that a neutral stimulus is easier to share than a traumatic one. Such neutral stimulus could be a specific type of music, a view, a flavor, or anything that will not trigger any traumatic material. It is important to check with all the parts, since an apparently harmless stimulus, considered neutral by one part, may trigger a traumatic memory in another one.

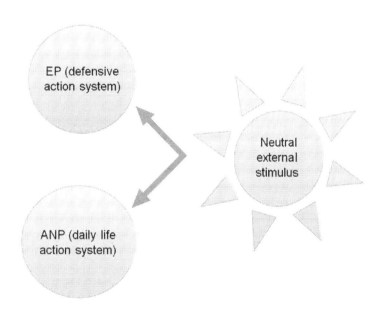

Fig. 1. Experiencing a neutral stimulus in the external world together.

With this exercise, dissociative parts are oriented toward the external world from the early stages of treatment. Exercises based on collaboration usually decrease phobia between dissociative parts.

Some parts have never been in contact with daily life, and many are focused on the internal conflict. Connecting these parts with daily life can be very scary for clients, because they fear these parts can become activated and do terrible things in the outside world. They may react not wanting to do this exercise. Sometimes therapists are also afraid of doing these types of procedures because they think that the client may become hyperaroused by the uncontrolled activation of hostile parts. However, it is unlikely that things will become overwhelming if we begin with neutral stimuli.

We want the EP to peek into the real world and be able to see the things he is missing out on (e.g., feeling the sun on their skin). This exercise is always done at the therapist's office, where the client is safe and can be stabilized if necessary, but the idea is to have the client do this as homework, initially with neutral stimuli and, later on, with pleasant ones. The main idea of the exercise is for the EP to contact the "bright side of life," the good part of current life. This proposal is not about acting but about experiencing passive awareness, so that the possibility of dysfunctional activation in the EP is very low. When the effects are positive for the entire system, both in the office and the days after, we can propose it as homework. These techniques are generally well tolerated, even when high order mental functions are poorly developed.

If we do not help fearful EPs to get in touch with the external world from the beginning of the therapeutic process, the risk of getting stuck in the inner world for too long is high. The therapist can remain working with the internal system for years, fascinated with the complex world of the dissociative parts and infected by the client´s phobia of normal life. This way, the therapist becomes part of the dysfunctional system, and it can increase the chronicity of the disorder. When this happens, these parts will continue having influence and interfering with adequate functioning.

The aggressive, hostile parts may need to be convinced of their right to be happy and enjoy life and of their ability to see "the other side of life." They were born to carry the burden of trauma and this has been their mission for years. Their attention field was, and still is, focused on threatening or potentially damaging stimulus. It may sound strange, but comforting for them, to hear from the therapist that they have the right to simply enjoy a song, a view, or a flavor, the right to simply enjoy pleasant things. We do not start by telling the apparently normal part of the personality, or other trauma-avoidant parts, that they should get in touch with traumatic issues. We begin from the opposite perspective: proposing that the parts fixated on trauma experience other possible positive experiences.

In addition to the aspects we pointed out, fearful or damaged parts may believe that they do not deserve to enjoy life. This cognition is based on:

a) Traumatic assumptions of guilt or shame derived from the exposure to abuse.
b) The fear of becoming excited with good things.
c) The conviction that bad things always follow good ones.

When different parts agree with this exercise, it is advisable to practice it at the office explaining it to clients as "an experiment." It is useful to label this exercise as an experiment, so clients can understand that the results will not always be successful, meaning that we might have to try again or even try something different. This prevents the client from labeling the exercise as a failure and, by extension, from applying this same label to themselves (e.g., I´m a failure).

Reinforcing the connection between the parts and the neutral stimulus by using BLS can be another step in the progression of our work. However, the therapist should decide the convenience of adding BLS on a case-by-case and session-by-session basis.

After having worked on co-consciousness with a neutral stimulus, we can propose a homework task. We may suggest that the adult self (see chapter 5) or any ANP lets other parts know when neutral or pleasant stimuli are present and that all the parts allow themselves to feel it together.

We can gradually increase the complexity of this exercise from completely neutral stimulus to pleasant ones and finally interpersonal pleasant stimulus.

Sometimes, the parts have small bits of these co-consciousness experiences, and these experiences may be reinforced with bilateral stimulation. For example, a client has a dissociative part that is very reluctant to participate in therapy. The ANP describes three different experiences that she and the EP experienced together. We propose short sets of BLS targeting positive sensations and begin with the shared elements of the experience. We offer the EP the opportunity to participate in the exercise and have a direct experience, but being careful not to force her in anyway. The emotional part participates, and both ANP and EP experience the sensations associated with those moments and the enhancement of those sensations. The connection and collaboration between both parts increases, overcoming a recent conflict they were experiencing in the past days, without direct intervention in that conflict.

Sharing Adaptive Information Inside the System

To install resources in a system characterized by structural dissociation may not be entirely productive when it is not done with the agreement of the entire system. When we install a resource without this previous negotiation, it can remain limited to the ANP or can provoke a negative effect for different reasons. Resources can be more productive when we can extend them to more than one part, because we are not strengthening the ANP or any specific part, but enhancing co-consciousness and collaboration.

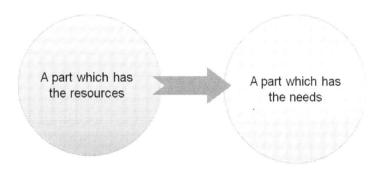

A part which has the resources → A part which has the needs

Fig. 2. Sharing resources.

We should carefully decide with the system which parts will participate. The resource may be contained in one part, and this part should agree on allowing other dissociative part or parts to connect with this resource. We can do it in different ways by using visualizations, imagery, drawings, etc.

Let´s see an example. A vulnerable EP has a need, and the stronger ANP has a resource. With their agreement, we can draw both issues (the need and the resource) and do eye movements alternating between both drawings. If some disturbance appears, we stop the exercise and focus on the disturbance, processing it with BLS. When the disturbance has disappeared, we return to the exercise with the drawings, until the vulnerable part is able to feel the connection with the resource. We can stop the procedure at different times, being more important to do the process progressively than to try to complete it in a single session.

The EMDR drawing protocol (Baita & Gonzalez, 2008) can be used to achieve the goals stated above. The procedure includes the following steps:

1. The therapist explains the exercise and asks for agreement from both parts, making sure that the entire system does not show opposition.
2. The therapist asks the client to make a drawing about the emotional part (EP) that contains a distressing emotion she wants to change.
3. Then, asks her to draw a resource that the client may use to cope with this emotion and that responds to the EP´s needs; as we explained before, the resource may be contained in a stronger part or the ANP.
4. The client does eye movements alternating between both drawings, looking at each one for a while in order to make contact with sensations in each part.
5. If any disturbance appears during the process, we stop the procedure and focus on that disturbance and the associated somatic sensation, processing it with BLS.
6. If traumatic content emerges, we manage it verbally or with any other technique, working with both parts involved in the exercise or with other parts in the internal system that can be of help. We stop the procedure and stabilize the client.
7. Once the client becomes stabilized, the therapist checks if the EP feels more in touch with the resource.
8. The procedure can continue or end at this point, but less is always better than too much, especially the first time we are trying out any intervention.
9. Depending on the post-session effects, we can repeat the intervention or postpone it for further stages of therapy.

We can stimulate not only the sharing of resources, but also of healthy cognitions, achievements, or any adaptive information. We can introduce this element in any intervention. For example, we can "share the improvements." Each time one part experiences any type of improvement (e.g., a realization about trauma, a change in a dysfunctional belief, the development of a new ability), we can propose that "all the parts in the internal system share this new resource for the system." The message that indirectly gets across is: what is good for one part is good for the system. Whenever possible, we can reinforce this collective experiencing with BLS. It is useful to remark the improvements, being careful not to trigger the phobia of change. By adding a collective experiencing, we are enhancing co-consciousness; by reframing the resource of one as good for all, we are increasing inner collaboration (and decreasing conflict); and with BLS we are multiplying the effect. The global intervention is much more powerful in such a way.

This exercise can be implemented in the early stages of therapy. The addition of BLS increases the resonance of the information in each individual part and reinforces the connections between parts based on adaptive information instead of traumatic assumptions. However, the therapist must be cautious and keep in mind that BLS could promote the emergence of traumatic material. Thus, very short sets of BLS should be used, testing the effects of the intervention in the inner system before repeating it or continuing with the procedure. Both positive and negative outcomes of any intervention may only be evident some days after the session.

Acting Together in the External World

We introduce action gradually, once they can co-experience external non-threatening issues, and parts can interchange resources and positive information. In order to work on an external task, more complex mental actions are needed. The client (as internal system) should learn to reflect before acting, instead of acting impulsively. Trauma survivors often experience blockages and difficulties in performing adaptive actions, especially when they require different action systems, and when they are still focused on their inner world and a lot of energy is consumed dealing with internal conflict.

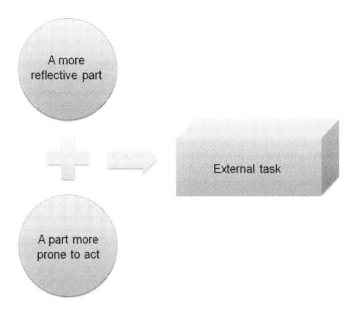

Fig. 3. Sharing tasks.

Collaborative exercises among parts develop communication and collaboration within the inner system. Dissociative parts evolve from being "enemies," lost inside the mental conflict, to being a "team" focused on present, daily aspects of life. In order to achieve motivation within the system to engage in this complex process, we should find a goal that is shared by different parts. We need a horizon and we need a plan.

Whenever there is a situation that needs to be solved and different parts or the entire system if possible agree (first step), we should decide which parts could collaborate (second step). Then we would represent the conflict, the problem outside the system (third step). When we are working from the meeting place, we use the screen strategy to represent a situation in the outside world, and we observe which parts become activated when faced with the situation. This strategy also helps differentiate between outside and inside worlds, something not easy for many survivors of early traumatization.

For some clients, it can be useful to use concrete representations, such as objects, drawings, etc., since there is a smaller chance of being triggered than if they have to visualize this situation internally, as Ostacoli & Bertino (2010) have described.

Another possibility is to identify an outside situation and represent it, along with the inner system of parts, through drawings, puppets, or objects. This representation toolkit (1) allows to take distance and perspective, (2) stimulates the development of "meta" functions (self-reflection, an observational stance), (3) gives the client a feeling of control, and (4) when we are working with child EPs with low order action tendencies, the use of these procedures is more adequate for this part´s level of functioning.

Let´s see how we can address this issue through a case example: Diana´s ANP wanted to engage in some social contact. She had been isolated for a while, taking care of her father who had a terminal illness. But an EP was afraid of what would happen if this social contact took place. This part was terrified about the idea of being seduced and the possibility of getting paralyzed with no chance to escape from a tricky and abusive relationship. The first step was to externalize the problem and, if possible, have the client explore the different options that might help her solve this situation, developing her capacity to make choices. In this case, Diana made a list of different solutions: she could just go out for coffee during daylight, instead of going out to dinner; she could choose a place she knew well, rather than letting the person take her somewhere else; she could ask her best friend to be available over the phone, just in case Diana, as an EP, felt she was in danger.

We used little dolls to represent the scene with all possible outcomes, while Diana, as ANP, was asked to pay attention to her feelings and somatic sensations, as well as those of her EP.

Once both parts agreed on one of the solutions, short sets of BLS were added, checking for possible disturbances. After doing this in the external representation with the dolls, Diana was asked to close her eyes and visualize herself in this situation, while paying attention to her EP´s reactions. In this case, the EP also had the resource of their shared internal place of calm, in case she might need it. Short sets of BLS were added, and the client was asked for her feedback, adding more BLS with each positive comment or feeling that arose.

On follow up, the client was asked about the results of this exercise in real life. The resolution of this conflict led to an improvement in the ANP´s quality of life.

Another exercise is the EMDR work with puppets, which fosters collaboration when accomplishing an external task (Baita & Gonzalez, 2008). Once all parts agree to work on this exercise, the instructions are as follows:

1. The client is asked to select one puppet to represent each part.
2. Two parts agree to cooperate in facing a daily life situation.
3. The client chooses the two collaborating parts and places each one in a different hand, imagining the situation or looking at a drawing of the situation.
4. The client takes the EMDR tactile bilateral stimulators or does eye movements alternating between the puppets.
5. The client looks at and connects with each part, while the tactile stimulators are connected or while she is looking at the puppet.
6. If any disturbing element arises, and depending on the client´s characteristics, it can be processed with BLS.
7. Any improvement, realization, or positive sensation can be installed with BLS.
8. When the process is more complex, dissociative phobias or blockages emerge, or the client tends to prematurely contact traumatic material, we can just focus on that element without BLS, in order to not stimulate the possible emergence of more disturbing information.

Different procedures can be designed for the same purpose. They are not simple tasks, as we have already commented. Clients are making choices, thinking about their feelings and thoughts, developing metacognitive capacities, and planning a reaction reflectively, instead of acting impulsively. Different parts, which are usually active at different times, can be present at the same time in a fluent and collaborative way. The internal system may shift from competition to team work. Although this is not a procedure that can be completed in a single session, these exercises will not only have positive effects in adaptive functioning, they will also set the conditions for further effective trauma work.

Co-Consciousness in Trauma Work

Once we have worked on co-consciousness, processed the dissociative phobias, and consolidated a good therapeutic relationship, we can consider using the standard EMDR procedure to work on a traumatic memory. Whenever possible, the EMDR standard protocol is a good integrative procedure (see more about trauma work on chapter 12). We should check that all elements have been processed and how things went with all the internal system´s parts.

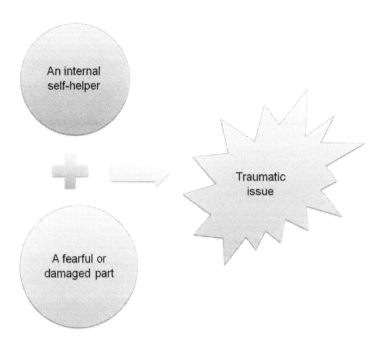

Fig. 4. Sharing trauma work.

When the client has the experience of working with the meeting place, we can return to it when the processing becomes blocked in any way. For many clients, it is necessary to plan the therapeutic work with the internal system, placing some parts in safe places and selecting only those who can and want to process a specific memory.

As a part of the necessary synthesis of traumatic elements, a lot of useful tools have been developed: Double Screen (Krakauer, 2006), different versions of screen techniques, Guided Synthesis (Van der Hart, Nijenhuis, & Steele, 2006), and different tools to "join what was dissociated."

Enhancing Connection

With highly functioning clients, or when the therapy is advancing, we can install the connection between all parts or just those who are willing to.

This connection may be related to self-care procedures (see chapter 6) or the transmission of adaptive information. In the next case example, we can see a task with drawings. The therapist proposes that the client draws a journey through a rainbow, in order for the ANP to be able to tell the little girl (EP) that the abuse is over, that the abuser is not present, and that the client is older and can protect herself. Each piece of knowledge is accompanied with short sets of BLS.

Fig. 5. Enhancing connection.

We can suggest that the adult self notices where she feels a specific EP on her body. By touching this area we promote "contact with this part," while the therapist reminds her about or explains adaptive information, which the adult part will transmit to the EP.

We can also help the client to have experiences of positive connection, once some traumatic issues have been resolved, even if core trauma is not completely processed. We can propose this with suggestions such as: "Feel the connection, how some parts compensate others, the experience of being together, the strength and energy that the connection gives to the system." The therapist can suggest that, during times of minimal stress, they continue to maintain this co-conscious state. We must be cautious with this procedure, because even when we are not focusing on exchange of traumatic material, connection between dissociative parts may precipitate the emergence of contents that the client is not prepared to integrate. In some cases, in spite of this awareness of traumatic memories, it allows the processing of part of these elements, and this is followed by a deep realization and elaboration of these memories or advances along this line.

Case example:

Therapist: Just be aware of the intensity of your connection with this part now. Let her (EP) notice this with you.

BLS.

Client: I am embarrassed to say what just came to my mind (surprised). I can't believe what just came up. I don't know if it's something from my conscious mind, this makes no sense... She (a voice representing the EP) tells me "Do you know he raped you?" I answered her (avoidance defense), "This is not related to the topic we were working on." I don't want to ask her about it.

In this case, connection makes the ANP contact a core traumatic memory (sexual abuse by her father). The phobia of traumatic memories is activated in the ANP, which cannot realize the meaning of the voice.

T: What sensation do you notice when you hear this?

C: It's as if something was blocked.

T (processing the phobia in the ANP): Open your eyes.

BLS.

C (holding her neck and crying): She is shouting "HE RAPED YOU, HE RAPED YOU, HE RAPED YOU!!! Aren't you going to react?"

T: Let me help her. Let her relieve part of this disturbance (client continues crying)... Ask her to talk to me, take a breath (orienting to present reality)... Observe where you are now, you are here with me... Look at me, are you here?

C (calmer): Yes, yes... Yes, I am here.

T: Ask this part how she feels.

C: She talks to me in a male voice... "How do you expect me to be? I am fucked!"

T: Ask her if she wants us to try to relieve this pain.

We know that this client can tolerate moments of high emotional intensity without serious decompensation. Progress with this kind of processing was higher than during a previous period in which BLS was not introduced, so we decide to continue. This proposal to the EP *is the tip of the finger strategy*, described in chapters 8 and 12. We try to reduce activation in the EP.

C: He said this cannot be solved.

The patient touches her neck. This somatic sensation seems to be an element of the core traumatic memory of the abuse.

T: Wounds can heal and cicatrize, scars don't hurt. Of course it can be solved (client cries comforted). Until now, this was the only way, but it can be over... It can stop hurting... You are a 40-year-old woman now, and you can protect yourself. Can you realize that?

C (nodding): It's possible.

T: Can this part realize this?

C (holding her neck): She is asking, "Who is going to guarantee that no bastard will hurt me again?"

T: This could happen, but you are an adult woman, able to protect yourself. This is what makes the difference. A girl cannot do it, an adult can. You have grown, you have learned many things.

C: This has happened so many times...

T: But by being together, you and this part, things will change. Your mental blockage made you helpless in many situations. Now you are behaving differently, coping better with situations that happen with your partner. You have clear proof of these changes. (Therapist is introducing adaptive information.) This part is helping a lot, you are changing...

The part agrees on working on her disturbance now.

C: I asked him if he wants this help and he says he does... He does (nodding)... He does...

After BLS, the activation in the EP decreased, but the ANP continues showing her non-realization about core trauma.

C: I can't actually understand what has happened... I am surprised, I can't understand why this came up. I feel guilty, as if I was making up all these things. I feel guilty for going in that direction, I don't know why, I know I should erase it...

T (processing the phobia in the ANP): Go with that.

This processing of dissociative phobias between parts is better tolerated than the initial enhancing of connection between parts. More work on peripheral aspects is needed prior to reinforcing this connection. After processing the phobia in the ANP, both ANP and EP can increase realization.

C: I asked him, "Is my denial bothering you?" He said, "A lot."

T (focusing on the phobia in the EP toward the ANP): Ask her to notice this annoyance. When she feels that annoyance, open your eyes...

We change the gender when we talk about this part, in spite of the client identifying the part with a male figure, because in Spanish the word "part" has a female gender. The therapist uses this trick to promote adaptive changes in the system.

BLS

Client's face shows suffering.

T: Open your eyes, let me help you with that.

BLS. (Therapist talks during eye movements to maintain dual attention.) You are here with me...

T: Ask her if she understands that you (the ANP) needed to do this (avoid memories) for survival. Can she understand this?

C: She (the EP) says I (the ANP) had to do it to be recognized, by being abused.

She refers to a submissive response toward the abuser, in order to achieve his love and recognition, as she will explain after a set of EM.

BLS.

C: By letting others abuse me, somebody could love me. They could see how good I was… I was really good… They could maltreat me and I wouldn´t react against them.

T: At that moment this had to be that way.

C: That´s how it always was.

BLS.

C: I am asking him (the EP) what he feels… He says I am beginning to realize we cannot live in this maltreatment (her current partner relationship is verbally abusive)… It´s unbearable.

We can see that the ANP has improved her level of realization. Empathy between dissociative parts has increased, and the general capacity for dealing with abusive relationship has developed. Contact between ANP and EP makes this traumatic content emerge. We should have in mind the ANP´s capacity for dealing with traumatic content, which in this session was initially overestimated by the therapist. It is crucial to carefully titrate this intervention.

Before integration takes place, we can propose "micro-fusions" to the client. Some survivors experience fear toward integration, or some parts may think that this will make them disappear. We should explain that integration will be a new experience where all the parts will be present and no one will disappear. In this procedure, we encourage two or more parts to blend with each other. We can facilitate this process through imagery, suggesting that both parts hold one another, or take each other´s hands, or merge in a common point. The selected metaphor should be adapted to the client characteristics and preferences. The micro-fusions are proposed as short and reversible exercises, where the client can achieve a real experience of what integration means. After doing this, even when they cannot maintain this state until the inner conflict and the traumatic issues are completely resolved, the client is more motivated to continue the process toward integration.

Full integration sometimes happens spontaneously when therapy evolves. Parts become more blurred, less defined, they begin to share characteristics, contents, and functions, and the client has difficulties differentiating them. During this process, sometimes more dysfunctional parts, such as perpetrator imitating parts, appear, while others are improving in collaboration or even integration. That is not a worsening of the problem, but proof that the integrative process is moving ahead. With time, when most of the traumatic issues have been processed, integration happens as a natural consequence. The previous work on increasing integrative capacity and diminishing internal conflict and blockages shows its effect when trauma is over.

The Integrative Movie Procedure

Other times we can propose specific exercises similar to those described for micro-fusions. A useful tool is the integrative movie procedure that helps to reinforce a new perspective on the client´s history and the development of a narrative memory and a full realization about past, present, and future. In this procedure:

1. The fusion of two parts or the entire system, after the main traumatic issues have been processed, is promoted and reinforced with BLS.
2. The client plays the movie of his life from birth to present and the imagined future.
3. While the movie is playing, therapist or client does tapping continuously.
4. The client stops the movie if he notices disturbance at any time.
5. Depending on the level of disturbance, the material, and the situation related to this disturbance, we can process it directly or decide to stop the procedure and proceed with a complete standard protocol.
6. When this disturbance has been processed, the movie continues with the same indications.

The procedure is repeated several times in the sessions, and at the end of the therapy, when all the parts are integrated and the client can do it maintaining stability, the client can do this exercise as homework.

Post-Integration Work

The inner world becomes especially relevant in early and severe traumatization, because the difficulties of severely traumatized clients in the external world may generate secondary traumatization, which worsens the pathology. And sometimes, the client has so many problems in relationships that "inner relationships" between parts replace outside relationships. In fact, DID or DDNOS clients frequently experience integration as "loneliness" and grieve for their lost inner world. Their inner system may compensate them when faced with a very poor real life.

Sometimes, we need to do additional work for some time after integration. In the following case, the client had recovered from a conversion disorder characterized by paralysis of the legs and pseudo-seizures for a year. After a conflict at work, she experienced a short relapse from which she recovered spontaneously. She has an emotional part that was related to her symptoms, more clearly with the paralysis than with the pseudo-seizures. Both parts had been integrated before, but in this session the integration did not seem to be complete.

We decided to use the *integrative movie procedure* in order to increase connection and develop a narrative memory of her past history.

> Client: The last time I came, we had already merged. We are not separated, we think the same things, before this was different. I don´t just see myself.

Therapist: There are still two parts, but more alike.

C: Yes. We feel alike, and there is no rage as there was before.

T. Ask her if she thinks it´s a good idea to become just one.

Client nods.

T: Feel each sensation of your body together. When you are entirely blended and feeling each body sensation at the same time… Play your life´s movie through your mind, and stop when you notice that there is the need to unite sensations… And you will do BLS with your hands while you are watching the movie… Take all the time you need for joining all that you and the part have experienced, to completely mix all the sensations, to entirely experience them.

C: For now everything seems okay.

T: You can repeat this exercise at home, every day, to feel the sensations of your body at the same time, together, feeling the fusion. Are you noticing now the fusion?

C: More than before, I don´t know why.

T: Can you still see the other part?

C: I don´t see her anymore.

T: Is she looking through your eyes?

Client nods.

After playing the movie a second time:

C: Okay.

T: What are you noticing?

C: Like I have something heavy on my head, I don´t know why, on my head and on my belly.

T: Just notice those sensations (client does tapping).

Client´s breathing is heavier.

T: Allow those sensations to be there, just notice them.

C: It´s a weird sensation, like being anxious, a stomach ache. It´s like having a ball in my stomach.

Based on the client´s history, we think this sensation is related to a preverbal EP. When she was born, she was seriously ill and spent three months in an incubator. Her parents did not visit her very much. Her father did not go at all, because the doctors had told them that the client would die for sure. The hypothesis is that the present discomfort is related to preverbal somatic memories, insufficiently processed, that are arising with the integration of both dissociative parts.

T: Take that stomach sensation. (The therapist places her hands on her own stomach modeling a posture of taking care of the sensation.)

C: This is the same sensation I get when I begin to have a seizure... It´s as if I needed to discharge something.

T: Hold this sensation imagining it´s a baby... Imagine that sensation in the baby and imagine you are taking care of this baby (no BLS).

C: The sensation doesn´t disappear.

T: Don´t try to make it disappear. Babies sometimes need hours to become regulated. And they modulate their emotions because there is an adult with them, calming them...

C: I do this (taking a deep breath) because it´s what I usually do when I´m going to have one (seizure).

T: Okay... When you are taking care of a baby, you don´t fight with her (client is caressing the sensation)... You can tell her, "I know you are nervous, It doesn´t matter, I am here... I know you will become calm" (client is becoming calmer)... We don´t become desperate, we give her time... We have a lot of patience, you know, it´s important when babies are distressed...

C: It´s okay.

T: It´s important to give them time.

C: Yes.

T: Emotions are sometimes long-lasting, like babies crying and having difficulties becoming calm. When you dissociate an emotion, it vanishes. And you learned to manage emotions by making them disappear. This is another way of managing emotions. I can feel this emotion, I can tolerate it. I am feeling anxious, I can notice it, but I can manage it... How is the sensation now?

C: I am feeling it a little bit, it´s disappearing.

T: Take the baby, notice her in your body, and talk to her.

C: Nodding and taking a deep breath... Yes.

Now we repeat the movie exercise, while the client does the tapping.

T: Feel the strength you get by being one (integrated self)... Notice how this feels in your body.

C: I am feeling really strong.

T: Feel it.

C: As if it was saying, "Now it´s really true" (that we are integrated).

T: Feel that strength (client continues tapping).

C: It´s as if I wasn´t afraid anymore. It´s as if I am who I was before the paralysis, before I was 18, when I had strength.

T: Feel that deeply... View the movie of your life again and observe how your emotions change when you feel them from this place of strength... from this experience of being integrated.

C: Now I am looking at all these moments in a very positive way, as if everything could be solved, I don't know why... Thank you.

Summary

Different procedures described in this book are thought to promote integration. By enhancing high order mental functions (see chapter 5), we promote the integrative capacity of the individual. By processing dissociative phobias (see chapter 8), we decrease separation between parts. By working from the meeting place, we increase the acceptance of previously disowned parts of the self. All these different interventions contribute to synthesis, differentiation, and realization.

We can also promote co-consciousness and integration with specific interventions. Some EMDR procedures oriented to increase co-consciousness have been described in this chapter, but integration is much more than isolated procedures or the final point of the therapy. It represents a main goal in structural dissociation, and the entire therapeutic process is actually a process of enhancing co-consciousness and integration.

Chapter 8
Overcoming Dissociative Phobias

Anabel Gonzalez & Dolores Mosquera

The term "phobia" is frequently used in the context of anxiety disorders, and it is understood as directly related to external elements (animals, social situations, etc). But Janet (1904) described phobic reactions directed toward internal experiences, such as thoughts, feelings, fantasies, etc. Chronically traumatized individuals are often extraordinarily fearful of internal mental contents as well as of external cues that trigger traumatic experiences (Steele, Van der Hart, & Nijenhuis, 2005).

Including dissociative phobias in the therapeutic plan can help us understand some of the difficulties we will encounter in our work with severely traumatized individuals. To illustrate what we mean by "dissociative phobias," we will describe several clinical situations.

Case examples

David agrees with processing a traumatic memory. He even asks his therapist directly to work on it, but he repeatedly cancels his appointments. When he manages to come to session, he is almost 30 minutes late because "something happened." This makes it impossible to have an EMDR session as scheduled. During another session, he anxiously talks about a problem that is worrying him, even though the week before, he had asked once again to work on a traumatizing event from his early childhood. His therapist experiences an uncomfortable sensation and thinks that the problem the client is talking about is not actually relevant and that he is being "resistant." Moved by this sensation, the therapist reminds the client that it is important to be on time and insists on working with the memory that they had selected initially. The client expresses high commitment and agrees. Some days after this session, he cancels future appointments arguing financial problems. Understanding that David may have had a strong phobia of traumatic memories, which can be underlying this situation, is crucial in order to structure interventions with this client.

Anna refers the existence of a dissociative emotional part (EP) that is very aggressive and constantly critical. This part is sometimes hostile toward the apparently normal part (ANP). As ANP, the client is afraid of this EP and indicates that this part does not want to talk to the therapist or participate in therapy. When the therapist asks the ANP to ask the EP directly, this part expresses her own opinion with fewer problems than expected. The ANP reacts showing distrust and judging the EP severely. In this case, we can detect a clear hostile attitude from the EP toward the ANP, but also a more hidden and complex fear, distrust, and rejection from the ANP toward the EP.

Therapy is evolving adequately, and suddenly, Peter burns his arm at home with an iron. When he comes to session, he does not remember doing this. He thinks an angry EP wanted to give him the message, "Don't get too confident." Several days before this incident, his general practitioner was very surprised to see the improvements and told him that he looked very well, that he was improving a lot. Although Peter as ANP was pleased with this comment, a certain dissociative part (EP) got upset. For this EP, the improvement and the possibility of changing was a trigger because a strong phobia of change and normal life was underneath. Another EP also got triggered because "getting better" meant "getting closer" to the processing of early traumatizing events (phobia of traumatic memories).

Diana refers a negative attitude from her boss as her only problem. She states that everything else is fine, that she does not have any difficulties in life. She describes a supportive partner and an excellent relationship with her old mother. The therapist explores possible core events related to the present problem, but none were found. When we begin with EMDR reprocessing, the client experiences extremely fast relief regarding the uncomfortable sensation with her boss, and after two sessions, she decides to end therapy. She expresses a lot of gratitude toward the therapist and says wonderful things about EMDR. The therapist does not understand why she does not feel fully comfortable with the "good" results that the client indicated.

The first difficulty with dissociative phobias is to identify them, to understand what is happening. The case examples we described in previous paragraphs can be interpreted as a simple lack of interest or motivation from the client (see chapter 11). However, to fully understand the relevance of dissociative phobias, it is very important to structure a therapeutic plan and prevent possible problems. EMDR gives us the possibility of processing these phobias, which can be targeted with modified EMDR procedures. This is a powerful way to enhance the therapeutic progress. We will develop these interventions in further paragraphs.

Maintenance of Structural Dissociation: Dissociative Phobias

Structural dissociation of the personality starts during early traumatizing events, but is predominantly maintained by a series of phobias that characterize trauma survivors and by a lack of social support (Nijenhuis, Van der Hart, & Steele, 2002; Steele, Van der Hart, & Nijenhuis, 2001, 2005; Van der Hart, Nijenhuis, & Steele 2006).

Janet (1904) described the core phobia as the phobia of traumatic memories, which consists of an avoidance of full realization of trauma and its effects on one's life. From this fundamental phobia ensue others: phobia of attachment and attachment loss (in particular with regard to the therapist), phobia of trauma-derived mental actions, phobia of dissociative parts, phobia of normal life, phobia of healthy risk-taking and change, and phobia of intimacy (emotional and sexual).

Gradually overcoming these phobias is essential for a successful treatment, in particular when treating traumatic memories in Phase 2 (Nijenhuis et al., 2002; Steele et al., 2001, 2005; Van der Hart et al., 2006). This aspect is very relevant for EMDR therapy. Usually, the phobias that emerge first are the phobia of attachment, such as difficulties to establish the therapeutic relationship and to trust the therapist; the phobia of dissociative parts (fear, rejection, distrust, and other negative emotions between dissociative parts); and the phobia of mental actions and contents related to the traumatic memories. For example, a client who distrusts the therapist and has a lot of problems when it comes to developing a working alliance (phobia of attachment to the therapist), or one dissociative part who is afraid of other dissociative parts because he thinks they are enemies.

Therapeutic relationships are usually disrupted in severely traumatized people. In the preparatory phase, therapists should develop a working alliance with the client's different dissociative parts and promote empathy among them. In order to be able to work with the traumatic past, we need to gradually decrease attachment problems with the therapist and important present relationships. Without repairing these relationships, the client will lack the necessary support from the environment and from the therapist to be able to deal with traumatic issues like chronic childhood neglect and abuse.

We understand EMDR treatment as a progressive approach to the core trauma, where different situations appear at different stages. Many mental structures are there to protect the client, to avoid contact with unbearable memories. Some of these issues are related to dissociative phobias, and they usually appear progressively throughout the therapeutic process:

1. In early stages, the therapeutic relationship is the most challenging issue, because relationships in general are extremely difficult for people who grew up in severely traumatizing and neglecting environments. The phobias of attachment are manifested in many ways, but in therapy they will be focused mainly on the therapist.

2. The client may be phobic toward many necessary procedures in psychotherapy. They may avoid thinking, feeling, or noticing their bodies. This is related to the phobia of trauma-derived mental actions, and it is usually more evident in early stages of therapy.

3. When we approach the internal system of parts, some degree of conflict between these parts is often present. In order to overcome this conflict, it is necessary to achieve a minimum of stabilization and prepare a collaborative attitude in the system. This will allow a safe containment and, later on, the work on traumatic contents.

4. As we get closer to the core trauma, more profound phobias appear. Aspects related to the perpetrator and the difficulties in attachment to this figure are more complicated to assimilate for the client (as ANP). Some parts who imitate the perpetrator tend to show after more acceptable parts are evident. This makes sense if we understand that, for many clients, it is very difficult to accept that some parts of them are reproducing certain aspects from the abuser, or that they feel attached to such a harmful figure. So at this point, since we are closer to very sensible material, to the most unbearable memories, some emotional parts may present new difficulties in the therapeutic relationship.

The process of uncovering layers is present in different degrees in different clients. The sequence we are describing is not a linear one. The schema in graphic 1 can be useful to be attentive to these situations. We must keep in mind that they can appear in a very subtle and hidden way, as we explained in chapter 4 on dissociative language. In the following graphic, dissociative phobias are described in their most frequent order of appearance, from top to bottom.

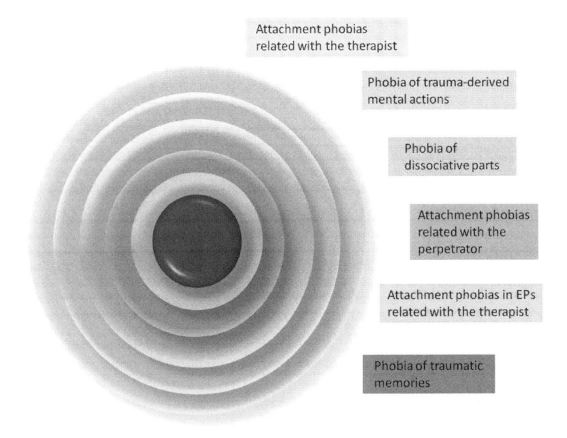

Attachment phobias related with the therapist

Phobia of trauma-derived mental actions

Phobia of dissociative parts

Attachment phobias related with the perpetrator

Attachment phobias in EPs related with the therapist

Phobia of traumatic memories

Dissociative Phobias

The concept of dissociative phobias is very relevant in EMDR therapy. If we try to reprocess core trauma, without realizing the presence of these "protective layers," we will probably encounter various problems. These layers should be carefully removed (and eventually reprocessed) in a step-by-step procedure, approaching the extreme pain that the client is feeling in a gradual, safe, and careful way.

There are other phobias that are related to the external world. People who grew up in severely traumatizing and neglectful environments have extreme difficulties in dealing with normal life, having intimate relationships, trusting and believing in a possible healthy future, and risking change. These phobias help us understand why some clients, for example, decompensate after improving.

In terms of the categories that we proposed in the AIP model (chapter 3), the dissociative phobias can be understood as interoceptively generated dysfunctionally stored information (I-DSI). To overcome these phobias is something we should do along the entire therapy process, but it is crucial during the preparation phase.

Classical conditioning of interoceptive stimuli is key in the maintenance of structural dissociation (Van der Hart, Nijenhuis, & Steele, 2006). This conditioning primarily occurs when the survivor, as ANP, experiences an unexpected intrusion of a traumatic memory. The intrusion, often experienced as confusing, overwhelming, and ego-dystonic (Van der Hart & Steele, 1999), involves three mayor series of mental actions:

1. The survivor as EP relieves a traumatic experience.
2. The survivor as ANP cannot fully synthesize and realize the memory (integrative actions).
3. The ANP takes mental flight from the traumatic memory and the associate EP, because experiencing the memory is inherently aversive.

It is already evident that these avoidant or mental flight actions that stem from the ANP can interfere with EMDR work. As we have mentioned, we can consider these elements as interoceptively generated dysfunctionally stored information (I-DSI). So, we can focus on this I-DSI as a target for EMDR reprocessing (for instance, aversive emotions in the ANP toward the EP or an intrusive symptom). Specific EMDR procedures can be used to overcome these phobias and allow a safe and progressive approach to the traumatic memories.

Some mental actions, which evolve in the aftermath of trauma - for example, the interaction between two dissociative parts in the inner world - have enough relevance to generate high emotional activation and block the internal information processing system, becoming themselves dysfunctionally stored elements (see figure 3 on chapter 3).

EMDR Active Ingredients and Processing of Dysfunctional Elements

Empirical research is showing that some effects of bilateral stimulation are relevant for our proposal on working with dissociative phobias. The first one is a de-arousal effect of BLS. It could be related to activating cholinergic and inhibiting sympathetic systems (Elofsson, Von Scheele, Theorell, & Sondergaard, 2008; Sack, Lempa, & Lamprecht, 2007; Wilson, Silver, Covi, & Foster, 1996). However, in clinical situations we observe that bilateral stimulation sometimes increases disturbing emotions. So, what happens in these cases? One hypothesis is that when structural dissociation is present, and we focus on the traumatic memory as a target, a neural network that contains highly charged memories is usually linked to it and becomes activated (EP). Another frequent situation is that a protector part (EP) emerges as a way to avoid facing traumatic issues. The situation is different when we specifically access this EP's neural network; then de-arousal is the norm.

Solomon & Shapiro (2008) state that "processing is understood to involve the forging of new associations and connections... facilitating dynamic linkages to adaptive memory networks." Based on session transcripts (Shapiro, 2001, 2002; Shapiro & Forrest, 1997) the authors indicate that "processing generally occurs through a rapid progression of intrapsychic connections in the session as emotions, insights, sensations, and memories surface and change with each new set of bilateral stimulation. The proposed mechanisms of action include the assimilation of adaptive information found in other memory networks linking into the network holding the previously isolated disturbing event. After successful treatment, it is proposed that the memory is no longer isolated, because it appears to be appropriately integrated within the larger memory network." This enhancing in connections when we are working with structural dissociation implies improving connections between dissociative parts that contain the dysfunctionally stored information. Without trying to completely process these DSI, we can use this "connection-enhancing effect" to increase connection between dissociative parts when this is appropriate for therapy.

The effect of BLS is probably related to memory reconsolidation and not to extinction, which have different neurobiological mechanisms (Suzuki et al, 2004). This process of memory reconsolidation would be related to previous de-arousal, in a way that has not been entirely established at this moment (Solomon & Shapiro, 2008). The authors state that further studies are needed to evaluate the relationship between reported changes and treatment outcome. In other words, we do not yet know the sequential order of these effects and cannot assume causality. Does heart rate decrease because the memory is becoming less distressing due to processing? Or does the decreased arousal facilitate processing of the memory so that it becomes less distressing? Only randomized controlled research under the appropriate conditions can give an answer to these questions.

With the lowering of arousal, information from other memory networks may be able to link to the network holding the dysfunctionally stored information (Shapiro, 1995, 2001). Our clinical experience is in line with this theory. When bilateral stimulation is used on a dysfunctional element (for example, the ANP's phobia of another dissociative part), the disturbing emotions often decrease. So the initial effect tends to be a calming sensation. Frequently, a dissociative part's perspective toward another part changes spontaneously. When bilateral stimulation is continued, we observe further associations with elements that were contained in different dissociative parts. This is consistent with the linking in of adaptive information as formulated by the AIP model.

The same reasoning is used with the tip of the finger strategy, mentioned in the introduction and described in detail in chapter 12 on trauma processing. Sometimes we may be interested in decreasing a dysfunctional emotion, which can be understood as a consequence of the traumatic memory contained in an EP. This intervention is included in this chapter, because the processing of dissociative phobias, as we understand it, can be combined with the tip of the finger strategy in a dynamic way. In our experience, some difficulties that EPs may present in engaging in a collaborative dialogue may come from high internal pressure. Even when the part is not ready to approach traumatic events, we can decrease part of this pressure with the tip of the finger strategy.

We have observed that BLS can help, but only initially, because if we continue stimulating, the initial de-arousal can switch to hyper-arousal when the client begins to contact traumatic content. It could reflect that the de-arousal effect is not present in every client in the same way or that, in some clients, de-arousal can happen before the connection with disturbing material, but this happens so fast that we cannot observe it. This seems to be the case, at least with some clients: We obtain a de-arousal effect with three sets of BLS, but the opposite when we continue BLS for more than three sets. Knowing this, we must use fewer sets of BLS initially and rule out the intervention when clients tend to hyperarousal. In these cases, we would need to stabilize them using different procedures. This does not imply that we definitely rule out BLS or even this specific procedure. BLS can be used on other targets or even with the same one at a different moment. By using an experimental and tentative attitude, we can decide how to proceed in each session with each client.

It is very important to check the internal process carefully and alternate this intervention with others, such as working with dissociative parts (negotiation, communication, collaboration), psychoeducation, reflective and collaborative analysis of what is happening, resource installation, etc. It is relevant to keep in mind that the associative process may begin or continue after the therapy session, especially in people with complex trauma. This intervention must be carefully titrated, and in the first sessions, we recommend using a very tentative and minimalist style. It implies starting with a tiny bit of disturbing information and gradually increasing this type of work, as the client is able to handle it.

In other cases, we may be interested in enhancing connections, and this can also help to overcome phobias between dissociative parts. This procedure is described in chapter 7 on integration. This effect may allow increased internal collaboration, alternating the processing of dysfunctional elements with the promotion of internal connection (Gonzalez, Seijo, & Mosquera, 2009). In clients with strong barriers between dissociative parts, or in very early phases of therapy, installing the internal connection may generate contact with traumatic material that some dissociative parts are not prepared to deal with. This is a powerful intervention that we must adequately titrate.

Processing Phobias Procedure

Phobia of Dissociative Parts

The procedure for processing phobias consists of focusing on the emotion and somatic sensation that a dissociative part (ANP or EP) is experiencing towards another part. We ask the part who is active in the therapist's office (frequently an ANP) to ask the other part (frequently an EP) if she wants relief from the dysfunctional emotion(s) she is feeling towards any other part.

Working on the phobia of dissociative parts may be a huge task for some clients. It is essential to go at a pace that the client can handle and do work that will gradually facilitate and enhance internal communication and collaboration. Some clients understand that internal communication is a problem, and they wish to change it, but they feel "it's impossible." Others are terrified of what might happen. Some EMDR active ingredients may be used to foster the negotiation process.

This modified EMDR procedure has been used in several cases with DID and DDNOS type I diagnoses. Positive effects at different levels were found in many of them. Sometimes, the procedure resulted in increased contact with disturbing emotions or traumatic memories, which could usually be managed during the session, without negative effects during and after the session.

One client experienced overwhelming contact between previously phobic parts, and four sessions were needed to recover stability. But her general functioning was maintained, and she continued improving. Another client spontaneously recovered previously amnesic memories outside the therapy session, resulting in therapeutic insight and significant improvement in her general functioning.

Some of the clients experienced intense changes, fatigue, and some uncomfortable sensations during the following weeks after the session, but none of them talked about this in a negative way. This was due to the fact that they experienced significant positive changes in their functioning, changes that they had never experienced with other approaches.

Some of our clients explained, "We (the dissociative part and the ANP) know we need some days to digest all these changes, it's like having a hangover. But when all these sensations settle, we feel much better. And since we know what is happening, we simply give ourselves the time we need to do it." The same may happen after a standard EMDR procedure with a simple trauma case. However, with complex trauma, we should keep in mind that very small bits of processing can have a very intense effect, and this may happen outside the therapist's office.

Positive changes were a frequent outcome. Even a client with severe DID improved, when there was no consistent compliance with therapy sessions and long unproductive work with the internal system. The extreme emotional deregulation and decompensation contraindicated introducing EMDR trauma reprocessing. But after processing dissociative phobias, she improved significantly and described the EMDR session as the most useful intervention in four years of therapy. Another client, whose dissociative phobia was processed, reported feeling more "connected inside" and less scared of his reactions toward himself. For the first time in years, he felt he could verbalize what was haunting him, and he began to understand his problems as an attempt to adapt to his difficult childhood circumstances, instead of hating himself for his reactions.

Not all clients experienced such spectacular results. However, processing phobias resulted in increased realization about aspects of themselves and their traumatic history, a more integrated functioning, and an enhanced internal collaboration and communication. In clients who were already being treated with standard EMDR procedures and other interventions, this procedure strengthened the previous work. Interestingly, in clients who had previously worked with the dissociative parts without introducing BLS, when BLS was introduced to re-process the dissociative phobias, changes were not only quantitative (faster and deeper effect) but also qualitative (changes not previously achieved in other areas).

The dissociative part we are working with should agree with the procedure and understand its goals. We may begin with the ANP, by processing the rejection and the somatic correlate in the ANP toward the EP, or with an EP, focusing on its emotion/sensation toward the ANP or other EP. We can alternate work between parts during the session, adapting to the client's situation. We introduce BLS when we observe a blockage in the process of developing empathy, communication, and collaboration among parts, or to increase a positive change in this direction. We can see this dynamic process in the following case example:

> Therapist: Please, ask the part who contains the rage to think if she needs all this rage, or if she feels that it would be best to relieve part of it (proposing the tip of the finger strategy).
>
> Client: She said that it would be better for her to let go of some of this rage.
>
> T: Ask her if she agrees with processing some of this rage with EMDR.
>
> C: She said okay.
>
> T: Then tell her to focus on the part of the rage that she wants to let go of. She doesn't need to share the contents that appear.
>
> C: She is ready.
>
> T: Then follow my fingers (few and slow eye movements). Ask her how she feels.
>
> C: She said "better" but... I have a comment about her attitude (the ANP feels disappointed, which is an indirect manifestation of the phobia of dissociative parts).
>
> T: Well, now we will work with you. Focus on the sensation that you are feeling about this part.
>
> C: I am noticing a somatic tension in my chest.
>
> T: Go with that (four eye movements).
>
> C: Really, this part is associated with my father (increase in realization).
>
> T: And how is your tension now.
>
> C: It has disappeared.

When we target the phobia in the dissociative part, we focus on the emotion and somatic sensation. We do not recommend accepting an emotion without a somatic correlate because the "name" of an emotion may just be a rationalization. Focusing on this element, we do a short set of bilateral stimulation and check the effect on the part. Applied in this way, BLS usually has the effect of decreasing the disturbing emotion. The initial dysfunctional sensation may change to a more adaptive one or shift a little bit in this direction. The perceived image of the dissociative part may change to a less threatening or negative one. The phobic reaction in the ANP usually changes and often decreases or disappears without direct intervention from the therapist.

Let's see another example:

A DID woman comes to therapy because her partner is worried about her health because an EP tried to choke her on several occasions. The client as ANP is not aware of the risk, saying, "I cannot be worried since I love life and I would never kill myself." Initially, she was able to identify two emotional parts that she described as "bug," usually felt in the genital area, like a harpoon; and "ball," usually felt as a ball in her throat that does not allow her to breath or swallow. In this session, we ask her to draw her inner system. She said she could not do this, since she was reluctant to consider them "part of her," and just thinking about them terrified her, expressing a strong phobia of these dissociative parts.

C (talking about "ball"): It would be like something that is trying to make a knot.

T: Could you describe this "something"?

C: No, it doesn't have any attributes; let´s see (thinking)...

T: Could you draw "bug" and "ball"?

C: I have a lot of drawings, but you know what happens... every time I try to draw bug, I draw some type of bird. (She is very phobic of birds, to the point that she throws up when she sees one. Here a phobia of an external object is associated with an inner phobia toward a mental element.) And I can´t draw ball, I would like to draw the tension but I can´t.

Exploring the phobia in the ANP toward the EPS:

T: Would you like to understand them?

C: No I wouldn't, I´m not curious at all, I just want them to disappear (clear phobia of these dissociative parts).

T: When you talk about "bug" and "ball" you seem to feel contempt.

C (thinking): Contempt... well... they are unpleasant elements.

T (trying to define a specific focus to target): Unpleasant elements... How does that feel? What feeling is predominant towards the unpleasant elements?

C: Attack... I feel fear.

T: Fear.

C: Yes, because they hurt me physically.

T: Okay, and now, talking about "bug" and "ball," are you distressed?

C: I´m making an effort not to feel distressed (client seems distressed).

T: Would you like to relieve a bit of the tension you feel towards them?

C: Yes, but what I would really like is to be able to suppress them when they come... next time they come I will put my hands down my throat, and if it´s necessary, I will do an exploration (vaginal exploration).

T: But you can hurt yourself and this is not our goal.

The therapist tries to explore the possibility of processing only part of the dysfunctional emotion in the EPs (tip of the finger strategy). Since direct communication with these parts, which are very rudimentary, is not possible, the procedure will be performed focusing on an unspecific sensation associated with these parts. At this point, it would also be possible to focus on the rejection that the ANP is experiencing toward these two EPs, but the therapist preferred to not start from this point because the ANP is far from understanding that to change her negative reaction toward these parts is good for her.

T: Where does that sensation come from? Does it come from "bug," "ball," or both?

C: The origin is from both "bug" and "ball," and at a certain point, I just don´t remember what happened... people tell me I squeezed my neck with my scarf... I remember having the "ball" sensation, so my guess is that I do that to get rid of "ball."

T: Are you feeling any uncomfortable sensations right now?

C: Yes, a little bit of "ball." (She touches her throat.)

T: Could we try to relieve part of this sensation?

Focusing on the somatic sensation.

C: Yes, what should I do?

T: Just follow my fingers with your eyes without moving your head.

C: Okay.

T: Focus on the sensation.

BLS (short set).

T: What is coming?

C: It went down, it switched places.

T: Where to?

C: Near my clavicles.

T: Can you focus on that for a bit more?

C: Yes.

BLS.

T: What do you notice?

C: I feel better. I swallow better.

After processing the phobia of the EPs, she was able to draw the internal system (see picture below):

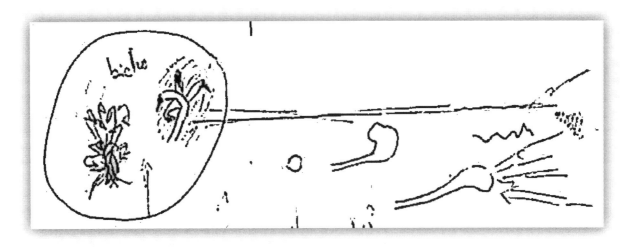

Sometimes the client as ANP does not realize about her own phobia. When there is fluent communication in the internal system, we can see it more clearly. For example, when we ask a supposedly hostile EP about her feelings toward the ANP, she answers, "She (the ANP) is the one who has negative feelings towards me (the EP)." This disclosure was extremely surprising for the ANP, who was convinced that the EP was the one that had problems with her.

Hostility tends to be reciprocal in severe traumatization, and frequently EPs also experience phobic reactions towards the ANP. The ANP may be aware or not of this negative reaction from the EP, but even when the ANP knows it, it does not necessarily imply that she fully realizes what this reaction means. For example, a therapist asks an EP to focus on her sensation towards her (the ANP). The EP expresses an intense and disturbing fear. The ANP was not only surprised by the EP´s fear towards her, but also because after processing this fear with BLS, she realized this fear was a reflection of the fear toward the abuser.

We can use this procedure even when the dissociative parts do not realize they are experiencing a phobia of another part. This lack of realization is just another manifestation of this phobia, more extreme than a clear rejection. When the dissociative parts can notice distrust, fear, or rage towards other parts, the degree of realization increases. This is why it can be very useful to focus on the somatic sensation, which can be present even when the part is not aware of the underlying emotion or the meaning of this sensation. However, even when parts deny the existence of a phobic reaction towards other parts, we can propose to process the somatic sensation that they are experiencing toward other parts. After BLS, parts usually understand the motives and meaning of their reactions. It is always important to ask for permission for any procedure we want to try.

Phobia of Attachment to the Therapist

The client-therapist relationship is a very important issue along the entire therapeutic process, but it is crucial in early stages. Dworkin (2005) developed various EMDR procedures to overcome relational problems during the processing of traumatic memories. He proposes a "relational interweave" to solve difficulties that arise from client-therapist issues while applying the standard protocol. We can also process relational targets with BLS, although we will delve deeper into relational issues in chapter 10. Our proposal in this chapter is to work on relational issues during the stabilization phase, introducing BLS on relational targets, before the processing of traumatic memories. If the client is ready, we can also work on memories that are feeding the client-therapist problems. The following are some examples of ways in which we can use this procedure.

If the client can tolerate to connect with traumatic elements, we can use the "relational bridge" procedure (Gonzalez, Seijo, & Mosquera, 2009) to search for the feeding memories connected with problems in the therapeutic relationship. After identifying the memory, we can use the standard EMDR protocol to process it.

If the client can partially tolerate traumatic contents, but we consider it is too early for standard protocol, we can introduce work with dissociative parts, bearing in mind the client´s specific characteristics. We may promote an interaction between the adult client (ANP) and his image at the age of the traumatic memory (EP). We can introduce BLS to process dysfunctional elements in this procedure.

If the client cannot tolerate contact with traumatic memories or even to remember them, we can use the tip of the finger strategy, targeting directly the dysfunctional emotion/sensation that is being activated during the relational situation. This dysfunctional emotion/sensation may be contained in a specific dissociative part (ANP or EP). The procedure is similar to the one we previously described, using as the target the emotion and somatic sensation that the part is feeling toward the therapist or the therapy. The emotion/sensation may be a present one or a past one, with actual or past therapist and therapies.

As we will explain in chapter 10, the relevance of relational issues is higher in the treatment of severely traumatized clients. Difficulties in the therapeutic relationship are not only good examples of interpersonal difficulties that clients have in their current life, but are also good clues for the EMDR therapist. They are a way to search for relevant past experiences that are contributing to the client´s present problems. For instance, the client may have difficulties opening up and giving personal information, being alert to every word or gesture from the therapist, or analyzing the therapist´s intentions. These reactions feed on traumatic experiences (keeping the secret, attachment issues, the abuser´s unpredictable behavior, etc.). The client frequently hides, these aspects, because the direct expression of feelings, concerns, and needs was not the norm in the unstructured and disorganized childhood environment. They need an attentive therapist who can identify these issues and not personalize them. Clients need a guide to overcome these difficulties. For therapists who are not used to "searching" for the clues, the use of specific screening questionnaires (Gonzalez, Seijo, & Mosquera, 2009), such as the Relational Problems Questionnaire (Mosquera & Gonzalez, 2009), may be useful.

Let´s see an example of managing attachment difficulties:

During supervision, a colleague commented that one of her clients was trying to "play" with her by not talking about important information and by making jokes when he felt pressured. The therapist believed he could benefit from EMDR but could not manage to follow the protocol in the "expected way." The client would leave out information, change subjects, or stop the processing because he was getting "nothing." His therapist thought they had a good relationship, but for some reason, she was not confident enough to do this work. We attended several sessions to observe how the work was being done and picked up on some relational aspects between therapist and client that could be interfering with the processing.

After this, the supervisor had a short meeting with both therapist and client and spoke about several things that could be happening in the session. We scheduled for an EMDR session with the supervisor. The client quickly idealized the supervisor, and from there, by processing dysfunctional elements, we got to core beliefs about himself that were interfering with therapy. The client had been in therapy for over 20 years with very minor changes. During the session, the client seemed uncomfortable and quite tense. We asked him if he was nervous and he said yes, that he had a weird sensation that he could not explain. When we asked if this had something to do with the new therapist, he said yes.

> Therapist: Okay, just go with the sensation you have now (with the therapist). Can you?
>
> Client: Yes.
>
> BLS.
>
> T: What is coming?
>
> C: What is coming (thoughtfully)… the first day you came into the session, when I was with L (his therapist) you said something like "I know you tend to make jokes but this won´t work with me" (client smiles). At that moment, I think I thought of you like as of higher category, like an authority figure. Since then, things began to work better for me. I began to function better. Then, when you supervised the sessions from behind the mirror (supervision mirror), the conversation (referring to therapy and therapist) changed, things were more focused.
>
> T: Okay, and somehow this is associated to an authority figure.
>
> C: Yes.
>
> T: Go with that (BLS).
>
> T: What is coming?
>
> C: That I am not totally confident that this will work out.
>
> T: Go with that (BLS). What is coming now?
>
> C: This uncertainty is not because of a failure in the method (referring to EMDR) or the therapy… this lack of trust has to do with me…. because I don´t do the homework, and this happens with you and with everyone, with everything.
>
> T: Go with that (BLS). What is coming now?
>
> C: That it is another boycott, another defense.

We can see that this dynamic introduction of BLS at certain points increases the client´s realization about his behavior. Minimization with the first therapist was as problematic as the supervisor´s idealization, and both are defensive behaviors linked to his traumatic history. The client could be partially aware of what his behavior meant, but after BLS, his perspective became clearer, and the therapeutic stance changed.

Phobia of Attachment

Attachment is a core aspect in severe traumatization. Leeds (2001, 2009) has thoughtfully conceptualized the EMDR approach integrating attachment theories, and he has proposed alternative ways to conceptualize cases and work with EMDR from this perspective. Other authors have proposed EMDR interventions that are useful to overcome attachment issues (Crow, 2007; Wesselmann, 2007; Parnell, 2013). Knipe´s loving eyes protocol (2008) and the procedures to install a healthy self-care pattern (Gonzalez, Mosquera, & Seijo, 2009), which are extensively described in chapter 6, are also useful interventions to overcome attachment problems in present relationships. Working on specific events from early relationships with caregivers, both the traumatic and the idealized ones (Knipe, 2006), we are processing the dysfunctionally stored information that is feeding current attachment difficulties.

We can also work on current interpersonal problems, since this may be more tolerable for some clients than to deal with past issues. This covers relationships with partners, friends, colleagues, and relatives. Depending on the client´s characteristics and the stage of therapy, we can process these situations with the standard EMDR procedure. However, we must keep in mind that relational issues often trigger early core memories of attachment with primary caregivers, so this must be managed carefully.

An especially relevant issue is how clients can establish an attachment relationship with their own children. In order to treat this, it is important to improve the client´s difficulties, prevent further problems in the children and future adults, and interrupt the trans-generational transmission of abuse.

We can see an example of this type of procedure in the following clinical case. This client explains her difficulties with her son:

> Client: When he presented certain behaviors, I became really aggressive, I couldn´t manage my authority. But after this, when he wanted to cry, I didn´t tolerate it; I didn´t allow him to do this. In some occasions I even put a towel in his mouth...

> Therapist: Imagine a really intimate relationship with your son, where he can show you his vulnerability, his emotions. To be able to actually see him... Notice what sensation you feel while you imagine this.

> We process with BLS this disturbing emotion in the ANP toward her son, and she can realize more relevant issues.

C: When he was little and expressed emotions, I would sometimes cover his mouth with my hand. Seeing his emotions was like looking at my own emotions... and the rage emerged as an automatic reaction.

At this point, we use BLS to install the differentiation between the vulnerable child inside her son and the vulnerable EP inside her, which is activated by her son's emotions.

Her capacity of having perspective, of being focused while she was feeling rage, was also reinforced with BLS. At this point her father's introject appeared, with a core belief, "You do everything wrong, you are stupid." After another set of BLS, she connected with the idealized figure of the father and her need of attachment with the abusive caregiver. Finally a realization about "I am now an adult, and my father was reacting toward his own issues, not against me" emerged, and this intervention helped her to develop a more calm and supportive attitude toward her son.

Phobia of Traumatic Memories

This is the core phobia in structural dissociation. To overcome this phobia is a central part of the therapy, but it is also the most difficult issue. The phobia of trauma and the phobia of attachment described below constitute the core of structural dissociation.

The work with the phobia of traumatic memories has to be approached after the work on the phobia of dissociative parts and attachment with the therapist, although different aspects are present, and different phobias can be simultaneously activated. The phobia of traumatic memories must be carefully planned, keeping in mind the client's resilience and timing. A progressive style should be the norm, fractionating the trauma work (Forgash & Copeley, 2008; Paulsen, 2007, 2009; Twombly, 2005, 2008), as we will describe in chapter 12. Knipe's CIPOS method (2008), where reality orientation is installed with bilateral stimulation, and a progressive approach to traumatic memories is alternated with reality orientation, is also an intervention that can help to overcome the phobia of trauma.

We can also target the phobia of traumatic memories itself, focusing on the negative reaction towards contacting traumatic content. We can say to the client: "Please, look at this part's eyes and feel in your body what it would mean to you to make contact with what this part contains."

Sometimes we need to help the ANP to follow this instruction, because the phobia itself may make it difficult. The first target, when the client has important difficulties performing the task, would be to focus on the difficulty to imagine it, to look into the part's eyes, or to establish contact with emotions or sensations. All these aspects may be expressions of the phobia of traumatic memories.

When processing the phobia of traumatic memories, we should be especially careful, because it is the core dissociative phobia. This work can be very intense, even when it is not evident. We need to apply very small dosages of BLS, always less than the client might appear to tolerate. If clients make contact with elements they are not prepared to cope with or assimilate, they may become de-compensated. Our goal is to help the client overcome trauma in the safest possible way.

As we already mentioned, the effects of this intervention can be intense. One DID client had suffered sexual abuse by her father when she was a young girl, but only some of the dissociative parts could remember it. An ANP presented a phobia of this traumatic memory. She did not fully make contact with the abuse memory in the session. But after the session, she started to hear a voice in her head telling her, "Kill him, kill him." She was very afraid because she thought the voice was asking her to kill her son. She had heard this voice many times in the past, bur then she realized for the first time that the voices (coming from different EPs) were talking about her father. She imagined herself hugging a 7-year-old EP while she told this part, "It´s over, you are now here with me, in the present, it´s not happening anymore, never again." This was very useful but very hard for the client. We knew that this client had enough strength to start working on these memories. But the most relevant change happened outside the therapeutic setting, and this same situation in a more vulnerable client could be intolerable. The most important aspect of any technique is not only how to implement it, but when and how much. One way of titrating this intervention is to use the "inner scan" and learn to translate indirect stop signals, which were described in chapter 4.

Phobia of Change, Intimacy, and Normal Life

The previous types of phobias are related to approaching core trauma. In this section we will describe phobias that are related to the outside world. These phobias usually emerge later in therapy, but it is useful to anticipate this, introducing the idea of "change as renewal" from the first sessions. It can also be useful to explain how, after an initial positive change, the client may feel pressured or overwhelmed, being prone to get worse, since they are used to their past way of functioning and relating. It is important to explain that we do not expect this to be easy, since it is something new and unknown to them. Clients that are used to being "inside-focused" and investing a lot of energy in their inner world may be afraid of an external world that they perceive as dangerous. People with frequent interactions with dissociative parts may experience integration as terrible loneliness. One DID client expressed it very clearly when she realized her inner helper part was actually a part of her mind, "I am alone!!!" For severely traumatized people, inner relationships can substitute relations with other people, since they have difficulties dealing with relationships in general.

In a psychoeducational program for borderline clients (Mosquera, 2004), one of the sessions is used to explain the phobia of change and normal life. This usually takes place after a few other sessions, when the client is doing better. Most clients feel relief when the subject is pointed out and recognize feeling pressured, scared, and even terrified of their "new life." Most have doubts about their capability to function better for prolonged periods of time and feel tempted to "go back to what they know best." These phobias can be processed with EMDR just as we have seen in previous paragraphs, since there are usually dysfunctionally stored elements that are interfering with the client´s ability to function better.

After several sessions processing phobias between parts, dysfunctional emotions in some parts, and a lot of modified EMDR processing of traumatic memories, one client told us:

Client: "What about my Self?" (She is referring to the "core Self," a central part of the system developed along the therapeutic process.)

Therapist: What is happening with your Self?

C: He is very tired, despondent... He doesn't know how things will be from now one... He is afraid about the future...

T: It's very common. It's been many years functioning that way, now he must learn to function in a different way, a completely new way. But does he understand these changes will be positive?

C: He doesn't know, he can't feel things this way.

T: Then, ask him to focus on what he is feeling and experiencing now... and let me know when he is ready.

Client nods.

BLS.

With each set of bilateral stimulation the "Self" experiences the change from the dysfunctional emotion to a more hopeful and positive sensation about changes and future.

T: Then, you and all the parts in the system may now hold your hands and feel the connection among all. You (the adult self) can feel how you are connected with all the parts and how this connection will give you strength and resources to cope with any situation in the present and the future. Feel it together.

We check that the internal sensation is entirely positive, and then we do bilateral stimulation to install it. The phrase "feel it together" is intended to increase co-consciousness.

In EMDR therapy, we usually work with a past-present-future perspective. Aspects of intimacy and normal life are equivalent to the processing of present situations. The phobia of change is related to the future template. Hofmann (2004) proposes to work on the future template as one of the first interventions. Hopelessness is a frequent experience in severely traumatized people. To install the possibility of positive change, improvement, or a good future for the client in the early phase of the therapy may be a good way to minimize the phobia of change.

Summary

Dissociative phobias are main factors maintaining structural dissociation. Working on these phobias is important throughout the therapeutic process, and its structure presents differences with traumatic memories processing.

The introduction of specific EMDR procedures can enhance and potentiate the strategy for working on dissociative phobias proposed by the theory of structural dissociation of the personality. This work is a way to stabilize the client in the early phase of the therapy and to overcome specifics points of blockage throughout the therapeutic process.

Chapter 9
Working on Blockages or "Stuck Points"

Dolores Mosquera, Anabel Gonzalez, & Andrew M. Leeds

With survivors of severe neglect and abuse, a host of problems in daily living disrupt their lives. In such cases, we cannot - and should not - begin by attempting to directly confront core traumatic memories. As first described by Janet (1919), issues of impaired self-care, high-risk and self-injurious behaviors, and a range of dissociative phobias must first be addressed in an extended preparation phase. In such cases, many intrapsychic elements surround the core traumatic events and remain dysfunctionally stored in isolated neuro-networks. As we commented in chapters 8 & 9, only after overcoming peripheral DSI elements, we can approach traumatic issues effectively and safely.

In some highly functional dissociative clients, the preparation and stabilization process seems to be clear and easy to structure. We can establish contact with dissociative parts easily and communicate with them. Relational issues are not too complex, and mental efficiency is high.

But other clients present a "blurred" aspect that can sometimes resemble a low IQ, a lack of motivation, or a non-collaborative attitude. In severely traumatized clients, sometimes there is so much conflict in the inner system that most of the available mental energy is depleted with internal struggles, and the consequence is a very low level of mental efficiency.

Other clients can seem to be disconnected. They can come to consultation and tell us about their traumas, but it is as if they were talking about somebody else's history. Sometimes they cannot realize or even remember any trauma at all, showing a "flat" personality without emotional resonance. In these cases, we can even elicit all the elements of phase 3, but most of the time, their statements will just be rationalizations, not here-and-now self-assessments, felt emotions, or fully perceived somatic sensations. So when we proceed with phase 4, we find apparently normal reprocessing that remains at a cognitive level, but nothing really moves. There are no emotional shifts, no psychophysiological relief, no lasting realizations.

Still other clients present "stuck points" at different moments of the therapeutic process, some at the beginning of therapy, others after an initial improvement that somehow is interrupted or becomes slower. Sometimes we can understand what is happening by exploring within the inner system. We may find that a part or group of parts is involved with this situation. We can also identify problems in the therapeutic relationship or daily life problems. But in some cases, the reason for this stuck point is not clear.

When we do not have a clear target to reprocess or all the elements that we consider necessary to begin standard EMDR reprocessing, we should think about the resources we can use with the elements that we do have. For example, clinical experience is telling us that the effects of BLS are wider than they were initially supposed to be. As we described in the chapter about the AIP model, we can work not only on memories of external traumatizing experiences, but also on dysfunctionally stored information for intrapsychic experiences that is generated in the inner world (see chapter 3). Some examples were mentioned in prior chapters: the work on defenses by Knipe (2006), the procedures for processing affect phobia from Leeds (2001), the DeTUR for addictions (Popky, 2005), or the processing of dissociative phobias that we propose in chapter 8.

But, could we extend this possibility even more? In standard EMDR protocol for PTSD, we can work with material that the client does not want to disclose. Could we work with material that the client not only does not want to disclose, but does not even understand? Could we use modified EMDR BLS procedures for other purposes, even if it still is not clearly defined in basic research? Actually EMDR was born that way: The clinical observations of the effects of BLS came first (Shapiro, 1989, 1995), yet even after extensive evidence for EMDR´s treatment effect has led to international acceptance of EMDR as an evidence based treatment for PTSD, researchers are trying to understand the basic mechanism for its effectiveness.

Two aspects could be considered. The first one is the possible effect of modified EMDR BLS procedures in improving mental efficiency. The second one is an apparently unblocking effect of modified EMDR BLS procedures. Some clinical findings point in that direction.

Mental Efficiency

EMDR BLS procedures increase mental efficiency. During the desensitization phase, we often observe how clients experienced many insights, and they can realize aspects about themselves that were not accessible to them before. More connections and probably more integrative capacity seem to be a consequence of EMDR procedures including BLS. This effect may be interesting in complex trauma clients, as we can see in the following example:

A low-functioning DID client has communication difficulties. Even when asked simple questions, she frequently answers, "I don´t know. I never learned to read or write, I can´t think about complicated issues." Her severe dissociative symptoms were evident to other people since she presented variable behaviors and memory lapses, but she was not aware of these occurrences. The only symptoms she described were auditory hallucinations, but she could not identify any characteristic of her voices nor establish an inner communication with them.

We asked her to focus on her sensation of "being unable to think" and did two short sets of BLS. After this, her thoughts seemed to be more fluent:

> Client: I can´t think about anything, I am very silly.
>
> Therapist: I don´t think you are silly... Focus on your sensation of being unable of thinking.
>
> BLS.
>
> T: Can you hear the voices right now?
>
> C: They are shouting.
>
> T: Can you understand what they are saying?
>
> C (slapping her head): No, I can´t.
>
> T: Okay, focus on that (BLS)... Try to listen again.
>
> C: They say I am useless.

The interaction between the therapist, the ANP, and the EP continued, with an increasing in inner communication. With this client, we used continuous BLS in many sessions, after finding that this intervention facilitated higher-level mental activity, which was much more difficult or impossible without it. For example, we observed that she could draw a map of her inner system while under the effect of continuous BLS. Without this, the client became blocked in front of the paper.

Continuous BLS is not a routine recommended intervention for dissociative clients. The same caution applies to other procedures presented all along this book. Each procedure must be carefully selected and evaluated as appropriate in the unique situation of each client. With this specific client, continuous BLS was useful during a certain phase of her treatment. The client was stable during and after these interventions. But the same intervention with continuous BLS could provoke emotional dysregulation in another client. The use of continuous BLS should be viewed as investigational, and it should be considered only by appropriately trained clinicians with a good knowledge of complex traumatization and the specific characteristics of their clients. A progressive approach and a solid therapeutic relationship are needed to make this safe.

Using a tentative and progressive approach, we can introduce these procedures in a way that is destabilizing. If the client has an adverse response, we can re-stabilize the client in different ways. It is prudent to begin with a short intervention in the first part of the consultation to have time to redirect the session if the client becomes emotionally over-activated or experiences depersonalization. The benefits for the client can be important, as we will see in different examples along this chapter.

In complex cases, we can find ourselves facing a never-ending dilemma: to give it a try or not. There is no guaranteed safe intervention in therapy, and to just wait can sometimes be equivalent to neglect. As therapists, we are obliged to be cautious and not cause damage, but we cannot remain with crossed arms when the client´s condition is severe. We think that the solution for a dilemma is to look for an alternative option. In our opinion, the alternative is to use a tentative and progressive approach, asking for permission, making decisions with the client, using initially small fragments of any intervention, and depending on the results of each intervention, continue or not.

In this chapter, we will describe how to reprocess unspecific blockages with transcripts from a clinical case, so that the reader can see how these interventions are dynamically developed in a session. The general purpose of this chapter is to propose the dynamic use of short sets of BLS, during therapy sessions focused on blockages or unspecific stuck points. We can also choose to work on these issues without BLS, and many useful interventions could be done. However, our goal here is to show where modified EMDR BLS procedures can be used to increase therapeutic effectiveness.

As we get closer to working directly with traumatic memories, our modified EMDR BLS procedures will be more and more similar to the standard EMDR procedural steps. With the progressive approach that we are proposing, we will first work on unspecific targets (increasing mental efficiency or overcoming blockages) or peripheral elements (such as intrapsychic dissociative phobias) as part of the essential work of neurocognitive, developmental repair that precedes a more structured focus on core traumatic memories, which will take place in the later stages of therapy. When we propose adapting EMDR BLS procedures to the level that a client can achieve at any specific moment, we are in no way implying a lack of structure in therapy. In every case, we apply a thoughtful process to the selection of the degree of structure in methodology appropriate to the needs of the client. We contrast this with an "everything is okay" approach that can lead to a chaotic, indiscriminate, and unplanned use of BLS. With survivors of early chaotic environments, who lived in a continuous storm inside and sometimes in their daily life, therapy should be very structured. In this chapter, we describe how we approach the use of modified EMDR BLS procedures in a thoughtful, structured manner in the early phases of work on increasing mental efficiency, working through peripheral elements, and overcoming blockages.

Processing Unspecific Blockages

Some clients describe the effect of EMDR therapy as a major change after being blocked, sometimes for years, in previous therapy. In the most fortunate cases, this change can happen in a single session or after a short period of therapy.

After processing an unspecific blockage, a client who suffered sexual abuse during childhood by her father, describes this kind of effect very graphically:

> "This is absolutely amazing. I have been in therapy for years, talking about all these issues. The therapist who treated me for the past five years was very supportive and kind to me.
>
> She helped me very much. Along this therapy I could realize what had happened to me, at first I couldn't remember anything, I just had to get out my home, get divorced and leave my

son with my husband because I felt unable to take care of him… my heart was broken because of this, but I think that this was the best I could do for them at that moment…

After a long therapy I was able to remember. I could understand that it was not my fault, that what my father did to me was not my fault, but I couldn´t get out of my deep depressive state. I have a lot of good friends who love and care for me, and with their help and my therapist´s help, I could put a stop to my suicide attempts. But the depression didn´t improve in spite of many years of therapy and a lot of different medications. My therapist told me we should stop therapy, because my state had become chronic, she told me I should learn to live with it, and I was trying to.

Now, I can´t believe it! During the previous session, and during the following days I could feel happy, maybe I am feeling true happiness for the first time. It´s like a knot was undone and everything changed. Before I was blocked, and after the last session this blockage disappeared."

The effect of EMDR therapy is not always so evident and spectacular, but therapists who come from other approaches describe cases of clients who understand what their problem is and what could help them, but who are blocked, unable to make changes or to progress. This "unblocking" effect can be observed with standard EMDR PTSD procedure, but we hypothesize that a similar effect can be obtained with modified protocols, using the unspecific blockage perceived by the client as a target.

Some clients can identify this blocking sensation, even physically. In other cases, they can describe what is blocking them, but sometimes this is only a rationalization of a "stuck point," which is really placed at a more primitive level of functioning, such as the sensorimotor level. In other cases, they feel blocked, but they cannot find any explanation for this, nor can they understand why or what is happening. In spite of this, if we ask clients to locate this sensation of "being blocked" in their body, they usually find a spot. We can use this element as a target for reprocessing, and in some cases, we can ask for a rating of the blockage level, along the line of a SUD rating, if we think it can help. The main intervention here should be stated as: where do you notice that blockage in your body? This question helps to identify a concrete element of DSI, and it provides a sensory focus for increasing the mindful perspective in the client.

When to Use this Procedure

Over the course of a phase-oriented approach (Gelinas, 2003; Korn, 2009; Van der Kolk & Van der Hart, 1989) to working with complex cases involving chronic early relational neglect and trauma, we have many options for EMDR procedures we may consider and use. When there are specific traumatic memories, we can work on identified targets. We can install functional elements or reprocess dysfunctional ones. We can choose to work with the internal system of parts initially in order to stabilize the client. We can work with the standard protocol on a traumatic memory while maintaining client stability and daily functioning. When things progress adequately in any of these ways, the process is fluent. But sometimes we do not know (in spite of different attempts) how to approach a case, or at some point of therapy, progress becomes slower or stuck. The following are some examples.

We had been working with a client for three years. She had a third, serious relapse that required her to go to the hospital. After this last relapse, she was in a depressive state, and it was impossible to find any reason for this or a related target to reprocess. She had a sense of blockage that she associated with a somatic sensation in her stomach. Reprocessing that target, she connected with a lot of underlying guilt related to her history of drug abuse. After this session, her attitude changed, and she started to make positive changes.

Another client, a victim of incest and severe physical maltreatment by her father, seemed to be stuck in her therapy after two years. She was asked to reflect on what was impeding her full recovery. She noticed a sensation of "something inside," without any realization about what it might be. That unspecific sensation was used as a target. By focusing on it while attending to BLS, the client contacted negative feelings toward her victimized mother that she had never previously recognized.

A client came to therapy because his mother thought he needed help. She believed he had been traumatized by the critical and hostile attitude of his father. The client could not remember any episodes before his parents´ divorce, when his father became verbally abusive and aggressive. He had previously attempted doing EMDR with another therapist, but those sessions were unsuccessful because the client did not know why he was in therapy. He had difficulties connecting with his emotions. He could describe situations that he identified as problematic, such as difficulties in school, but when he described them, he neither showed nor described any disturbing emotions or sensations. He could not feel anything when thinking about personal resources or good situations and was not aware of any physical sensations linked to those positive experiences. In the face of these difficulties, one session that was especially productive was the work with "that which doesn´t allow me to become better." Paradoxically, the session itself did not initially appear to be effective. There were no relevant associations and many statements of "nothing is coming up." We returned several times to this very unspecific target, the only one that this client could access. After this session, the client said he felt worse, but for the first time he reported feeling many different emotions and a completely new one: rage. In the next session, he was able to express rage against his father, something that had never happened before. This "worsening" actually represented establishing an emotional contact that seemed strange for the client, since he had lacked this capacity previously. Obviously, the underlying emotions were not pleasant, but contacting them allowed a change in the therapeutic course. In subsequent sessions, he was gradually able to learn to make use of EMDR reprocessing to address the effects of the adverse experiences with his father.

A Clinical Case

Ania was a 27-year-old woman. She came to therapy because she could not walk. After many medical exams, the doctors could not find any medical explanation for her symptoms. She was diagnosed with a conversion disorder.

When she came to therapy for the first time, she had to walk with crutches, and for some time before this, she had been in a wheel chair. During the history taking, the client referred to psychological, physical, and sexual abuse, but when she spoke about these issues she seemed disconnected, as if she were speaking about something insignificant or neutral. There was no emotional resonance and no signs of disturbance when she explained how she was raped by a close relative during a wedding in front of his friends. She said, "This must have affected me, but I´m over it." When she got home her dress was torn. She had bruises all over her body and was very shaken up. When her parents found out what happened, they called her a "slut" and told her, "You must have done something to provoke him." She did not receive any medical attention and was kicked out of her house until her brother found out what happened and took her to the doctor. She was not allowed to press charges, and no one ever spoke about this again.

In this case, there were many "small" adverse experiences and several major traumatic experiences. In her experience of rape event, the most debilitating elements involved not just the rape itself, but how her cousin´s friends were laughing, how no one did anything, and how her parents reacted. By itself, this event could perhaps be severe enough to explain her dissociative symptoms (conversion and emotional disconnection), but she also had a childhood of many beatings and a pervasive lack of adequate care. She was often yelled at and called disgusting names. The most frequent messages she got from her parents were, "You are worthless" and "You can´t do anything right." Thus, the social messages during and after the rape recreated in a more extreme form the worst aspects of her childhood and triggered previously constellated emotional parts of her personality into a deeper state of decompensation.

In therapy, we tried to do EMDR in several occasions, but the client "didn´t get anything." We could do a perfect phase 3 and apparently normal reprocessing, but there was no real connection with the memory, emotions, or cognitions.

A week before this session, the client expressed suicidal thoughts to other people. She said she was afraid she would end up like her mother who had killed herself.

She did not express any emotional problems because she is not connected with her emotions.

> Therapist: How are you?
>
> Client: Fine!
>
> T (doubting): Really?
>
> C (laughs): Yes, why?

T: You are always fine. Are you really okay?

C: Yes, I am.

T: R (another therapist) told me you talked to her about important issues.

C: Yes.

T: Can you tell me about it?

C: ... What did I talk about? (She takes some time to think)... This has not happened in the last two days but it´s like a felt presence of other people, of my mother at home.

T (Silence, giving the client time.)

C: And... Wait! (She knocks her head, as if the information was stuck, and by hitting her head she could remember.) Well, I guess this happens to everyone who lives with somebody and then is suddenly gone.

Positive dissociative symptoms (walking disturbance) and negative dissociative symptoms (emotional numbing) speak to us more clearly than the client´s actual words.

T: How is the walking issue?

C: Some days are better than others.

T: How about the emotional blockage, the difficulty to feel emotions?

C: It´s the same.

With this information, we might ask ourselves, as EMDR therapists, if this client is prepared for EMDR reprocessing. As we commented before, it is possible to get all the elements for Phase 3, since the client can recall the memories. She may not be destabilized by such reprocessing. However, based on the degree of positive and negative dissociative symptoms, we believed that we were not likely to obtain much progress either with a direct approach. So the therapist decided to instead target the blockage itself, conceptualizing this as the targeting of the "peripheral" dissociative phobia or defense.

T: Do you think we could focus on that?

C: Yes.

Once we get permission, it is important to explore a bit more about this blockage. If we focus on it too soon or without understanding what it is related to, at least partially, the result might not be so helpful.

T: Can you describe this blockage to me? How do you know this is a blockage and not your usual way of being?

C: Because I used to cry, to feel bad. I laughed. I felt good... Now, it's as when something bad happens I cry and so on, but I don't really feel upset. It's as if I have... as if I was digesting things in a different way... as if... I don't know.

T: Once you told me you couldn't feel or cry, and that it felt weird to you.

C: Yes, I don't cry.

This client can compare her present state with a prior state. Some clients don't have a pre-trauma state or the capacity to mentalize about a contrast from prior to present state.

T: Do you think the blockage and the walking issue are related?

C: Yes I do... Sometimes I think it was due to a shock or due to something that I could not... what's the word... synthesize... some experience that marked me and my brain... it was a way to somatize this... Other times, I think it doesn't make any sense.

For now, the client cannot realize what experience is related to her symptoms, so we do a bit of preparation to help her connect the blockage with possible adverse situations.

T: Do you think you have been affected by hard situations?

C (convinced): Yes indeed.

T: Do you have any in your mind right now?

C: My mother's death... but I couldn't walk before her death.

T: I'm going to ask you to focus on that blocking sensation.

Client nods.

T: Just focus on the blocking itself. Just notice this blocking sensation you have both emotionally – to notice and express emotions – and physically – regarding your walking capacity – because you do think they are linked.

The blockage will be the target for EMDR processing. From similar prior clinical experience, it was thought likely that we would not be able to access and resolve the underlying traumatic memory without first overcoming this "peripheral" barrier. Before focusing on the target of "blocking," the therapist will first do some "preventive work" by giving mindful instructions and pointing out frequent, potential obstacles to effective reprocessing: over control, fear or shame to disclose, minimization and rationalization.

T: Allow whatever has to come to come. Remember you don't have to disclose issues that you don't want to talk about. I don't need to know details, if they are difficult for you to share. I just need to know where you are at in order to help you (client nods). Don't try to rationalize anything or minimize things... Comments such as "This also happens to other people," "It's normal to feel this way" (The client normally rationalizes and minimizes her experiences.) help you go on, but emotionally you still feel bad.

C: Yes, I notice I need relief from many things... (The client seems a bit more connected now.)

And we need to do a last step before we proceed with the target: the "Inner scan." We need to explore the degree of willingness or urge to avoid going forward with reprocessing.

T: Try to do an inner scan, you can close your eyes if you want and notice if you feel any reluctance or insecurity about what we are going to do now.

C (closing her eyes): I do feel reluctance and insecurity.

T: How can you tell? What do you notice?

C: To express feelings is not easy for me.

T: What are you noticing inside? (Therapist gives her time)... Is it as if something is telling you that this is not safe? Are you noticing physical sensations? What do you notice?

C: Rejection.

Since there is reluctance and insecurity, the therapist asks for permission. Asking the inner system for permission introduces very relevant information: boundaries will be respected.

T: Will this "rejection" that you notice be willing to give a try to what we want to do?

C: Yes.

With this statement of permission, we can start to reprocess the blockage.

T: Focus on that blockage and on those sensations that you are noticing. When you feel ready we will start with tapping.

Client nods as a sign that it's okay to begin.

BLS.

C: Fear.

BLS.

T: What is coming?

C: I'm on the verge of tears.

T: If you need to cry, just cry... whatever comes, let it come... and when you need to stop let me know.

C: Okay.

BLS.

C: Pain, incapacity.

BLS.

T: What is coming?

C: Being inexpressive.

T: Okay, go with that.

BLS.

T: What is coming?

C: I don´t know why: rationalization.

T: Go with that.

C (while doing BLS): Lack of understanding... tiredness... rejection... insensitivity.

We briefly explore the meaning of the associations.

T: What is going through your mind?

C: That I´m insensitive.

T: Go with that.

C: Lazy.

BLS.

C: Incoherent.

We explore again, we want to check if these words are coming from an EP.

T: Open your eyes for a moment.

Client opens her eyes.

T: What is coming? Single words?

C: Yes.

T: Where do those words come from?

C: From my inside.

T: Are you hearing a voice inside telling you these words?

C: No.

T: How can you describe what is happening?

C: It´s a thought.

T: Okay, so single words are coming from your inside.

C: Yes.

T: But, you can´t hear them?

C: No, I don´t think about them either, they just come.

T: Are there other sensations or images coming?

C: No, no images.

We explore how the client is experiencing the process.

T: How are you doing?

C: Fine.

T (doubtfully): Fine?

C: I don´t want to say "badly."

T: I know you have learned to say "fine" most of the time, but in this place, with me, try to connect with your true feelings, try not to just say "fine" automatically.

C: Actually, I feel terrible.

T: Okay, you feel bad right now. What are you noticing?

C: I feel pain.

T: Physical pain?

C: Yes, physical pain.

T: Where are you noticing that?

C: In my back.

T: Were you feeling this pain when you came in today?

C: Yes.

T: Are you feeling it more now?

C: No, but I still feel it.

At this point, we will switch and ask the client to focus on the somatic sensation.

T: Focus on that pain. Are you noticing it now?

C: Yes.

BLS.

C: It never ends... It´s something that´s much bigger than I am (She knocks her head again.)

T: Unbearable?

C: Yes, unbearable... at this moment I can tolerate the pain, but tomorrow I will go to the doctor. It´s probably due to the weather... It doesn´t matter. They will give me anti-inflammatory meds. I have taken a lot.

T: We can focus on the pain a little bit more. If we don´t observe any change we will return to the blockage.

Client nods.

T: Focus on the point where you are noticing it most.

C: In my back.

T: Pay attention to this place and don´t say anything until I ask you, unless you need to talk.

BLS.

T: What is coming?

C: Unbearable.

T: Go with that.

BLS.

C: Now my neck hurts.

T: Go with that, notice that.

BLS.

C (while doing EMDR): Incurable, immovable…. Histrionic… I don´t know why… This is very strange. Why would I say the word histrionic?

T: You are getting words again.

C: Yes.

T: What do you notice when those words come?

C: It´s just something that comes and I just say it, but I don´t feel anything.

T: Okay, so it´s automatic and you don´t feel anything when you say those words.

C: Right.

T: How is the pain now?

C: It hurts, but it didn´t increase.

T: You are still noticing it (Client nods). Are you noticing any other physical sensation?

C: My legs hurt less than yesterday.

The physical pain decreased. We return to our target: the blockage.

T: Let´s return to the blockage. Try to think about that reluctance that you notice and when you notice that the reluctance agrees to begin, let me know.

C (takes her time): It agrees.

BLS.

C: It´s as if there is a... membrane.

BLS.

T: What is coming?

C: A thought about being covered by a membrane or something like that.

T: Go with that (BLS).

C: It (membrane) helps to bounce all the problems off.

T: Go with that (BLS).

C: I don´t allow many people to go beyond.

T: Go with that (BLS).

C: Lack of feelings.

BLS.

C: Loneliness.

BLS.

T: What do you get now?

C: Fear.

C (while doing EMDR): Incontinence... confusion... discomfort... insouciance... shame... insecurity... fear.

Once again the client gets words while we do BLS. This time they are sensations and feelings.

T: What do you get now?

C: Happiness, I don´t know why.

T: Go with that (BLS).

C: Freshness.

BLS.

T: What do you get now?

C: Nothing.

T: How are you feeling now?

C: Good. My back even hurts less.

We explore the internal experience.

T: Was the experience similar to before, words coming?

C: Yes.

T: Were they linked to feelings this time?

C: No, because the words I said were feelings themselves.

T: So this time, feelings came up.

We return to the target of the membrane as a blockage.

T: Can you go back to the membrane?

C: Yes... I feel like "Alien."

Both client and therapist laugh.

T: Okay, when you notice the time is right (to continue) let me know.

C: The time is right.

C (while doing BLS): Somatization... Lack of perspective... Irregularity... Dissatisfaction... Comfort... Disturbance... I don´t know why... Fat.

She realizes some aspects related to her blockage.

C: I don´t see any advantages of being this way, but it´s as if I got used to being this way.

T: Go with that (BLS).

C: Frivolity, wrapping oneself up.

BLS.

C: Being tangled... How weird!!

T: Allow whatever has to come to come (BLS).

C: Powerlessness.

BLS.

T: What is coming?

C: Bad mood. I don´t know why.

T: Focus on that (BLS).

C: Foul mood... (BLS)... Lack of organization, fear, distrust.

We explore issues related to the therapist.

T: Open your eyes. (Client opens her eyes.) Are your fear and distrust related to us (therapeutic relationship)?

C: No, it´s related to me.

T: Can you explain this to me?

C: I´m concerned about not being able to walk again... but on the other hand I´m sure I will be able to... If I can stand, I can walk... I don´t trust myself.

T: Focus on that distrust.

BLS.

T: What is coming?

C: Nothing.

T: Okay, go with that (BLS).

C: Blank page.

BLS.

C: Pen, writing.

BLS.

C: No ideas come to my mind.

T: How do you feel now?

C: Fine (both laugh). Okay, fine, "fairly well."

T: How do you feel inside?

C: Not too well.

T: Can you describe "not too well"? What are you noticing?

C: Maybe I need to cry, to allow many things to come out.

The client seems more in contact with her emotions and can now realize when her problem appeared.

T: Why do you think you have difficulties allowing these things to come out?

C: This happens since my father died.

T: Did something about your father come up?

C: No, I´m just thinking about this. They always told me, "You have to be strong." So in order to be strong, you get to a point where you don´t allow things to affect you... You have like a protective layer around you... When my mother died, I cried many times... My brother asked me, "Why are you crying?" and I said, "Because it hurts, obviously"... Insensitive (pointing to her head).

T: When you think about these comments they made to you, "You have to be strong," what do you feel inside?

C: That it´s hard for me to be strong. I was 18 years old.

T: Can you link "You have to be strong" with that barrier that you were noticing before?

By linking the sensation with the image and cognition, we are helping the client to do the basic element of integration: synthesis.

C: Yes.

T: Okay, focus on that (BLS).

C: I should demolish the wall.

T: It will demolish when the time is right (BLS).

C: It´s done in my mind.

BLS.

C: Lack of understanding, lack of gentleness.

BLS.

C: I´m thinking that all guys are bastards.

The client is approaching the core trauma: being raped when she was a teenager.

T: You get this and it seems weird to you...

C: No, because my mother told me... I´m not sure about this... She said I was like this (conversion symptoms) because of a past boyfriend... The first time (first conversion symptoms) I had a hard time because of him, and the second time (second conversion symptoms) it was because of another guy.

T: And what do you think?

C: That I´m not so stupid as to let a guy affect me like that.

The client needs help from the therapist to face this issue.

T: How much do you believe what you just said?

C: I don´t believe it at all.

T: You don´t believe, it but you say it.

C: Yes.

T: Is this comment helping you? Is this comment trying to protect you?

C: It isn´t.

T: What do you actually believe?

C: It had to be something worse than that... Breaking up with a boyfriend can be hard, but it´s not a reason for not walking... I think it is more related to my father´s and mother´s death... to his surgery (her father´s leg amputation)...

T: If I asked you to think about an image that represents something very hard for you... take your time... something that has been affecting you for years and that can be related to your problems...

C: Any image that is difficult for me?

T: Or a situation.

C: From years ago?

T: Yes... (Client is thinking.) When you say there must be harder situations, what do you think about? What do you think has really affected you?

C: My father´s death itself.

T: This often comes up. Do you want us to focus on that? Do you want to try?

C: Oh, I don´t know... The rape when I was 16 is strongly related to it.

T (searching for emotions and sensations): Just by thinking about that, what physical sensations did you notice? Because your face changed...

C: Disgust.

Should we try to do a standard protocol with this event? In this case, we thought it was a good moment for the client. This is where our knowledge about each client can guide us regarding what is best for this particular client and moment. Of course, we should also ask the client, important choice points should be agreed with the inner system.

T: Do you think it´s the right moment to approach this issue?

C: To try to remember all those things?

T: It´s not so much about remembering, but about this event not hurting anymore.

C: Okay.

T: I want you to do the same as before, check by doing an inner scan... your safety is the most important aspect. Take your time. We have all the time you need... if you notice any signal from your mind saying "no," we should respect it (client nods). Do an inner scan and observe if you notice that the time is right or if there is anything saying "no." Can you do this?

Client nods and closes her eyes.

T: Take all the time you need.

C: It´s very unpleasant... very, very unpleasant (client has tears in her eyes).

T: It´s very unpleasant and it´s there...

C: Right.

T: And you have been suffering because of this for a long time.

C: A lot.

T: Do you think it´s helping you to have this issue there, without being reprocessed?

C: It doesn´t.

T: But you are afraid of getting into this.

Client nods, still upset.

T: We can do it step by step... you are getting nervous. This issue is upsetting you.

Client nods, swallowing nervously.

T: Would you prefer not to get into this today?

C: No, I want to.

T: So you are getting upset, because it´s a difficult issue.

C: Yes.

T: Do you feel secure enough to do this?

C (confident): Yes.

T: Okay, we will try then.

At this point, one question we could ask ourselves as EMDR therapists is whether or not we should use a standard procedure for trauma processing at this point. Asking for permission, giving time, and not forcing the client to make a fast decision are crucial steps before proceeding with trauma processing.

Phase 3

T: So the event would be the rape, is this right?

C: Yes.

T: Can you tell me what´s the worst part of the incident?

C: Not being able to defend myself.

T: What picture represents the most traumatic part of the incident?

C: The hardest part... the penetration. I was a virgin.

T: Having this picture in your mind, what words express a negative belief about yourself now?

Client is thinking.

T: A belief about yourself when you think about that... What do you say to yourself?

C: I could have stopped it.

T: Anything else? Do you feel guilty about it?

The therapist understands that there is guilt behind the client's statement. A client who is not well connected needs more help from the therapist to achieve a core negative belief.

C: Not anymore.

T: Do you entirely believe the words "not anymore"?

C: Yes.

T: But you say, "I could have stopped it." Do you actually believe you could have stopped it?

C: If I hadn´t gone with him.

T: So in a way, you feel responsible.

C: Yes.

T: So at a rational level, you know you are not guilty.

C: Yes.

T: But at an emotional level...

C: No.

T: Emotionally you feel "I´m guilty."

C: Yes.

T: So this is a negative belief about yourself, "I´m guilty, I could have stopped it."

C: Yes.

T: When you bring up that picture, what would you like to believe about yourself now?

C (takes time to think): I got over it.

Notice that the NC and the PC are not aligned. "I am guilty" is probably the NC from the EP. "I can bear this" and "I´m weak" are the PC and NC from the ANP.

T: When you bring up that picture and the words "I could have stopped it, I´m guilty," what emotions do you feel now?

C: Disgust and fear.

SUDS= 9

T: Where do you feel it in your body?

C: All over my body.

Phase 4

T: Hold all 3 elements in your mind and let me know when you are ready to begin.

C: I´m ready.

BLS.

C: Fear, misunderstanding... anguish... disappointment... pain... disgust.

T: Open your eyes... What is coming?

C: When it was happening.

T: Go with that.

BLS.

T: What is coming?

C: I got blocked.

T: Do you want to continue?

C: I do.

T: Focus on that blockage.

BLS.

C: It´s as if there was a wall between that image and me.

T: Do you think it´s ok to go on?

C: Yes.

T: Ok, go with that.

BLS.

At this point we will switch and ask the client to focus on the somatic sensation.

C: I am demolishing the wall.

T: Good, go with that (BLS).

C: Terror.

T: (While doing BLS.) Remember those are things from your past, they can´t hurt you anymore... Allow whatever comes to come.

C: Ridiculous... misunderstanding.

BLS.

C: His friends made fun of me (while she was being raped).

T: Go with that (BLS).

C: All the events that happened afterwards... when my family kicked me out of my home... reporting it to the court...

T: Okay, go with that, we will do a longer set of tapping... Let all those things pass by, as if you were watching a movie... We will try that this old material, all these things that happened a long time ago, stay in the past, just let them pass by.

C: Okay.

BLS.

After several sets of BLS.

T: What is coming?

C: Blurred.

BLS.

T: What is coming?

C: It´s in the past.

T: Go with that.

BLS.

T: What is coming now?

C: It´s over.

T: Okay, go with that.

BLS.

T: What is coming now?

C: Nothing.

Phase 5

The PC emerges spontaneously, so the therapist decides to follow this associative chain. The client´s brain is going spontaneously toward integration of a new perspective, phase 5.

C: It was something very unpleasant. I was afraid, but this happened a long time ago and should not bother me now.

We can wonder if the client´s statement represents presentification: I am in the here and now. The situation was in the past. Or if on the contrary, it may represent a new disconnection of the client (as ANP) in the face of a very difficult issue.

T: Is this rational or emotional?

C: Rational.

T: And at an emotional level, is this what is coming?

C (calm): Yes. It doesn´t affect me now.

T: How true do the words "It´s over, it´s in the past" feel, on a scale from 1-7?

C: 7.

T: Notice that. Notice the memory and the words "It´s over, It´s in the past."

BLS.

C: The memory is blurred.

BLS.

T: What do you get now?

C: It almost disappeared.

BLS.

T: And now?

C: It´s not there anymore.

Phase 6

T: Notice the memory and the words "It´s over, It´s in the past" and scan your body for any discomfort or negative sensations

C: None.

Phase 7

A new "fine" emerges in Phase 7.

T: How do you feel now?

C: Fine (laughs). I´m really fine.

T: Was it hard?

C: A little bit.

T: Remember what I always tell you... Log any sensation you get, any memory, any nightmare, anything... After an EMDR session, the process can continue for some days. Sometimes it evolves in a positive way, feeling better day-by-day... Other times, new issues can become activated. If this happens, it´s very relevant information for us. So take notes and bring them to the next session.

C: Sometimes I can´t remember my dreams.

T: I don´t want you to search or make special efforts. Just observe what happens during these days. If you feel better, great. If you notice any weird sensation, unpleasant things, thoughts... write them down.

Client nods.

Phase 8: Next Session

The client arrives for the next session walking. She explains she is feeling better, "I'm tired from walking so much. I walk a lot now. I walk everywhere." The client stands for a while to show the therapist how well she can stand.

Follow-up

Two years after the session described in this chapter, the client was stable. She did not have any walking difficulties again. She had been in a romantic relationship for over a year.

Summary

With survivors of severe neglect and abuse, we cannot begin by directly confronting core traumatic memories. Many peripheral intrapsychic elements surround these core traumatic events and remain dysfunctionally stored in isolated neuro-networks – intrapsychic DSI. These peripheral elements include a variety of dissociative defenses and phobias, which must be carefully and sequentially addressed before moving to directly address the dysfunctionally stored traumatic memories that remain sources of current symptoms.

In some cases, working through these peripheral issues may be a simple prelude to resolving traumatic memories. In other cases, work with peripheral issues may constitute the essential and more prolonged elements of the therapy.

Whether in addressing peripheral or core traumatic material, survivors of severe neglect and abuse often present "stuck points" at certain moments in the therapeutic process. These moments in which blockages emerge may occur at the beginning of therapy. Others emerge after an initial phase of improvement that is interrupted, or becomes increasingly slow. These moments can lead to a sense of impasse unless we have tools for working through what may turn out to be hidden and subtle elements of intrapsychic defense. In this chapter, we have offered some tools for addressing these moments of blockage, especially when the reasons for the blockage are unclear.

Chapter 10
Working on Therapeutic Relationship Problems with EMDR

Dolores Mosquera, Anabel Gonzalez, & Andrew M. Leeds

Severely neglected and traumatized people need a long time before they feel safe in the therapeutic relationship. In childhood, they never formed a basic sense of interpersonal trust (Erikson, 1950, 1968), and many essential elements in therapy function as traumatic triggers. The therapist must confront the paradox of needing to interact with the client's social engagement system, which is underdeveloped and needs to be rehabilitated. In these cases, the therapeutic relationship can be very complex. To deepen our understanding of the different interactive relational processes, which are typically activated in therapy, we will incorporate perspectives from attachment theory (Bowlby, 1973, 1980; Main, 1996, 1999) and the theory of structural dissociation of the personality (Van der Hart et al., 2006) with our knowledge of mental function impairments in people who experienced early, chronic interpersonal trauma. Together, attachment theory, the theory of structural dissociation of the personality, and cognitive analytic theory (Ryle & Kerr, 2002) offer us comprehensive concepts that we will try to integrate with the Adaptive Information Processing model of EMDR (Shapiro, 2001).

Attachment theory gives us essential guidance for understanding how clients approach intimate relational situations. Clients with predominantly dismissing attachment orientation as adults experienced significant emotional neglect with a lack of mindsight (Siegel, 1999, 2010) with one or more caregivers in early childhood. Consequently, they tend to present difficulties in connection with their own emotions, sensations, and needs, which they poorly understand and manage. They also have trouble activating their social engagement system. For these clients, to establish a safe therapeutic relationship, and to learn to tolerate the intimacy that develops with proximity in therapy, will often require a long time and a careful and patient approach from the therapist. People with a preoccupied attachment style as adults experienced overly intrusive and often shaming caregiving that only rarely met their emotional needs for relatedness with one or more caregivers in early childhood. As a result, they will have difficulties with boundaries in their relationships. They oscillate between the urge to approach and demand support from the other, which is never enough, and the urge to withdraw to protect themselves from the risks or perception of being hurt, shamed, or rejected as "too needy." Disorganized attachment orientation in adults, which is related with secondary and tertiary structural dissociation, is often seen in those who experienced an early lack of maternal-infant play, parent-child role reversals, and a later failure to protect them from significant physical or sexual trauma. These clients are characterized by paradoxical and simultaneous opposing and extreme reactions, as we will describe later in this chapter.

Characteristic narrative styles and difficulties that arise in the therapeutic relationship give us relevant information about the organization of the client's early experiences. Not infrequently, these relational patterns may be a more significant guide than what we can learn from client's verbal reports of early memories. Sometimes, clients cannot tell us about issues they are not aware of. Other times they are aware, but do not want to disclose because they believe some experiences should be kept secret or are too embarrassing to reveal, especially before the therapist is perceived as a safe and trustworthy person.

From a neurobiological perspective, Porges (2003) describes that the social engagement system may serve as a regulator of physiological activity. People who grow up with secure attachment relationships can easily activate this system to contribute to self-regulation. On the contrary, severely traumatized people, with insecure or disorganized attachment, are stuck in more primitive levels of development in their action systems (with immobilization and fight/flight responses) that can easily be activated in the therapeutic relationship. Thus they cannot easily achieve a sense of relational security, even when the therapist is attentive and consistent. With them, the therapist is confronted with the paradox of needing to use a social engagement system that is underdeveloped and needs to be rehabilitated.

The theory of structural dissociation of the personality explains how different action systems, related to different dissociative parts of the personality, can be activated in the therapeutic relationship, both in the client and the therapist. As we explained in previous chapters, dysfunctionally stored information (DSI) can be stored in different parts of the personality. Intrapsychic elements, such as dissociative phobias, can serve to maintain this separation and lack of coherence. Paradoxical patterns of relating can be simultaneously activated during the therapeutic relationship. These patterns can manifest with changing attitudes and confusing behaviors and reactions. Different parts of the personality can react differently at different times in essentially the same relational situation, and these reactions may or may not be readily observed. In order for us to be prepared to identify these types of relational triggers, we must keep in mind at all times, not only the apparently normal part of the personality (ANP) present in the session, but also the hidden presence of an inner system of parts. In order for us to be able to establish a good therapeutic relation with a client with secondary or tertiary structural dissociation, we need to establish a working alliance with all the parts of the personality. This therapeutic task requires that we draw up resources and strategies from group and family systems management.

The theory of structural dissociation of the personality is an approach focused on the individual and intrapsychic phenomena, but dyadic relationships and system relationships are dynamic processes subject to principles that an understanding of individual psychology cannot fully explain. The concept of reciprocal role procedures from cognitive analytic therapy (Ryle & Kerr, 2002) can assist us with case conceptualization on these complex cases by shedding light on how early experiences are connected with relational patterns in adulthood. It focuses on the concept of circularity in the therapist-client relationship. From this model, we can identify different kind of interactions that might be connected with the client's and the therapist's neural networks. Ryle (1995) remarks that, in both the inner life and the outer life, we can find reenactments of early traumatic scenery, but these reenactments are not "literal copies" of those experiences. Severely traumatized people tend to engage in entrapment relationships, partly because they choose to relate to people who have personality characteristics similar to those early attachment figures. In addition, survivors frequently elicit in other people the complementary role, pushing them to perform the same pattern of reciprocal roles that they experienced in early traumatic scenes.

These situations are specific of each client-therapist dyad. Nevertheless, commonly occurring elements can be observed in many survivors of early trauma. In this chapter, we will describe different types of reciprocal role procedures that can help us identify common relational problems and understand the connection between these situations and the dysfunctionally stored information, in both client and therapist.

In each section, we will first describe possible relational situations that correspond with sets of items that are part of the Relational Problems Questionnaire (Mosquera & Gonzalez, 2009). We believe this strategy will help clinicians to have a clear point of departure to identify underlying patterns. Next, we will present the related reciprocal role procedure, linking each one with dysfunctionally stored information (DSI) from possible early experiences. From the AIP perspective, it is the DSI that lies behind the recurring relational problems the client keeps reproducing in both daily functioning and in the therapeutic relationship. The world of severely traumatized people is a world of extreme and opposite roles, living in the constant dilemma of choice between one extreme and the other. When aspects associated with the opposite role are triggered, the client switches to the contrary role. Each role is organized with an action system that is dysfunctionally linked through early traumatic scenes with affective states, physical sensations, sensory cues, and maladaptive beliefs. Together, these elements of DSI are organized into compartmentalized roles which recursively re-enact early scenes of neglect, betrayal, and trauma in developmentally primitive attempts to cope.

The Relational Problems Questionnaire (RPQ) can be found in the appendix of the book, but we will outline the items we explore in each section so the reader can understand the relevance of each of the reciprocal roles we will encounter in therapy when working with complex trauma.

Frequent Relational Situations and Reciprocal Roles in Therapy

Helpless Child vs. Idealized Omnipotent Rescuer

Has any client told you how special you are for him?

Do you remember any client telling you, "You are the only one who can help me, I am very disappointed with all my previous therapists, but I know you are different"… And after some time, saying, "You are just like the others… I thought you were different but I was wrong… Don´t you care about me?"

Did you ever find yourself thinking or speaking about your good-for-nothing colleagues? Did you ever feel you were the "only one" who could save a client´s life or effectively treat him? And after some time, feeling useless or unable to carry the therapy through? Trying not to disappoint that client, who depends on you to survive or improve?

A frequent way to overcome an oppressive and devastating environment is to idealize parents, family, and reality itself. When the client becomes an adult, he may describe a perfect family and a childhood history with no traumatic issues. To realize the actuality of trauma provokes grief for the idealized parent, the only one with which the client could at least dream of a perfect attachment. In Phase 1 of the EMDR standard protocol, this client will tend to minimize or hide these relevant memories, because the childhood situation will not be considered inadequate by the client without psychoeducation by the therapist about what is natural and adequate in a childhood caregiver.

Another possibility related to this dyad is the experience of not having resources to cope with the situation. Growing up in an extremely adverse environment, with the impossibility for the child to escape from his family, generates learned hopelessness. This "dead end" situation leads to fantasy as the only escape. The child dreams of a rescuer who will take him away from the hell he lives in and avenge the injustice.

The role of a rescuer can be placed on the therapist, who may be pleased to hear, "You are the only one who understands me. Only you can help me." The therapist may imagine that this is evidence of a growing therapeutic alliance and fail to recognize the elements of re-enactment offered in this imaginary role.

Fig. 1: Idealization.

A therapist with unresolved narcissistic issues is in danger of over-representing this role and becomes more vulnerable to future and probable discrediting from the client. The inevitable evidence of the therapist's imperfections, or the inability to fill huge client demands, can trigger once more the same fight/flight action systems in the client that were activated in childhood in response to the abusive parent. The early memories that need to be reprocessed with EMDR are not only the worst memories related to the abusive parent, but also the best memories with the abuser. These become an idealization defense, which can be reprocessed as Jim Knipe proposes (2008). The apparently "good" memories are false positive memories that generate disturbing emotions or the client feels as initially good, but quickly after targeting with BLS will be associated to negative aspects of experience. When we select a target for reprocessing, it should be a dysfunctional element, but some apparently positive issues can be also dysfunctional, as in this case.

Needy Child vs. Perfect Caregiver

Do some clients seem so vulnerable that you are moved to do a lot of things for them?

Have you found yourself doing things for a client and feeling that you were going beyond adequate limits? Or doing more and more for a client, so much so that you became exhausted and even then, you could not meet the client's needs?

Did you ever go out of your way and do things you did not want to do, hoping this would make things in the relationship go better or trying not to disappoint a client?

Did any of your clients end up as friends or having a work relationship with you?

Have you had the experience of making a lot of concessions (saving more time for sessions, extra sessions, favors...) and, after some time, feeling unjustly treated by them, for not reciprocating your generosity?

Have you found yourself disclosing personal information or your problems to a client? Did you let the client help you in any personal way?

Some clients have terrible overwhelming histories. As therapists, we feel moved to help, but this is sometimes a delicate issue in severe traumatization. A needy client may activate in the therapist a corresponding caregiver role, reacting from the caregiver's system independently of the therapist's reflective mind. This situation will be further complicated when therapists have a hypertrophic caregiver role, based on their own attachment history, or when therapists compensate for shortages in their personal life by excessive care giving in their relationships with their clients. This readiness to overextend the caregiver role may increase the client's dependency and powerlessness, which will then become an important obstacle for the therapy (Herman, 1997).

This situation may evolve differently depending on the client's attachment style:

If the client has an avoidant attachment style, when the client allows the therapist to get closer and is starting to be a relevant attachment figure, the client's phobia of attachment may emerge. The activation of attachment phobias can create different situations: passive reactions from the client, missing appointments, abandonment of the therapy, therapist's burnout from the lack of results and the client's non-compliant attitude, and consequently, open or hidden aversive reactions toward the client.

This situation can manifest differently if the client has an ambivalent attachment organization. These clients tend to express an extreme need for attachment, asking for more attention from the therapist in the form of longer sessions, any special gesture, or more interest and effort. These needs can never be adequately met. Nothing will be enough. Any attempt from the therapist to limit the client's demands can trigger early experiences of abandonment and neglect in the client.

Dysfunctionally stored traumatic early memories trigger action systems in both client and therapist. Each action system performs a different role, which stimulates the enactment of a reciprocal role in the relationship partner.

Fig. 2. Side A. Increasing of the caregiving attitude.

Fig. 3. Side B. Client's defensive aggression toward the therapist.

These reciprocal role procedures may be unstable systems, which tend to switch, or become stable and chronic. As we can see in the picture immediately above, when the therapist performs a hypertrophic caregiver role that the client seems to need, the phobia of attachment can become activated in the client, leading to a negative reaction toward the therapist. When this happens, therapists tend to respond in three different ways: 1) extending the caregiver role to the extreme, 2) expressing overt or covert aggression, and 3) seeking supervision and getting perspective about what is going on and how this pattern can be related to the early histories of client and therapist. Of course, option 3 is the most useful and therapeutic response.

The Reverse Situation: The Client Taking Care of the Therapist

A client who has grown up with neglect and maltreatment tends to invert reciprocal roles with the caregiver. The child is constantly focused on the parent's emotions and discomfort and is constantly attentive to their needs. On the contrary, their own needs are systematically ignored (by caregiver and child), and as an adult, this person may even fail to detect them. Here, a therapist with a personal history of early experiences of neglect or lack of care may have unmet needs that the client (hyper-sensitive to these clues) may detect and meet perfectly. The possibility of an inadequate pattern in this situation is high. The vignette below exemplifies this situation:

Fig. 4: Patient taking care of the therapist.

Repeating the parentified relational pattern that the client learned as a child:

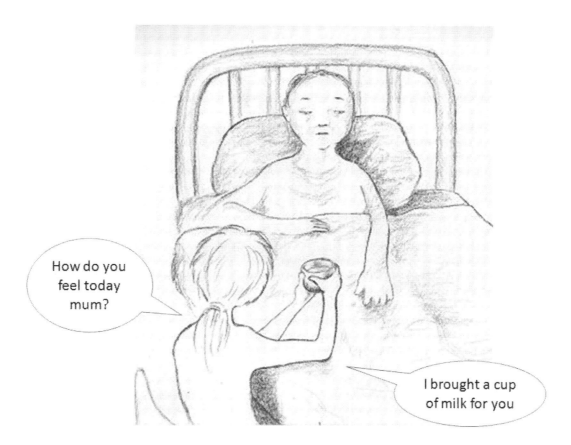

Fig. 5: Child taking care of her mother.

The following client gives us a good example of this situation:

"I think I was constantly concerned about how others felt and about not making them feel bad. I always felt responsible for their feelings.

My last therapy ended like that: My therapist pouted and was moved many times when I talked. This man had over 20 years of experience. I thought that something was happening to him, and finally, he became my only concern and I didn't want to worry him... The reasons why I was in therapy lost relevance, I only wanted to help him. I wanted to help him, but I was afraid of him at the same time. My social phobia and my desperation to get out of my home made me end up focusing on him, and I was afraid to run into him in the street. Finally, I ended the therapy because I was feeling worse and worse."

Submission vs. Domination

Have you ever found clients extremely interested in pleasing you?

Did clients ever tell you they were very relaxed or experienced a fast relief with EMDR, when you had a much different sensation... only to find out later that they became worse after the session?

Did any clients offer or give you valuable gifts?

What kind of clients do you prefer to treat? Do you prefer clients that tend to be compliant, do the homework, and agree with every proposal you suggest?

Have you ever found yourself "challenged" by a client? Have you ever thought a client was not really motivated because he did not follow your instructions?

The total submission action system substitutes for the impossible-to-activate, proactive responses of the fight/fight action system. The child cannot fight against the abusive parent, and if he tries, he will probably suffer serious retaliation. Neither can he fight against the non-abusive caregiver who fails to protect him, because this would be "blaming a defenseless and victimized person." The flight response is also impossible: a child does not have autonomy to live on his own.

Submission in these environments is the only possible chance for survival and often also reproduces characteristics from the non-abusive parent, who is frequently the most acceptable figure for the client. The child may tend to be the perfect child, doing everything right in order to obtain love, which never comes, or to avoid punishment. As an adult, this client easily will perform the role of "the perfect client" to get approval and be accepted. This is a client who will follow submissively the therapist's indications and who will consistently agree without discrepancy with the therapist's comments and observations. A therapist who has difficulties tolerating clients with ambivalent or conflictual relationship patterns may be pleased with this kind of relationship. But a therapeutic alliance with an emotional part of the personality acting from the submission action system is not compatible with an active engagement of the adult self of the client in therapy. Interestingly, these submissive clients seldom, if ever, switch in the way clients in the borderline spectrum do, but rather fall deeper into compliance and tend to show their problems with increasing symptoms. The therapist loses a sense of collaboration and is drawn into greater and greater sense of having to direct the therapy blindly.

Soon or later, it will emerge that the therapy has been ineffective. The client may put in a lot of effort trying to do or say what he thinks is expected, "the right thing," like controlling what is being reported during EMDR reprocessing. But this attitude of accomplishment and effort is not compatible with the spontaneity and the synthesis with adaptive memory networks and adult capacities, which are the hallmark of effective reprocessing in the EMDR standard protocol. If this client is overwhelmed during reprocessing, he will find a way to continue and will avoid telling the therapist "stop." He will leave the session still overwhelmed. At home, this client may feel disappointed for not being able to "control" the symptoms. When he has bad moments, he does not mention them to the therapist because he tries to show his "best side." This leaves targets incomplete and leads to the loss of opportunities to reprocess present triggers. If the client is uncomfortable with the therapist's attitude, it will be difficult for him to communicate it. Some of his symptoms will get worse, but this may be blamed on medication not working as well as it did before.

As we have mentioned before, a client who has grown up in neglect and maltreatment tends to become aware of the parents' emotions and discomfort and is constantly attentive to their needs. Since nobody looked after his needs, the client, as a child, learned to ignore them and as an adult cannot recognize them easily.

Let's see the following example: A client is progressing adequately with her EMDR therapist, working on reprocessing targets involving present situations. Then, the therapist starts to reprocess past traumatic memories. The client agrees, but suddenly begins to present depersonalization during the session. As they continue, depersonalization symptoms emerge some days before and after the reprocessing sessions. Finally, depersonalization persists during the entire month. Her therapist understands that things are not progressing adequately, but does not entirely realize the meaning of this situation, continuing with standard EMDR protocol on traumatic memories in hopes of "completing" the work they began.

Another possibility is that the submissive action system represents an emotional part that usually is present during the sessions if the therapist tends to act in a dominating or demanding role. Other parts, based on the proactive action system (fight or flight), may be underdeveloped or may only act in the internal system against the ANP or the submissive EPs, creating more subtle internal symptoms. For example, a client agrees with a proposal from the therapist regarding some tasks, but after the session two internal voices will not stop bothering her. Different problems that the ANP cannot explain may also emerge when there is an EP based on a fight action system. Here, the client insists that nothing is working, but there is objective data showing effective progress. In this example, the client presents "passive-aggressive" patterns.

The therapist may react to these situations in different ways. One possibility is that the therapist labels the client as "resistant," as not being motivated for therapy, or thinking that the client has some kind of secondary benefit by maintaining symptoms. These clinical impressions may actually be expressions of the therapist's unconscious frustration and rage in response to the lack of therapy progress. The client may increase his efforts performing the role of the perfect client, which worsens the relational problem. For example, a client can try to be the perfect client telling us what she thinks we want to hear, but systematically fails to come to her appointments. The therapist does not understand what is underneath this attitude, and the third time she "forgets" to come, the therapist confronts her with some hostility. The client may react to this perceived aggression, turning to a different reciprocal role procedure, mediated by a different emotional part, for example, accusing the therapist of being cold and inattentive or taking an overdose of pills for being a "bad client."

Victimization vs. Aggression

Have you been mistreated by a client? Unjustly accused of something? Physically assaulted?

Have you felt manipulated? Fooled? Used?

Have you ever achieved a strong alliance with a client, while a hostile dissociative part kept creating problems?

Have you ever felt that "no matter what you would say or do" it would be used against you?

Have you ever found yourself subtly challenged or threatened by a client?

Did a client ever give you a compliment that sounded odd and felt like an attack?

Have you ever thought, "I hope he does not come to session today"?

Have you found yourself feeling angry with a client?

Have you ever felt annoyed thinking, "He is theatrical, hysteric, a bad person, selfish"?

Have you ever confronted a client in an extremely harsh way?

Have you ever felt like saying rude things to a client? Have you ever felt like saying or doing "terrible things" to a client?

Have you ever experienced negative visceral responses toward apparently nice clients?

These items represent other typical situations in the reenactment of the aggressor-victim dyad. Aggression in the therapy setting is usually emotional, but it may be physical or sexual, as we will comment in the next reciprocal roles. The client may adopt the role of victim with great intensity. Positions of extreme victimization in the client can give rise to complementary aggressive reactions in the therapist. This influence is mediated by the tendency to function in complementary roles in relationships. But the client may send subliminal aggressive messages toward the therapist through the episodic activation of a hostile emotional part. This may be evident, but also may adopt a very subtle expression.

Fig. 6: Subtle aggression

The therapist may perceive clients as theatrical or exaggerated, labeling them as "hysteric" and distrusting them. The therapist may feel disappointed or angry, thinking in terms such as, "I can't stand this client," and may express it openly: "If you really want to kill yourself, why do you keep coming to therapy?" or in a hidden way, like postponing therapy sessions.

The world of extremes where the client grew up is revisited here once again. In some client's childhood, only victims and tyrants existed. If the client rejects the tyrant role, he only has one choice left, which is to exaggerate the victim role: "I want to be the opposite of what my father was." But this creates two different problems. On one hand, the more extreme the victim role is, the more the other person in the dyadic relationship will tend to adopt the opposite role. On the other hand, the abuser role contains an essential action system – fight. When the client needs to activate this defensive system, a different emotional part is activated that may exert his influence only in the internal system or outside, either clearly (getting into an argument, hitting someone) or in a hidden way (self-injury). In other client's childhoods, in addition to the victim and tyrant, there was an ineffective caregiver who failed to detect or to protect. When the client from this background imagines that the clinician has failed to protect him from an aggressive life partner or even from an aggressive EP, the client can switch from the victim role to the role of aggressor toward the therapist.

Opposite and complementary roles are frequent reproductions of parental models, such as the aggressive father who maltreated the helpless and victimized mother. The number of potential triggering memories that are dysfunctionally stored are diverse: being battered by the aggressive parent; good moments with the same aggressive parent; being concerned by the emotional state of the non-abusive parent; being angry because the non-abusive parent did not protect the client from the situation; and images of aggression by one parent toward the other (the victim/aggressor dyad reenacted).

These early scenarios and the related emotional parts may be successively activated in response to different interactions during a single session. The dyad may shift from a client who presents himself as a victim and a therapist who begins to feel hostility towards the client, to the opposite situation. For instance, a client who reacts against the perceived therapist's hostility with open or hidden aggression, demeaning the therapist or complaining about the ineffectiveness of the therapy, and the therapist victimized by the client's attitude.

Hidden in this relational pattern are other aspects of the client, who relishes frustrating the clever therapist as a form of covert revenge against the original perpetrator who was overly controlling. This internal dynamic within the client moves the therapist toward the same overly controlling role than the past abusive figure.

Seducer vs. Seduced

Have you ever felt attracted by a client, to the point of having difficulties focusing during the session?

Have you ever found yourself trying to look better or more attractive before seeing a certain client?

Have you ever found yourself inquiring about sexual details that are not relevant for therapy?

Have you ever thought about engaging in an intimate relation with a client?

Have you ever felt a client was trying to seduce you?

Has a client ever declared his love to you or expressed his wishes to be intimate with you?

Have any clients described their sex life in detail, even when it was not related to what you asked?

A particular but unfortunately frequent situation is seduction and romantic or sexual relationships between client and therapist (Pope, 1993). This reciprocal role is frequently a reenactment of sexual abuse. The client, or some dissociative part, may display open or hidden sexualized behaviors. This situation is more frequent between male therapists and female clients. The therapist may feel sexually aroused, incapable of gaining perspective over the interactive process. Sometimes this situation is so uncomfortable that the therapist abandons the client, stopping the therapy or referring the case to another professional. This might be a reenactment of the abandonment and neglect that the client has suffered, and it activates a different reciprocal role procedure. Even worse is the development of a romantic or sexual relationship with the client, as we can see in the following case example:

A borderline woman told her male therapist that she was not able to have orgasms while being with a man. She explained that she did not have difficulties when she masturbated, "I can by myself but not while having sex, not even just playing." At first, the therapist tried to work on this complaint as a current issue of sexual dysfunction, but nothing seemed to work. The client remained preoccupied with this issue and brought it up constantly during sessions. In one of the sessions, the client asked her therapist if this "had ever happened to him." He responded "of course not." In the next session, she asked him if he thought he could please her; he answered "of course, but I am your therapist."

After this session the client insisted on having sex, "so she could make sure there was nothing wrong with her." At first, the therapist said it was not possible, but the client kept insisting. During the next session, he touched her breasts without taking her clothes off, and said this was "okay" because the "clothes were on." He said it was only to show her that she could become excited with a man. After this, the therapist would delay seeing her in therapy, but would call her for "phone sessions" that ended up in "phone sex." Finally, he told her he could not keep seeing her because she did not have boundaries.

Cases such as this one can help us reflect about how important it is to be able to recognize the introduction of sexual issues and sexualized actions into the session as the starting point for exploring early scenarios. When this fails to occur, it may be due to inadequate training of the therapist. It can also reflect unresolved narcissistic issues in the therapist, which need to be addressed in consultation and in personal therapy.

When survivors of early neglect and early abuse introduce sexual concerns and sexualized attitudes or behaviors, these should be addressed not merely as difficulties in current adjustment, but also as starting points for identifying early material that may need to be addressed with EMDR. These behaviors can be indicators of relevant information from a client´s history. For example, a borderline client would lean constantly, trying to get the therapist´s attention towards her breast or legs. If he looked, she would suddenly shift into viewing him as a disgusting pig and would react in an out-of-control manner, insulting him. If he failed to look at her sexually, she would get upset, feel she was not important, and complain that "he did not care about her" or was not paying enough attention to her. This client was referred to a female therapist. Through a careful exploration of her history, it emerged that this client was normally not "seen" by her father. He would only notice her and be attentive to her while he was sexually abusing her. This client was re-enacting what was reinforced during her childhood and adolescence: "I felt disgusting after sleeping with him, but being invisible was much worse."

With EMDR, we have the possibility of reprocessing the early memories that are related to these reciprocal roles. For example, a borderline client with a homosexual orientation cancelled an appointment by text message explaining that she thought her therapist was not interested in her case. She complained to her therapist of being disappointed because she was not taking care of her as much as she needed. The therapist did not want to give her a clinical report in the terms that the client dictated. In recent months, the client tended to ask the therapist more personal questions and offer her gifts. The therapist had the impression that the client was trying to move the therapeutic relationship toward friendship or perhaps a romantic relationship. The therapist told the client that she respected her right to end the therapy, but she considered it necessary to talk about these boundary concerns directly. The client agreed to have this conversation and all these issues were discussed, but the client denied all of them. The therapist proposed working with EMDR on the client´s belief that she was being neglected by her therapist, and the client agreed to do so. Focusing on the somatic sensations that the client experienced in the presence of the therapist, and asking for her earliest memory with the same sensations, she associated a past situation with a previous therapist. In her last therapy, the client fell in love with her therapist, who after noticing it, decided to stop the therapy, explaining to the client that her feelings made it impossible to continue the treatment. After reprocessing that memory, the therapeutic impasse was overcome. To resolve this type of issue, the therapist must first be aware of the situation, picking up on the signals from both client´s behaviors and therapist´s inner responses. Well-timed and appropriate psychoeducation about the issue of romantic and sexual feelings in therapy can avoid implying a blaming attitude towards the client, which has the potential to reproduce earlier situations: "You were asking for it."

I do not Realize that Trauma has Happened to me vs. I Relive the Trauma

Have any of your clients wanted to avoid reprocessing traumatic issues?

Did any of them experience negative reactions during trauma reprocessing? Has a client ever asked you to work on a traumatic experience with EMDR, and when you are about to work on it, all you encountered were problems? Or has a client ever told you that he wanted to recover memories of his past, and when you agreed to try, he reacted negatively?

Have you ever felt so much curiosity about a client´s history that you acted in ways where you ended up feeling like an investigator?

Have you ever delayed reprocessing a specific memory because you found it was too hard or intense?

Have you ever felt distant or disconnected during a therapy session, not because you were tired, but because you "needed to distance yourself" or you "couldn´t help it"?

Have you ever thought in terms of "I hope the client doesn´t bring me that memory to work on it today!" or "I am starting to think the abuse was not real, but is just the client´s fantasy?"

Have you felt exhausted by so many traumatic histories?

Fig. 7: Non realization / Avoidance of trauma.

Primary structural dissociation is the basis of the posttraumatic response. The client's personality splits between an emotional part of the personality (EP), which contains the traumatic perceptions, emotions, cognitions, sensations, and defensive actions systems, and an apparently normal part of the personality (ANP) that avoids the traumatic contents and continues to cope with normal aspects of daily life. This division of the personality becomes more complex in secondary and tertiary structural dissociation, where more EPs appear to manage different aspects of recurrent trauma (secondary) or more ANPs emerge to cope with different situations of daily life (tertiary).

The client usually comes to therapy as an apparently normal part of the personality. In this mental state, the client may be partially or completely amnesic to the trauma history. Or the client may remember that traumatic events occurred, but not realize how much they are influencing present problems. Sometimes, clients express that they want to know "the truth" about their lives. If the therapist enacts an investigator role, parts that are "keeping the secret" may emerge and act against the therapist or the client. A novel therapist fascinated with her first dissociation cases, may over-act this investigator role (Chu, 1988).

Fig. 8 Trauma ghosts peeping out of the box.

To survive in a traumatic environment, the child must think that "this never happened" or "this has never happened to me." To realize the traumatic past entirely is emotionally intolerable. This lack of realization will continue being a main aspect of adult consequences of traumatization (Janet, 1935; Van der Hart, Nijenhuis, and Steele, 2006). "This has never happened to me," expressed by the client as ANP, alternates with trauma reliving, experienced in the client as EP. The therapist may also share these opposite reactions. On one hand, the therapist may fail to explore any trauma history, may distrust the client´s reported history of trauma, or consider that past traumatic events are not relevant to the client´s present problems. On the other hand, the therapist may become traumatized by the terrible histories that she hears. In this case, the therapist may stop or simply avoid EMDR reprocessing because she, not the client, cannot tolerate the EP´s intense emotions during the desensitization phase.

The therapist´s own wounds are very important at this point. To reprocess our own traumatic history is the best guarantee of being a well-tuned instrument and able to adequately help our clients. If we fail to acknowledge and resolve our own life histories, relationship situations in therapy will trigger our dysfunctionally stored memories and distort the therapeutic process. Even when therapists have managed to avoid or to fully work through a difficult history of their own, clients´ traumatic histories may in time generate vicarious trauma in the therapist. For all these reasons, therapists´ self-care is extremely necessary.

Control vs. Out of Control

Have you ever felt that the therapeutic process was out of control? That there were so many crisis and relapses that you could not work on the therapeutic goals? Have you found yourself performing a fire-extinguisher role?

Do the crisis in the client's current life contrast with a rigid attitude from the client during the sessions?

Have you sensed the client was trying to be in control during the EMDR reprocessing or trying to over-control their symptoms during the session?

Have you ever thought, "Is the client controlling the session instead of me?"

Have you ever said to a client, "If you don't stop this behavior, don't return to this consultation"?

Have you ever applied one protocol after another, trying to help the client in taking control over his symptoms without results?

Do you remember ever engaging in a power struggle with a client?

A traumatic environment is an unpredictable place, where the child is at the mercy of erratic and inconsistent adults. Faced with this situation, the child tries to introduce predictability in his chaotic world in order to live. Dissociation helps him do this, separating incompatible contexts and coping with them through different dissociative parts of the personality. Emotional parts deal with traumatic, abusive, or neglectful circumstances, and apparently normal parts do the same with more normalized, daily life situations.

A predictable and consistent therapist is the best emotionally corrective experience for the client. But extreme reactions from a client can push the therapist towards extreme reactions too. Severely traumatized people can generate changes and intense emotions in their therapists, reproducing the reciprocal emotional states from their early chaotic environments. Clients enact the roles that have helped them to cope with these situations, and the therapist responds with the complementary reciprocal roles.

Another way to deal with the absence of predictability is to intensify internal control, expressed in the control of symptoms, the suppression of traumatic memories, and as the basis for this, the control of some dissociative parts by others. The high amount of energy invested in maintaining internal control restricts that available for daily life situations, affecting the client's ability to function and leading to a lack of control in the outside world.

Fig. 9: Client controlling the process.

This may translate in different ways in therapy: the client trying to control the therapy or the therapist, or different parts showing an absence of control, alternating with an extremely controlling EP. The therapist in turn may enact different complementary reciprocal roles trying to control aspects that only the client can control, in this way being controlled by the client, rigidly controlling the therapy, which is an impossible goal, or functioning in a chaotic manner.

To overcome this situation, the therapist should take a position outside the conflict, taking perspective and saying, "I do not want to play this game. I am not trying to control you. My role is to support you in reflecting on your problems, to work with you, not to direct you." Or, "Sometimes I feel as I have no choices, no options… Have you ever felt that way before?" Regarding the internal conflict we can say, "I will not take sides in your internal fight for control. I think that you are losing too much energy in this fight. This is what you learned in the past, but I think that by working together, we can find other ways of relating without fights." Obviously the therapist´s actions should support her words.

The Holding of Hope vs. the Despair of Hopelessness

Has your client expressed hopelessness or distrust repeatedly during the therapy session, and you felt you should encourage him to continue? And yet, at the same time as you were overtly encouraging him, you could not avoid feeling frustration or distrust about the client really wanting to improve?

Have you thought, "This client is adopting an illness role" or "He doesn´t want to get better, he has no real motivation for therapy"?

Have you found yourself thinking, "This client is so damaged that he will never recover?" or "All the work we are doing is useless. Is it worth making such an effort?"

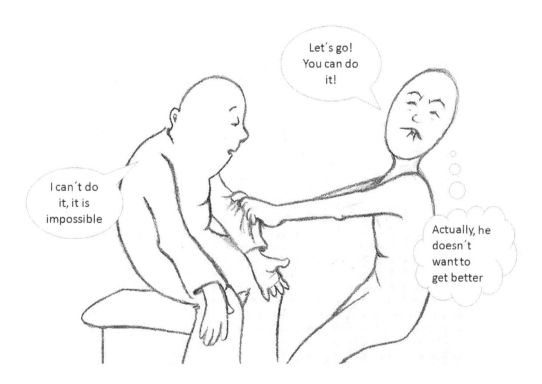

Fig. 10: Doing too much

Another frequent situation in this dyad is the polarity of illusion/disappointment. One of the parent´s responsibilities is to teach optimism, to sustain the child in the face of difficulties. When the parent fails to do this, the child may try on his own, but will experience insurmountable difficulties. In a family with severe neglect and abuse, the child ultimately must abandon such hope as irrational and too painful to maintain. Then again, later as an adult in therapy, the holding of hope becomes the therapist´s job, and the roles are reenacted in a way unfamiliar to the adult/child.

The child must survive in a long-lasting, hostile situation. For a child, the time is exponentially longer than for an adult. Each day is long, and a month might feel like an eternity. In that context, illusion hurts. When the child dreams for the nightmare to be over and then wakes up in the middle of an even worse version of it, the child learns not to dream. Killing the illusion is necessary for survival. Illusion is related to proactive flight and fight action systems, which he repeatedly had to block. When the child learns to avoid dreams and abandon hope, reality beats him to despair.

These dysfunctionally stored memories are re-activated by the need of hope that is implied in the therapeutic process. Using EMDR to reprocess these early memories of loss of hope is a powerful way to dismantle them. The therapist must be careful not to react to the frustration when faced with a client who periodically becomes disappointed with therapy, his current state, and the possibility of definitively overcoming his difficulties. The therapist must bring an active stance, not only of affect tolerance for this resurgent grief, but of compassionate welcoming of it as a sign of working through the childhood state of despair, as the necessary foundation for new dreams and a new sense of self.

For example, in the middle of the therapeutic process, a client was making many healthy changes and starting to reprocess core traumatic events. From time to time, she would have doubts regarding the possibility of recovering from her problems. But at that point in her therapy, these comments became more repetitive, and dealing with these issues took much time in each session. After a long conversation about what she thought had improved, and after recognizing many achievements, she again asked the therapist the same question, "Do you really think I´ll get to be okay some day?" The therapist felt desperate and did not understand why she was questioning her possibilities of healing, even after reviewing and recognizing her progress.

When client and therapist explored when the client felt that emotion for the first time, she realized that this hopelessness was a common feeling in her childhood. The reprocessing of some core traumatic memories was activating an old feeling that was pointing to new relevant early memories.

Extreme Guilt vs. Irresponsibility or Blaming Others

Have you ever felt too concerned about some of your clients?

Have you ever felt responsible for the client´s actions?

When your client gets worse, do you tend to think you are not doing things the right way?

Does your sense of responsibility increase as the client becomes more irresponsible?

Have you thought of any of your clients in these terms: "He is searching for trouble, so in some way he deserves his problems…" "He is always complaining about things that he caused."

Have you ever felt unjustly blamed by a client?

Have you ever found yourself in a "judging" role rather than in a therapeutic one?

Did a client ever apologize for not doing what was expected of him? Or for not progressing positively in therapy?

In a family where maltreatment and neglect are the norm, adequate responsibility is absent. Abusers blame the victimized family members for causing their bad mood, rage, or violence. Sometimes they apologize profusely for their conduct, only to repeat the same behavior sooner or later. Non-abusive parents do not assume any responsibility for allowing the child´s maltreatment, claiming it was not so bad, pleading they were not able to do anything, or blaming the abuser, but not doing anything about it. The child finds it difficult to blame the non-abusive, victimized caregiver, because, as we commented before, it places them in the same role as the abuser.

So in these types of situations, the child assumes all the responsibility and guilt that no one in the family wants to assume. Bearing all the guilt, the child is also preserving the possibility of maintaining some kind of attachment, often disorganized, with the abusive parent. He feels guilty and responsible for the abuser´s behavior, for chronic parental arguments or domestic abuse, for being sexually abused, and for not being able to protect siblings from the abuse. He feels responsible for the non-abusive parent´s emotional state and protection, or for the difficulties that other family members are experiencing.

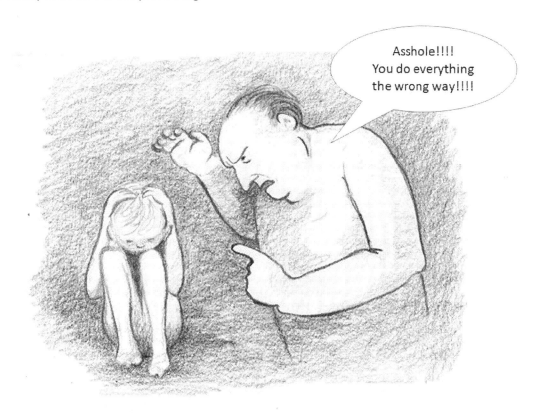

Fig. 11: Blaming parent.

In adulthood, the client can manifest an inadequate sense of responsibility about other people´s feelings or actions. In consequence, any criticism or non-judgmental comment from the therapist may activate the client and generate an out-of-proportion reaction. This reaction may not be explicit or apparent, like a relapse in the client´s problems. If the therapist feels frustrated by the client´s reaction, she may blame the client, reenacting the client´s childhood environment.

Fig. 12: Blaming therapist

Another possibility is that the client may disproportionately blame the therapist for issues regarding the therapy or for his current problems. These are the same reciprocal roles, but with an inverse distribution. The therapist may feel unjustly treated, degraded, and maltreated. But this client-therapist interaction is revealing the key elements of the client´s history and internal organization in a very significant way.

Responsibility and guilt may be irregularly distributed in the internal system. Aggressive emotional parts of the personality, which reproduce elements of the perpetrator´s behavior, may in the same way not assume any responsibility. The apparently normal part of the personality may feel the guilt that the emotional part fails to accept. Or the ANP may avoid a sense of guilt thinking, "It was not me." All these complex inner relationships can be reflected in the therapeutic relationship.

Interventions

Relational aspects of the therapy should not be viewed as merely "the client´s problems in relationships." They are dynamic situations where dysfunctionally stored information and elements of early attachment history and current attachment organization of both client and therapist are constantly interacting. The goal of this chapter is helping to do a differential diagnosis of relational situations to assist the therapist in establishing an adaptive perspective. Only after shifting to an adaptive relational perspective and identifying the relational triggers in both therapist and client, can appropriate interventions be selected and implemented:

a) Dworkin & Shapiro (2005) have described the *relational interview* to be used during the standard protocol of traumatic memories.

b) A *relational bridge* (Gonzalez, Seijo, & Mosquera, 2009) can help us find relevant core memories associated with issues manifesting in the current relational situation.

c) Work with the inner system is key in secondary and tertiary structural dissociation, as different, shifting attitudes toward the therapy, the therapist, and relationships in general can be found in various emotional parts of the personality, and the ANP may or may not be aware of them.

d) We can target the client´s somatic sensations at moments when the client experiences relational difficulties toward the therapist, along the lines of the work with ambivalence described in chapter 11.

When both sides of a conflict can be identified, it is possible to target the conflict itself. We can ask the client to put one facet of the conflict, or emotional part of the personality, to one side of the visual field and the other facet of the conflict to the other side. Then we can ask him to engage in sets of eye movements back and forth between these two positions and to notice what emerges. Sometimes, this will result in a spontaneous decrease of conflict between these parts. Other times, a problem or early memory shared by these two parts will emerge and the work can shift to a collaborative effort with the therapist to address this underlying material, which the conflict had masked.

Summary

Relational problems are not actually problems, but rather excellent points for deepening our understanding of our client´s difficulties. They provide rich opportunities to strengthen treatment planning and guide our selection of relational interventions that can further the central goals of therapy. Dealing with severely traumatized clients can generate strong emotions in therapists and, with time, it can be easy to lose perspective. Reflecting on how the elements of our own memory networks are activated by our clients – our own sensations, our own emotional, cognitive, and behavioral responses – is a crucial aspect for EMDR therapists.

In order to work with trauma survivors, we must work steadfastly to develop our capacities to be aware, reflective, and compassionate about the complex, ambivalent, and difficult relational situations our clients bring forward in therapy. In this direction, as therapists we must: develop a good knowledge of oneself, one´s history and triggers; be mindful and reflective with one´s own sensations, feelings, and thoughts; seek personal therapy when it is needed; continue education in areas of specialization; maintain steadfast, healthy management of boundaries and limits; cultivate consistent good personal self-care; and achieve balance of work, play (exercise), family, friends, and rest.

As therapists, we need to be well-grounded in our capacity to contain and reflect on our emotional responses, realizing when they are related to our own issues, and being able to use them as indicators of the client´s internal organization and early history. We need to maintain a steady awareness and focus on the main aspects of the therapy. In this challenging endeavor it is crucial to have a group of supportive colleagues and to receive regular consultation when working with survivors of severe neglect and traumatization.

Chapter 11
Working on Ambivalence, Defenses, and Motivation for Therapy

Dolores Mosquera, Anabel Gonzalez, & Andrew M. Leeds

Some patients identify an avoidance or ambivalence toward the therapy or the therapist. Sometimes they are aware of the resistance and its meaning, but at other times, they feel frustrated for not understanding and controlling their reactions. Specific interventions will be needed in order to realize what is happening.

A patient who is "avoidant" or who is being "defensive" should be analyzed, not only regarding intrapsychic mechanisms, but also regarding the dynamics of the therapeutic relationship. The information that emerges can be crucial to the development and re-evaluation of the case formulation and to the selection of appropriate therapeutic interventions.

Bilateral stimulation can be used to enhance this kind of intervention. Approaching the analysis of defensive avoidance through Socratic dialogue is often useful, but in cases of structural dissociation, we take the risk of conducting this conversation with just the apparently normal part of the personality (ANP), who can only tell us about those aspects which this part can realize. The most rejected aspects of the personality are often contained in dissociative parts that the ANP is very phobic of, such as a hostile emotional part (EP) containing some of the perpetrator's characteristics. These EPs can be entirely unknown by the ANP. Even when the ANP is aware of their existence, the ANP often does not have access to mental contents that are part of this EP. In these situations, the ANP may tell us about the avoidant or defensive behavior and give us a rationalization about it that is far from the actual underlying motives for it. Or, as ANP, the client can feel a lot of guilt for behaviors that the ANP experiences as "not me."

When we encounter evidence of avoidance or defenses, we may not yet have good access to the internal system. For example, the dissociative part may have a low first person perspective, and a dialogue with parts is not possible, or phobias of dissociative parts or mental actions may be very strong. In these situations, we can work in a more indirect way. In EMDR, we like to have a target as specific as possible, but in these cases, the client's physical sensation may provide a more specific point of access for the client than is immediately evident for the therapist. The client may not be able realize the actual reasons for the behavior, perhaps cannot even talk to us about it, but in many cases, can clearly feel an associated physical sensation. This will be our target.

The BLS used in EMDR seems to activate associative areas (Bergmann, 2000) and has an effect on memory retrieval (Parker, Relph, & Dagnall, 2008). This can be related to clinical observations where we notice that BLS can promote increased association to previously structurally dissociated underlying material. As early as 1995, both Lipke (p. 382) and Paulsen reported evidence indicating that sudden emergence of EPs and of dissociated and forgotten memories of adverse events occurred more commonly in EMDR than in other forms of therapy. In addition, BLS as used in EMDR seems to have an effect in promoting realization. When we work on a traditional target with the standard EMDR procedure, we can observe that clients develop an understanding of and give a sense of meaning to many aspects that previously could not be faced and assimilated. The material that emerges during EMDR sessions is often more relevant and meaningful than previous hypotheses that we, as therapists, may have elaborated or the reasons that clients have given for their present problems. Similar effects can be observed with modified EMDR procedures and targets when working with cases of secondary and tertiary structural dissociation.

We can see how to work on these issues in the following clinical cases:

Proactive Action Systems: a Defensive Attitude

A 47-year-old male client is ambivalent towards EMDR and the therapist. One part is eager to "know the truth," but another part is uncomfortable because he is afraid of "making up things." One part is very angry towards the father (fight action system) and thinks he sexually molested him. Another part thinks the client is "a bad son" for thinking and saying such things. After the previous EMDR session, the client got drunk because he could not manage his emotions (flight action system).

> Client: When I left the session, I had a weird sensation in my stomach... like wanting to cry, but I began to drink (a frequent way for the client to deal with his emotions) and the alcohol covered those sensations.
>
> Therapist: Can you tell me about these sensations?
>
> C: Intimidation... it´s such a paralyzing sensation (client explains how he feels when he is connected with his emotions)... I know I have many defenses and that they are very hard to demolish.
>
> T: It is not about demolishing defenses. I respect and value defenses very much... When there is an inner resistance, when there is a resistant part, it is usually a protective part (client nods)... It is an important part. The idea is to reduce the inner conflict so you can open up while you protect yourself (client listens with attention)... This can happen; not in one or two days, but we can get there.
>
> Client nods.

T: I appreciate you being clear about these defenses because it is important. It is important to keep this in mind. Tell me about the sensation you have now. Do you feel insecure here, with me?

C: Yes, a little.

T: Ok, can you think about this, about this insecurity you feel here with me? (Client nods).

T: Don´t judge anything that comes to your mind (client looks down)… John, this is important. Don´t question what comes, try not to worry about what I might think, ok? (Client nods)… Here, the least important one is me. I am here to help you; you are the one that matters, ok? (Client nods and seems more relaxed)… Try to focus on this insecurity you feel here with me; just focus on the sensation, can you?

C: Yes.

T (after BLS): What is coming?

C: Like I can`t breathe (chokes, suffocated), also I feel like running away from here.

T: Can you go with that?

C: I suppose I can.

T: Okay, great, go with that.

BLS.

T: What is coming?

C: Wanting the session to end.

T: Wanting the session to end?

C: Yes, but I also got mixed with "I would tell her (therapist) this and that." (A part of the client wanted to disclose his early memories, but other parts were not ready for this step.)

T: Okay, so in order for me to understand, it got emotionally mixed with…?

C: More sex.

T: More sex?

C: Yes, at earlier ages (the client seems disturbed).

T: Right now, from 0 to 10, how much do you want the session to end?

C: 70%

T: Okay, I think it is an intense enough signal; we should listen to it and stop here for today.

C: Yes.

T: Remember it is important not to force yourself. I will be here, I will listen to everything you have to say, but this should be at a pace you can handle (client agrees).

So when "more sex" came up, the therapist crucially kept the focus on the client's phobic and defensive urge to avoid emergence of the material that had been triggered in the previous session and identified through the client's drinking behavior. It would have been a serious mistake to merely say, "Go with that" and continue BLS with a focus on the previously avoided memories. Although the client felt like running away, he knew he could stay. He learned that we would not go into the traumatic material too fast. This invites future communication about these phobias as an alternative to acting out by drinking.

In this case, the client clearly identified his defensive reaction and with help was able to disclose its meaning to the therapist. In other cases, this information may be subtler and can be indirectly indicated during reprocessing with symptoms such as sudden tiredness, headache, switching topics, or reporting, "Nothing is coming" or "This is not working." Another cue could be what appears to be apparently normal reprocessing but which, in contrast to other reprocessing sessions, strikes the experienced EMDR clinician as too simple and too fast.

Reactive Action Systems: Passive Resistance

A 30-year-old client comes to therapy because he has been depressed for over 10 years. He has been to many therapies and taken all different types of medication without significant results. He explains he has an ambivalent relationship with his mother since he loves her and hates her at the same time. He frequently has nightmares where he murders her.

During the history taking, the client talks about different situations that bother him, although he cannot understand why. One of the memories he wants to work on is from when he was an adolescent and still "played with his mother in bed." They used to play the "kissing game." His mother would tickle him and kiss him on the mouth. At the time, it was a pleasant sensation and he did not think there was anything wrong, until one day his father walked in the bedroom and gave him an angry look. When he looks back at this moment, he thinks that he was too old to play this "game." When we tried to reprocess this memory, he would get images where he would hurt his mother and his reprocessing became blocked. He explained that something in inside was pulling him back and "blocking what was coming." "I was getting something important, but it's as if something erases it when I want to speak about it and I can't remember it."

In the previous EMDR session, he became suddenly tired. After exploring this sudden symptom, he realized that he felt an inner resistance to allowing the material to emerge. We agreed it was important to listen to this resistance and stop. In the next session, we checked on the resistance and then we agreed to work with it as a target.

> Therapist: Do you still feel this inner resistance?
>
> Client: Yes I do feel resistance (seems upset about this)... there is something that for some reason doesn't want to... I don't know, doesn't want to be commented.
>
> T: Okay, and you notice this resistance.

C: Yes.

T: In a scale from 0 to 10, how strong is this resistance? Being 10 the highest and 0 neutral.

C: A 7 maybe.

T: So it's quite high.

C: Yes it is.

T: Is this related to a lack of trust?

C: No, it has nothing to do with that... To talk about this is like unpleasant and shameful, something like that, that's the sensation I get.

T: explained that one of the great things about EMDR is that you don't need to go into details (client nods). I don't need to know all the details. All I need to know is where you are at, what is coming, but without the need to give details, unless you want to comment on these details because you think it would help you.

C: Aha.

T: How about working with this resistance sensation today?

C: Ok.

T: How do you notice this resistance? Is it a physical sensation?

C: It's nothing personal; it's not lack of trust either.

T: I know it's not personal, I think you do show trust in many ways, but the point is whether this trust is shared with all of you.

C: Sincerely, I feel good talking about some things, but there is something in my body, in my mind, that doesn't want to talk, it becomes like a person... It becomes like... there is something that... How can I explain this? It's not... what is the word? Let me think... it's not spontaneous, it's... like when you do something, but you don't do it consciously...

T: Automatic?

C: Yes, it's automatic but it has another name... you do it because the body tells you... it's like a cerebral order.

T: Like an internal impulse?

C: Yes.

T: Okay, do you think it would be possible for you to focus on this "resistance 7" and in this "something" (probably an EP) that holds you back?

Client nods.

T: Are you okay with this?

C: Yes.

T: Is this "something" okay with this?

C: Yes.

T: You know we can stop whenever you want.

C: I want to try. I don´t know if I will be able to open up or not. That is complicated, but I can try.

T: Okay, let´s try. Focus on this resistance you notice and on this "internal something" that holds you back. Don´t try to justify or rationalize what you get. (The client tends to do this.)

Client takes his time and when he and "this something" are ready, he nods as a sign that it is okay to begin.

BLS.

T: What is coming?

C: I got the word I wanted to say before: *involuntary*, it´s totally involuntary. It´s not something I want to do but for some reason, my mind reacts that way and there are certain things that it doesn´t want to let out, even with people who I trust a lot.

T: Okay, I remind you that the idea is to go at a pace you can tolerate and are willing to follow.

Client nods.

T: Can you go with this?

C: Yes, for now I don´t have any "alarm signals" active.

T: If alarm signals get activated and you feel we can go on, we proceed; if not, we stop.

C: Okay.

BLS

T: What is coming?

C: Pornographic images.

BLS.

After several sets of BLS, we measure the resistance again.

C: I don´t notice as much resistance as other times... This resistance is more "silent" than the other one. With the other one, I would get very anxious and distressed, what this resistance does is make my "senses go to sleep," like "turned off."

T: Okay, focus on this resistance.

After several sets of BLS targeting the resistance, the level went down.

T: Right now, what would be the level of resistance from 0 to 10?

C: Less than usual, I´m less anxious.

In this case, the client was able to start to explore aspects of the phobic avoidance by taking small steps into the traumatic material. The clinician did not press either to fully identify or to resolve the emerging material, but instead returned to assessing the degree of the urge to avoid the material. Keeping the focus on slowly working through the defensive avoidance is crucial to progress in these cases. Slipping too quickly into the frame of mind of the standard reprocessing of traumatic material risks breaching the client's existing defenses, and overtaxing the client's available capacities for mentalization and realization. In such situations, going "slower" is much more efficient that trying to go "quickly."

Another intervention we use is to ask the client to think about the resistance and how it helps or how much it is needed. After doing this with the same client, he realized something relevant:

> C: It's as if I didn't want to face certain problems... So problems are still there, but they temporarily don't affect me. It's some type of barrier that keeps me in the same position (no change).

By targeting this defensive "barrier," the client was later able to reprocess a traumatizing memory with his mother.

Working on Motivation

Some clients do not regularly come to their appointments, do not take their medications, and do not do their homework. Sometimes they are apparently collaborative, but over time they find problems with each task that the therapist proposes. Some of these clients will insist that "nothing works with them" and maintain contradictory attitudes toward the therapy. In other cases, they are overtly oppositional and defiant, arguing with the therapist about the utility of therapy in general or of a specific intervention.

Their motivation towards therapy is not always clear and can fluctuate widely. Some therapeutic approaches select only clients who are "motivated" for therapy, but what happens when this "lack of motivation" is part of the main problem?

A severe DDNOS client was evaluated during research on dissociative disorders and referred to the psychologist in her area. The day she went to therapy, the apparently normal part (ANP) was in charge, and the conversation was focused on current problems with her brother that, in the client's opinion (as ANP), she had overcome. The psychologist concluded that the client did not have any clinical issues and told her that she was (apparently) "okay" at that moment, and that she could return when she considered it necessary. When she came to the next research evaluation, she told the interviewer that the psychologist's attitude represented a lack of interest in her and her problems and, for this reason, she decided not return.

To seek out and ask for professional help and to maintain continuity in therapy sessions is not a simple or easy issue with trauma survivors. We need a client who comes to therapy, and then we can try to help in different ways. But we cannot help a client who does not show up for the sessions. Working on these issues in the early phase of the therapy is crucial.

During these first sessions, we can be attentive to the client's goals in therapy with psychoeducational interventions regarding how early traumatization affects the capacity of asking for help, exploring feelings of hopelessness about possible recovery, and many other aspects. To anticipate these reactions, and to help the client to express them openly to the therapist, is essential to the client's long-term success in therapy. It is crucial to explore from the beginning of therapy different attitudes toward the treatment from each dissociative part, because the therapeutic contract should be entered into with the entire system when this is possible.

A client with a severe DID did not show up for her appointments with different practitioners and sometimes forgot to take medications and vitamins that she needed for a malabsorption issue, which caused her serious physical problems. These factors were negatively influencing the therapeutic process.

> Therapist: We need to understand reluctances from different points of view. I wonder if your physical problems could be influenced by psychological aspects, if there is any part of you that doesn't want you to become better.

> Client: Yes, I always think about it. Sometimes I feel that something is pushing me down, is keeping me in... I want to stand up and there is something there (nodding).

> T: Okay, it's very relevant to explore this, because there is a chance you won't come to the sessions. Do you associate this sensation to any particular part?

> C: I know about one part because others have told me about her... my friend John is the only one who knows her... He said that she is like me when I was a child. When she appears, he has to hold her hand, so she becomes calm. If he doesn't, she makes a big fuss!

> T: Is it a very little child?

> C: Yes.

> T: Can you identify other parts?

> C: Yes.

> T: How many parts can you identify?

> C: We know that there is a male personality, who writes on my diary. There are others, who are not really personalities, but attempts, and they are very integrated in my personality. I am not sure about it. One is like me, but absolutely sad and devastated. She can't see anything. All she can see is negative. The other one is the contrary, she is full of energy. People have told me that I suddenly change from "I am dying" to "let's do things."

> T: I think it is relevant to identify what parts are more related with not going to therapy.

C: I believe that nothing is holding me back. I think I don´t go just because I feel very depressed. Before, even if I was tired, I went to the therapy. My therapist would help me feel my feet on the ground. Now I can´t do it, even when the sessions are near my house.

At this point, we may think that the depressive state is actually influencing the behavior. But we have three aspects to reflect on. First, when we ask for a part that can be influencing the behavior of not coming to therapy, she talks about the child part. She is not realizing a connection between the behavior and the part, but the association could be something to explore. Second, she explains that before she was able go to the session, even when she was still tired and depressed, so the depression would not be a relevant factor. We know that the previous therapist had minimized a disclosure from the client regarding sexual abuse, as well as the dissociative diagnosis itself. This could be a something else to explore. Third, we know that typically the apparently normal part of the personality cannot realize elements contained in other dissociative parts. So, the behavior should be explored with the entire system. But in this case, the capacity to contact with other parts is still underdeveloped, and the phobia of dissociative parts is very strong, so we must proceed with caution.

If we have the opportunity to work step by step, the inner communication should come first, and if the result is positive, we should continue working slowly. But with this client, a more patient approach could imply another six months without regular appointments. We chose to use bilateral stimulation to more quickly locate the more relevant association with the therapy avoiding behavior.

T: So is it okay if we explore this, because we may not be aware of other aspects. We could try to do a little bit with EMDR. Maybe it could help you. Using eye movements, sometimes we can unblock things. We would take one step at a time. What do you think?

C: We can try.

T: So, try to notice what is preventing you to come to therapy…

C: It´s like tiredness, like a: "I´ve had it! Why should I continue trying?"

T: Can you notice that in your body?

C: It is as if something was pushing me, as an enormous weight on me…

T: Are you noticing that sensation now?

C: Yes, like cold. (Notice that the sensation described and felt are not the same.)

T: Just notice that, and follow my fingers (BLS).

C: I am noticing much more cold and like foggy.

T: Is there any thought coming to your mind?

C: Right now, I feel like crying.

T: Do you associate this sensation with any part?

C: I always associate this cold with the "little girl." She is always cold.

After this sequence, the association between the attitude towards therapy and this child part seems clearer. A strong phobia between ANP and EP could be decreased during the session. Due to the intense effect of BLS, the therapist decides that it was enough BLS for that session and turned to work on self-care procedures. The session finished with an agreement from the child part to come to therapy. The client went to her next appointment, a specific group therapy for dissociative disorders, and had difficulties managing the group interaction, which probably provoked a new disconnection from the therapeutic process. We are aware that the therapy of a severe DID case is not a simple issue, but a complex process with plenty of choice points. We are not talking about magic solutions, just about using BLS as one more tool that we can use to clarify the organization and lessen the degree of phobic avoidance or specific blockage points, as we have commented in the previous chapter. Whether to use BLS or not should be decided with clinical judgment.

Motivation at Different Stages of the Therapeutic Process

The Early Stage

As we commented in the previous clinical case, to explore initially negative or ambivalent and contradictory attitudes toward the therapy is crucial in establishing a therapeutic contract that includes all the client´s tendencies. Another related aspect to work on in the initial sessions is to explore self-care patterns, as we explain in chapter 5. Understanding the client´s difficulties to commit to therapy as unhealthy self-care patterns based on early experiences, and redefining therapy as healthy care is one of our proposed initial interventions. This approach tends to be well tolerated even by very disorganized clients, and in some cases, it generates a relevant change regarding attitude toward therapy.

The Middle Phase

Some specifics problems about motivation emerge in the middle phase of therapy. Hopelessness can arise after early progress on inner communication has taken place. Clients are more in contact with their emotions, and traumatic content starts to emerge. This hopelessness used to be a feeling that characterized the client´s entire childhood, time passed by slowly and the pain seemed to be never-ending, like there was no exit. Thinking about these issues may trigger experiences of frustration or re-emergence of resignation, which helped the client to survive in such an adverse environment. Hopelessness is the basic feeling of learned helplessness and is a central part of the trauma material. One problem with working through this hopelessness is when the therapist becomes emotionally infected with that feeling, thinking, "Therapy doesn´t work" or, depending on the therapist´s own dysfunctionally stored information, "I am a failure as therapist. I should refer this client to another colleague." The client needs a therapist who can maintain realistic hope and confidence in the client's possibilities. If the therapist gives up, it can be experienced by the client as a new abandonment. When these challenges arise, it can be a good time for case consultation.

The Trauma Work Phase

New difficulties may appear, adopting the form of relapses, sudden improvements, abandonment of therapy, and many others, when therapy is approaching the work with core traumatic events. We should be attentive to subtle manifestations of this phobia. For example, a client suddenly has a lot of activities that do not allow her to come to therapy, just after the last session where she started to experience disgust when thinking of her father's image. These aspects were described more extensively in chapter 12, about trauma work.

Later Phases of Therapy

When therapy is successful in generating relevant improvements in daily life or is drawing close to the end, phobias of change, of normal life, and of intimacy may appear, as well as grief about the impending loss of the therapeutic relationship. When integration happens (see chapter 7), the client must still cope with difficulties in current relationships, while experiencing the "loneliness of being one" that may come from integration. The inner world is not yet fully stable, and the outside world is still a challenge. Use of the inverted protocol described by Hofmann (2010) may be useful to reduce these problems from the beginning of the therapy. By starting with identifying and addressing future challenges, and installing resources specifically oriented to these issues, we can partially prevent the appearance of phobic reactions for normal life. With this advance preparation, as the client expands social engagement and pursues wider life goals, he or she will have more tools to manage emerging interpersonal difficulties.

Knowing the typical issues that tend to present at specific stages, we may be able to prevent crises, by working on them even before they begin to cause problems. But other situations are specific to each client. The use of BLS may help us, as we commented in previous paragraphs, to explore relevant connections with a behavior that could be interpreted as lack of motivation. We can see an example:

This client has a dissociative disorder with an intense depersonalization symptom, which was activated previously when she approached core traumatic events in therapy. After this crisis, she was referred to us and her case progressed well during the last year. Two months ago, she again abandoned taking her medication, after a previous experience of relapse for the same reason some time ago. She "forgot" the last appointment and experienced doubts about continuing therapy. She explains the reasons for this behavior:

> Client: It was stubbornness. It just got in my head.

> Therapist: Think about what happened before you stopped taking the medication.

> C: It may be because we are approaching a topic that terrifies me.

T: If you don´t want to go into this issue, you don´t need to become worse. You can say, "I can´t do it" or "I don´t want to go into this for now," and we won´t go there.

C: It´s as if I want to solve this by myself.

What could we think about these statements? The client (as ANP) is offering different, unrelated possibilities and does not seem to come to a full realization about underlying reasons. The first one (phobia of traumatic memories) seems to be a reproduction of some elements commented in previous sessions, and the second one (phobia of attachment) lacks a solid logic. In this client, contact with dissociative parts is difficult, and direct communication with the inner system has not been possible, because even the most minimal attempt to establish contact provoked an intense re-experiencing of traumatic material that the client (as ANP) cannot tolerate or manage. Based on other good experiences working with modified EMDR procedures, we believe that by managing it carefully, BLS could be used to clarify the origin of the phobic avoidance and prevent another crisis.

T: It sounds like there are different options.

C: Maybe I can´t tolerate the situation, I can´t tell you why, but I don´t know. I feel bad with everybody.

T: Was this before or after you stopped taking the medication?

C: It started before.

T: It seems like there is something that is not allowing you to search for a constructive solution. Do you notice something inside you, something that is blocking you, like a resistance?

C: I feel the desire of overcoming this.

T: Do you notice any physical sensation associated to this?

C: I am terrified.

Since the client has difficulties focusing on this issue and being specific, we ask her to draw her sensation, facilitating a symbolic expression of her difficulty. Such symbolic expression can help externalize material in cases with low levels of mentalization.

T: Can you draw the difficulty itself?

Client doodles.

T: Looking at the drawing, get a sense of your inner sensations and tell me if you think that it´s a good idea to work on this (asking the inner system for permission).

C: I am afraid. I don´t know. I blame others around me. I can´t look at me. I am looking at them.

Usually, this client easily makes contact with her body sensations. During this session, she is not able to make this contact, probably in part because of the lack of medication, but maybe because she is not being able to think reflectively. We try with BLS.

T: Look at the drawing and notice if you want to draw some more (tapping on shoulders).

C: Things from the outside (she draws people from her environment) crash against this (a barrier). This tries to stop it....

T: Focus on that (BLS).

C: (She draws herself, probably as EP.) I can´t go backwards. I sit here, closed in myself, in a white room, and protected.

T: Focus on that drawing (BLS).

C: I don´t hear. I don´t see anything... I will be there forever.

T: Focus on that (BLS).

C: But there I am sad. I want to cry... this is not the solution.

T: See what happens if you stay there.

C: I can´t bear it.

T: We can work on this sensation if you want.

C: It has to do with my students. (She teaches little children.) I am insufferable with them. There is something about them that reminds me of something that´s mine, especially a little girl in my classroom.

T: Okay, go with that (BLS).

C: I can´t bear this. Becoming depressed helps me hide deeper in my suffering, so all of this (points at the dark part of the drawing, representing traumatic memories) doesn´t affect me.

What could seem initially a lack of motivation was finally understood as a problem with boundaries. An EP within this client, who as ANP was an efficient teacher in spite of her disorder, was activated by one of her students, who had triggered a childhood part. This led to work on developing and installing a "filter" to protect herself from the environment and to assist her to differentiate between herself and the outside world. After these interventions, this client no longer needed to be depressed in order to protect herself. She returned to being medication compliant and continued coming to therapy sessions on a regular basis.

In this case, using a modified EMDR procedure led us to an understanding that was very different from those that the client initially could give, and even from those that the therapist could think of.

This procedure is not a step-by-step protocol, but rather is a dynamic procedure of applying BLS while the client is focusing on specific sensations associated with an issue, in order to increase realization.

A Therapeutic Contract with the Dissociative Client: Negotiating with a Hostile Part

One of the first interventions to do with any client is to establish a therapeutic contract where as many parts as possible agree with the main goals of the therapy. One difficult part of this intervention with dissociative clients is dealing with negative, critical, or hostile parts. The client as ANP can agree and be willing to do therapy, but if some of the ANP's goals are perceived as a threat from any EP, things can get complicated, for instance, when the ANP wants the hostile or critical voices to disappear. The ANP should accept that even the more hostile or apparently negative EP is part of the client, and that the therapy will be directed to the entire person. The EPs may have the belief that the therapist, probably as many previous therapists did, will want to get rid of them or make them disappear or become weaker. From the inner conflict between EP and ANP, the figure of the therapist can be seen as a threat. When this configuration is active, there will be much interference and conflict between the ANP and the EP or EPs. So one of the central responsibilities we have as therapists is to help the client to think of the inner system as a cooperative team, where all parts will win if they help each other.

Some useful tools to create this "therapeutic team" are to:

1. Define a new collaborative context for therapy, instead the previous competitive one.

2. Recognize the adaptive function of apparently negative parts.

3. Express interest and empathy with the suffering in these parts. Sometimes, they may reject these comments from the therapist because they have associated that showing their suffering makes them weak. We should work to dismantle this belief, explaining that a lack of understanding and empathy with their suffering actually makes them weaker. These statements should come from a true understanding of what we believe lies beneath the hostility in the EP: They were frequently protective parts who had to bear the worst part of the traumatic experience.

4. Remark their importance and key role in the system.

5. Make them part of the therapy from the beginning.

6. Identify and be sensitive to the specific goals in each part, keeping in mind that each is driven by what that part feels. For example, a part can define that its main goal is to be strong, but we can see that its main agenda is to be in control of what other parts do. Rigidly controlling other parts is just a substitute action for real control in current external situations. Psychoeducation about learning to be in control of the external situation, regarding their behavior and their life, in an adaptive way is a good goal. But no one part should have main control over others. Instead, control should vest in the integrative functions of the emerging, meta-cognitive adult self.

7. Explain the advantages each part can get out of therapy. As we reduce the amount of conflict between parts, there will be much more energy to invest in achieving each part's objectives.

8. Explain to each part the advantages of working with the other parts. When there is a strong phobia between dissociative parts, this should be done little by little.

9. Help the client to separate this therapy from other therapies and differentiate the current therapist from other therapists and other people.

10. Show a deep respect for all parts of the system, even ones who are reluctant or negative towards therapy.

11. Ask and encourage each part to take the time they need to decide if they want to engage in therapy.

12. Do not ask for trust, but for time. Distrust, when it is not extreme, can be re-defined as precaution.

13. Explain that they are not going to disappear or die, that the therapist cannot do this and does not want to. The goal is to be more present in an adaptive way, not to eliminate parts.

It is very important to keep in mind that some of these parts function cognitively at a developmental level of little children or adolescents who may try to seem like terrible monsters, devils, or "bad boys" as a protective cover for intense feelings of fear or shame. Others are more complex and may reproduce some of the abuser's features as encoded in introjects via mirror neurons. But even with the most sadistic parts, we should work from the idea that they are relevant parts and can become positive aspects of the self.

Working with hostile parts is a crucial issue in the therapy of dissociative clients and is very relevant when we are working on motivation toward therapy in early sessions. The following example illustrates the first contact with a dissociative client with a hostile EP.

A 32-year-old woman was referred to our Trauma and Dissociation Program by a colleague, who identified severe behavioral problems. She presented with self-harming and aggressive behaviors that she only remembered partially. Sometimes, she presented total amnesia. After exploring these behaviors, we started to talk about an auditory hallucination that she related to these aggressive acts.

> Therapist: Can you tell me about your voices?
>
> Client: I don't just hear voices, I HAVE a voice... an internal voice. I have a person inside... His name is Ethan... He asks me to do things. He wants me to go to "his side."
>
> T: What kind of things does he ask you to do?

C: Always bad things, and when I feel bad, I usually listen to him and do these things. When I am strong, I try to avoid it, because when I am okay, I know those things are not appropriate. When I feel bad, I am not so conscious about what is right and what is wrong.

T: It seems like a male voice… (Client nods). How old is he?

C: He´s about 40.

T: Does he sound familiar?

C: No.

T: Can you ask him what he thinks about you being here?

C (quick answer, indicating no reflective thinking): Bad, he doesn´t like it.

T: Why?

C: Because he doesn´t want, he wants to have me only for himself. He doesn´t like when others try to take me away from him.

T: And why does he think I would want to do something like that?

C: Because he knows that if I have support from other people, they will try to separate us, to take me away from him.

T: How does he know this? We just met. I wonder why he thinks I would do that.

C: Because… he is not stupid… He knows that if I know the reality… He thinks that all of you are lying about him.

T: Okay, but I am wondering why he thinks this about me, because this is the first time that we meet.

C: Because you are psychologists and psychiatrists, and he thinks that you are not good people, that you try with medications…

T: Psychiatrists are not identical people…

C (smiling): I know, I understand. I am just saying what he thinks…

T: Please, ask him why he thinks that about me, not about other people.

C (more reflective): Because he believes that you will too, you will try to take me away from him.

T: And if this is not the case?

C: If this is not the case, he doesn´t have any problem with you.

T: Okay, I will explain how I understand your problem, but I want to know your opinion about my ideas, and his opinion also, because he is part of you.

C: Okay.

T: When a child grows up in a traumatic environment, her mind cannot tolerate all this stuff. This is logical, because she is very vulnerable. So in some cases, the mind has to be divided to deal with what is happening. On one hand, she has to go on with daily life, acting as if nothing happened, and on the other hand, a part of her has to bear the burden of these traumatic experiences. This part, the one that has to deal with all these memories, usually has a lot of rage, a lot of pain... it´s just too much to handle...

C: He is not another part.

T: Why does he say he is not another part?

C: Because he is another person inside me.

T: This is a sensation, right? We usually make hypothesis from our sensations and from some facts. My hypothesis about him being a part of you comes from other clients I have seen, who have similar problems... and also, from the fact of he is talking through you... He can have the sensation of being somebody completely different (client nods) and in some sense he is, but you are just one. Of course, this is just my opinion, but he is in your body, he is in your mind. I think that he feels completely different than how you feel and that´s why he concludes that he is a separate person.

C: Do you mean that he needs me for communicating?

T: From my point of view, he is a part of your mind, completely different from the other one, right? (Client nods). But for me, both parts are "you," both make a lot of sense, and are there for a reason.

C: Okay.

T: He may have a different perspective. I am not trying to indoctrinate you. This is just my view, and I would like to know if this makes sense for you and for him.

C: Okay.

T: What does he think about it?

C: He is listening.

T: Thoughts, experiences, and feelings can be very different in each part... (Client nods)... but all are valid and important information. One aspect that is frequently isolated is rage... Children can´t fight against the adults, because this can be dangerous... They have to contain the eagerness to fight, and that urge to fight creates a lot of pressure... Rage is good. We all need it. It helps us to fight for our needs, to say "no." But when there is a lot of "old rage," it´s often too much to bear... Do you have the sensation that there is a lot of "old rage" inside you?

Client smiles and nods.

T: Most of that rage is probably in this other part, and that was necessary for survival. Flight is another useful reaction that is also impossible during childhood. This urge for flight is more related with fear.

C: There is a lot of this also.

T: When you are a child, you only can engage in flight with your mind. That's your only chance.

C: Yes, I also have a parallel world.

T: All these aspects have been there for a long time, but sensations are as intense and clear as when they were happening for the first time. All these issues can change now, yet not disappear. For example, you shouldn't lose your fear. Fear is needed in order to protect ourselves. Fear, which is adequate for a certain situation, is caution, and adequate rage is strength.

Client nods.

T: The problem is the burden of the past, which doesn't allow you to improve and this burden maintains this division... If this part realizes that he is part of you, he can begin to work with you, and this constant conflict will diminish...

Client pays attention.

T: You know, I think this fight between both of you is consuming all your energy, and it's not allowing you to achieve goals.

C (nodding): This is destroying me.

T: Can you ask him what he thinks about this?

C: What do you think? That he doesn't agree with anything.

T: With what?

C: He wants me to go, he is not listening to you. He doesn't want you to help me. He wants to be there for ever...

T: He will always be there. What makes him think that I want him to disappear?

C: He would lose power.

T: Why is that?

C: Because when I am better, he is worse.

T: This doesn't always need to be that way. The goal is that he is better, and you are better.

C: But he is very evil.

T: I don't think so, I think he has a lot of rage because he had to carry the burden of so much pain. Does he believe that he can't become better?

C: He is happy that way.

T: Are you sure?

C: No, you can´t convince him. The only thing he can feel is evilness... He wants me to feel bad. He thinks that if I commit suicide, we will be finally united.

T: Would he agree to give us some time to think about all these issues?

C: If he doesn´t agree, fuck him!

T: This is not okay with me.

C: But it is with me.

T: He is part of you and I can´t treat half of a client... I need to work with him, I realize that you have difficulties with him, but in my mind, he is also "you." Both parts are you...

C: Well... what can we do?

T: How about we listen to what is he saying? Could you try to listen and tell me what he says, so we can reach an agreement?

C: He insists that you won´t separate him from me.

T: What makes him think I am trying to do this?

C: That you try to show me a different side of him... He thinks that you are trying to make him better than he is, and he doesn´t want to be good.

T: Trying to make him better... No, I think that everybody should be a little bit good and a little bit bad. I don´t believe that being completely good is representative of mental health. Extremely good people often crash. It´s better to be partially good and partially bad. The problem is fighting between being extremely good and extremely evil. This wastes a lot of your energy, and when it comes to dealing with the outside world, you are exhausted. (Client nods.) He has his function. He is there for a reason, and he should remain being there. Probably, he should be more present, because you are not caring for you in the best way you can.

C: Okay, we will try.

T: Does he agree?

C: Yes.

This negotiation with dissociative parts can be relatively easy with some clients, but might need many different interventions throughout the therapeutic process in other cases. Some parts can manifest later in treatment, communicating directly or through different symptoms or problems. This situation is frequent with perpetrator-imitator parts, which are the most difficult parts for the ANP to accept. A main rule for working on motivation with structural dissociation is to explore from the internal system, not only from the ANP or the most collaborative EPs. Participation of hostile emotional parts in therapy decision-making is necessary for an effective treatment. These parts can become powerful allies. They usually have more energy than vulnerable and submissive parts and are based in proactive defensive action systems, more prone to action. The client needs these parts to achieve changes, even when the ANP or some emotional parts do not realize this.

Summary

Ambivalence, defenses, and lack of motivation are not only therapeutic challenges, but often represent good points of departure for change. A client who always agrees with all our comments, with all our proposals, will not recover faster and deeper. Sometimes, the parts that are more accommodating to the therapeutic process present more problems with change, and parts that initially present more distrust, ambivalence, or hostility, can become excellent co-therapists.

Every apparent stuck point can be seen as an attempt to reveal highly relevant information. EMDR therapy provides a way to see this more clearly than some other approaches. These stuck points are often related to dysfunctionally stored information that, when reprocessed, generates deep changes. When our clients present problems in the office, we have an excellent opportunity to explore them and to offer clients an emotionally corrective experience that they can learn from. These experiences set example and help the client to manage aspects that are troubling them in their current life, as we commented in the relational aspects of therapy in chapter 10.

Chapter 12
Trauma Processing in Structural Dissociation

Anabel Gonzalez, Dolores Mosquera, & Janina Fisher

Controversy regarding the use of EMDR in dissociative disorders has continued since the first developments in EMDR therapy. Although at first EMDR was used applying the standard protocol for processing traumatic memories to all cases, problems quickly appeared in clients with complex trauma and dissociative disorders. In the last decade, EMDR therapists have been warned about the cautious use of the standard processing procedures with dissociative disorders. Resource development and installation (Korn & Leeds, 2002) has gained much attention for its usefulness in complex cases and has become one of the most frequent interventions used among EMDR therapists during the preparation phase. However, the problem of memory processing in dissociative disorders has not been fully addressed simply by using the RDI protocol.

These difficulties led to the creation of a task force for the treatment of dissociative disorders, which recommended extreme caution. The task force advised that the following be in place prior to proceeding with EMDR for trauma processing when a dissociative disorder is present: good affect tolerance, a stable life environment, willingness to undergo temporary discomfort for long-term relief, good ego strength, adequate social support and other resources, and history of treatment compliance (Shapiro, 1995).

In the description of some authors, EMDR is viewed as a procedure to work with trauma memories, more than a psychotherapeutic approach. Paulsen (2008) states that "failure to prepare or work with the structure of the self prior to doing EMDR can result in sudden and severe flooding, disorganization and decompensation." And although this statement is true, in this phrase the term EMDR is used as a synonym for phases 3 to 8 of the standard protocol (traumatic memories processing). For example, Lazrove & Fine (1996) state that "it is important to understand that EMDR should be considered a form of trauma work and should not be conducted until the initial stages of psychotherapy have been completed and the patient is ready for such work" (Fine, 1991; Herman, 1992; Kluft, 1993 1994; Van der Hart et al., 1993).

These prudent recommendations have generated an extremely cautious attitude in some EMDR therapists, even with dissociative disorder cases who meet the criteria for using it. Some authors advise (Leeds, 2006) therapists not to delay trauma processing unnecessarily. A significant number of clients with posttraumatic stress syndromes, who meet standard EMDR readiness criteria for ego strength and stability, have been offered RDI instead of standard EMDR reprocessing. This situation continues to be present in many countries, where EMDR has been relegated to a secondary technique when working with dissociative disorders and complex trauma, applicable only to a few selected cases, the most functional ones.

The present consensus about the treatment of trauma has its origins in the conceptualization of a three-stage phase-oriented treatment model described by Janet: First, stabilization; second, work with traumatic memory; and third, integration. Some authors are proposing non-linear models that seem to be more adapted to clinical reality (Courtois, 1999; Gonzalez, Seijo, & Mosquera, 2009; Van der Hart, Solomon, & Gonzalez, 2010; Van der Hart et al., 2013). Accepting the Hipocrates´ maxim "primum non nocere" (first, do no harm) and understanding that standard EMDR protocol on traumatic memories is just one of the EMDR procedures that we can use, Janet´s ideas can be improved and adapted for EMDR therapy.

The way EMDR works is not completely equivalent to other therapies, and complex trauma has many particularities that should be taken into account. So we need to think about complex trauma and structural dissociation from the EMDR perspective, integrating new developments and procedures. Our proposal of a "progressive approach" integrates some of Janet´s contributions, but uses the phase-oriented model in a less linear way, which, in our opinion, can be an obstacle regarding the possibilities EMDR has to offer. That is, at all times, the progressive approach adapts targets and procedures to ensure that the client is able to maintain functioning and affect tolerance, but it does not refrain from specific uses of EMDR until the client is fully stable. Different EMDR interventions may be implemented from the early phases of treatment, but instead of trying to adapt the client to procedures such as the standard protocol, we propose to adapt the interventions to each client, depending on their specific characteristics.

We are aware that processing traumatic memories in complex trauma is not a simple issue. In an all-or-nothing phase-oriented perspective, the preparation phase must be completed before we can proceed with trauma work. In the progressive approach that we are proposing, small fragments of processing can be introduced with many clients in early stages of treatment. Some authors have described similar interventions but reserve the term "EMDR" just for the standard protocol on a traumatic memory, and they call these other techniques "alternating bilateral stimulation" (Shapiro, 1995, 2001; Gelinas, 2003) or "the use of short sets of bilateral stimulation" (Fisher, 2000). We consider that the same underlying mechanism is operating both in a complete standard EMDR protocol, with all the phase 3 elements, and when we are processing peripheral elements of the traumatic memory, as in the "tip of the finger strategy." The tip of the finger strategy was briefly described in chapter 8 on dissociative phobias and will be explained below in more detail. So, in this chapter, we will use the word "processing" for both traditional memory processing and processing of peripheral elements, and we will consider the last one as a way to work on trauma, even when we are not focusing on a particular traumatic memory itself.

We can introduce processing of peripheral elements, such as the tip of the finger strategy or the processing of dissociative phobias, as we will comment upon in further chapters of this book, and we can combine titrated or graduated processing with interventions such as psychoeducation and resource installation. If we keep in mind each client's specific strengths, symptoms, and ability to tolerate emotions and arousal, we will be able to introduce more and more elements of the standard EMDR protocol and proceed with a complete EMDR procedure when the client is ready. The intermediate stages may require many adaptations and modifications of the standard procedure, and those will be explained in the section of this chapter about protocol modification.

When to move forward in this process is a matter of constant decision-making for both client and therapist. During this process, many aspects will need to be addressed, such as the client's empowerment to feel a growing mastery and control regarding the therapeutic process and therefore about his own life. Clients learn to observe their mental processes and reactions and to analyze how the therapeutic interventions influence them. In order to do this, the clients need to develop the capacity of being aware of their own feelings, sensations, and needs and the different options to address them. If we think about this, there is an important message implicit in this task, the possibility of having choices, a message that the client can learn and interiorize.

Processing Peripheral Elements: The Tip of the Finger Strategy (TFS)

Before targeting the traumatic memory, it is helpful to target those specific elements that can strongly enhance the process of increasing internal communication and collaboration between parts and prepare the client to further trauma work. Processing dissociative phobias, working on self-care patterns, and working on nonspecific blockages or defenses are all part of the preparatory process to strength the client and promote emotional regulation and daily life functioning. But even without searching for it, some traumatic elements are indirectly processed during these procedures. For example, by working on self-care patterns with the loving eyes procedure, many disturbing emotions and even some traumatic memories, mainly related to attachment issues, will be part of the associative chains and will be processed.

Among all these interventions for the preparation stage that we are proposing, which include BLS, the tip of the finger strategy is the only one that intentionally targets part of the traumatic content. The tip of the finger strategy term follows from the hand metaphor that we use to explain the processing of a traumatic memory. In the standard protocol, we start with the memory itself and follow different associative chains (the fingers), periodically returning to the initial memory (the back of the hand). Using the tip of the finger strategy, the target is not the traumatic memory, but a small part of a disturbing sensation or emotion that can be considered a peripheral consequence of the memory.

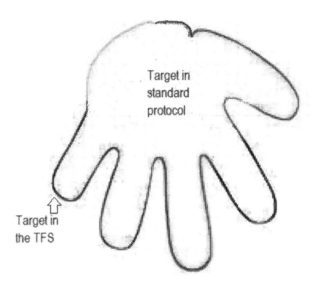

Fig. 1: Hand metaphor and the TFS

In the standard EMDR protocol, working with single traumatic events, we choose the worst part of the earliest or worst memory as the initial starting point. In severely traumatized people, an inverse strategy can be implemented. Using the hand metaphor of EMDR memory processing, we should start from the "tip of the little finger" (a peripheral element), rather than the "back of the hand" (the memory), to progressively approach the core traumatic events. We use an outside-to-inside perspective, starting from the periphery (e.g., the emotion) and slowly approaching the core aspects (e.g., the core memories). Metaphorically, this would be like peeling onion layers, little by little. Peripheral somatic sensations or emotions are ultimately the consequences of dysfunctionally stored memories, and we will first work with these peripheral elements. Direct work with traumatic memories will develop in the second phase of phase-oriented therapy. The processing of these peripheral elements in combination with the meeting place procedure constitutes an effective and useful intervention for the first phase of trauma therapy, stabilization and safety.

This concept is crucial in a progressive approach. Our goal is to progress toward a complete processing of the traumatic experience, but when this experience is extremely overwhelming, we need to approach those memories in small steps, starting from the most tolerable interventions and processing small amounts. In our opinion, the underlying mechanism of both this procedure and the standard protocol is exactly the same. We are activating the innate processing system in the brain, which has been blocked by the traumatic experience. To untangle a simple knot and a tangled ball of wool, we use similar movements: the first step in untangling a ball of wool will be to start from a more accessible, peripheral, and small knot.

Case example

A 34-year-old client comes to the Trauma and Dissociation Program after several severe suicide attempts and episodes of aggression that she hardly remembered. In the first session, the dissociative symptomatology was explored, paying primary attention to the establishment of a therapeutic relationship. The client described an auditory hallucination that she related to the self-harming and aggressive episodes: "He makes me do these things, he wants to get me to do bad things." A negotiation was immediately carried out with this part, and at the end of the session, the part agreed to stop harming the client and to participate in the therapeutic process.

However, a week after, in the next session, the client once again attempted suicide by taking pills. The client's adult self did not understand what had happened, so we asked the emotional part (EP), the one who had agreed to stop the suicide attempts, about why he did it after last session's no-harm agreement. He explained that the emotions were so overwhelming that he could not control his behavior.

This happens frequently in dissociative clients. The emotional parts may be open to making changes, but the traumatic content is stronger than their capacity for planning and decision making. In these cases, it is too early to process the traumatic memory itself, but it can be a good time to explore the possibility of using the Tip of the Finger Strategy (TFS).

Steps to Apply the Tip of the Finger Strategy (TFS)

Step 1: Psychoeducational Intervention

The therapist begins by giving the EP different options to explain the self-harm, including possible problems in the past session, any environmental factors that might have triggered the EP's reaction, and the possibility of being too overwhelmed and unable to do anything different.

> Therapist: Sometimes the parts are so disturbed by what is inside them, that even if they want to change, they cannot do it...
>
> Client nods.
>
> T: But we might be able to relieve a part of this internal pressure with specific therapies. Would he like that? Maybe we could try this today.
>
> It is important to ask the EP specifically, since the ANP might answer based on her own thoughts or feelings alone.
>
> T: Does he agree with doing a short test with this therapy?
>
> C: He doesn't want to talk.
>
> T: Okay, but I need to know his opinion. I don't want to force him. I need to know if he wants to do it or if he doesn't. A "yes" or "no" is enough. I will explain the test we can do.

Client nods.

Step 2: Explaining the Procedure

Next, the therapist explains EMDR to the ANP and EP in language both can understand.

Step 3: Explaining to the Dissociative Part how it can Help him

The EP previously recognized feeling pain inside and is willing to work on anything that could help with the pain.

Step 4: Explaining to the Adult Self what she might Gain from this Procedure

T: It´s good to feel control. You don´t need to lose it. But people who spend all their energy in this fight for control of the parts don´t have energy to control their lives. If this part becomes better, he will have more control, you will have more energy, and both of you will have more control in your life.

C: Okay, if he doesn´t agree, he´ll just have to put up with it!

T: This is not okay with me. For me, you are both important, and he is part of you. I can´t treat half of a client, do you understand?

The emotional part has his own objections:

C: He thinks that you want to change him, make him nicer than he is, and he doesn´t want to be good.

T: Why does he think I want to make him nicer?

C: It´s just what he thinks.

T: I really want him to help you become stronger. This part of you has your rage, and this is extremely important for saying "no" and asking for your needs.

After this psychoeducation, both the ANP and the EP agree with the procedure.

Step 5: Explaining the Specific Procedure

T: Ask this part to notice the disturbing sensations from which he wants relief. Sometimes after eye movements, these emotions decrease. Sometimes, the effect is that these emotions change. If any more memories or feelings come in, we can talk about it a little bit if you want, but our goal is not to go into past issues at this moment. Would it be okay with him?

C: Yes.

T: It´s very important that he tells me how he feels and what to do next (giving the part the control of the procedure). After each set, he should tell me what to do next, what effect he notices, and if we should continue or not.

Client nods.

Step 6: Selecting the Target

T: Okay, so ask this part to focus on the part of his sensation that he wants to relieve, this sensation inside him that is not allowing him to be well. Just a little bit, we don't want to work on all this stuff at once.

C: He feels hate.

T: Does he think that he needs all that rage? Or is it too much for him? Would he like some relief from it?

C: He thinks that he needs all his rage.

T: Why?

C: Because he suffered very much.

T: Yes, he did suffer very much, and does he worry that he needs his rage to protect himself from more suffering?

C: It is… it's the way he defends himself from the world.

T: And in order to protect himself, does he need all his rage? Or just the right amount of it? Rage is necessary to defend ourselves. But when rage is extreme, when there is too much hate, and he is controlled by this emotion, he cannot defend himself very well…

Client nods.

T: And usually such extreme rage is painful (client nods)… So he is suffering because of this. And maybe this is related to self-harm…

C: Yes.

T: If he wants, we can decrease the rage a little bit. Or focus on his suffering to relieve the part of the rage that makes him suffer.

C: He feels rage all the time, he feels hate, fury…

T: And is that painful?

C: It is.

T: Now we will try to help him. I don't want to take his rage away, I can't either. The goal is for him to have a level of rage that allows him to have the control of the situation (the client seems very interested in this explanation). When emotions are very high, we are not the ones who control things. Those emotions have the control. I am trying to help him maintain his control.

C: And how can you do this?

T: That's what we will try to work on with EMDR.

Step 7: Desensitization

T: So, ask this part to focus on the part of his sensation that he wants to relieve. When he is noticing it, he should let you know, and we will start with eye movements. When we stop, he will tell us what is he noticing, and then we will make decisions about how to proceed next.

C: Okay.

T: Let me know when he is noticing that negative sensation that he feels inside.

C: Now.

T: Okay, let´s go with that.

Six sets of eye movements.

Step 8: Checking the Effect on the Part

T: Take a deep breath... What is coming?

C: Hate.

T: Does he notice that the eye movements are bothering him? Or are they okay?

C: They are okay.

T: He notices all this rage inside...

C: Yes.

T: Is it okay for him to continue?

C: Yes.

T: Ask him to notice those sensations ... It´s normal he has all that rage... Now he is just noticing the sensations so they can slow down and settle.

A short set of EM. The therapist stops the movements when the client´s face begins to show sadness.

T: What is he experiencing with what we are doing?

C: He is suffering.

T: Is he noticing what underlies this rage? Some other feelings or sensations?

Client nods.

T: So the sensations are changing, even though he is still suffering. Now I need him to tell me how much to do. If we continue, we can digest more of this suffering, but I don´t want it to be too much. Tell him if he wants to continue for a little bit or if he rather stop now.

C (after a moment covering her face with her hands): He wants to continue a little bit more.

T: Ask him to notice his sensation.

Eye movements (short set).

C (taking a deep breath): Flying.

Step 9: Closure

This step is implemented when the therapist notices and/or the client and the EP decide that is good to stop or cannot continue. The main rule is: less is better than too much.

At this moment, the client seems to be relieving past memories. Reality orientation should be introduced in order to maintain dual attention.

T: Is this part of the memory? Or is he afraid of what is coming?

C: He is terrified; he wants to escape.

T: He is afraid of this memory… Does he realize that this is not happening now?

C: I don´t know…

T: Ask him to look around the room for a moment. Can he see where we are? You and him are here with me in the office… and his body is remembering how painful it was. He is remembering.

C: He is feeling bad.

T: I know it, of course, he is feeling bad. But can he see us? Can he see where we are?

It seems to be difficult for the client; she shakes her head.

T: Ask him to look through your eyes at where we are NOW. What does he see if he looks through your eyes?

C (looking around at different places in the room): We are here (covering her face with her hands).

T: What does this mean, for him to realize that all that pain he is remembering is just a memory?

C: He can´t understand it very well.

T: He has painful and frightening memories inside, right? (Client nods.) But at the same time he can be aware of being here… They are very vivid memories, but they are not happening now. Right now you are talking with me about this. The good thing is, it doesn´t matter how painful those memories are now, it´s possible to relieve all this pain in a near future.

Client nods.

T: I think that when he feels better inside, he will be much more secure than before. (The EP feels frustrated because he is feeling lack of control.) He will feel true strength. I understand that all these sensations are weird for him and for you. But working on it, we will achieve a better state than before.

Step 10: Stabilization

We should have enough time at the end of the session to stabilize the client. The TFS intervention should never be introduced in the last part of a session. Having time to stabilize the client is a relevant factor in deciding how much TFS we should apply.

In this case, fifteen more minutes were dedicated to psychoeducation, to explain the benefits of the intervention, and to think with the internal system what to do in the time in between sessions. The idea of "how the ANP and the EP can take care each other" was introduced.

The effect of this session was not immediate relief. In other cases, the effect is directly calming because the EP experiences a decrease in the disturbing sensation, or the client can understand more about her problem. Insights and an increase in empathy are frequent. Sometimes the effect is that the client can notice, maybe for the first time, the painful emotions contained in an emotional part. Even when disturbing for the ANP, it usually helps the adult self to realize what underlies the hostile attitude or the rejection from a dissociative part, previously judged as evil or negative.

But in the case that we are describing, we encounter the most difficult situation we can face with the TFS: The client and the EP contact with traumatic memories in the early phase of the therapy. They are not prepared to do it for now. We should be prepared to introduce reality orientation, psychoeducation, to explore how different parts in the internal system interpret this situation, and all the needed interventions to re-stabilize the client.

It is important, as in any EMDR session, to explain to the client that processing may continue after the session, and that she can experience tiredness, emotional changes, and even anxiety in the days after. Optional medications to control these symptoms can be prescribed, and tasks to calm down prepared. With the TFS, we explain to the clients that this intervention may have a "hangover effect" in the days or weeks after the session. We encourage the client to observe all the changes she notices without analyzing or judging them.

Step 11: Reevaluation

We could think that this intervention was unnecessarily overwhelming for the client. The previous session – negotiating with the system a no-harm contract - was better tolerated, and it would be preferable. But the most important issue is how the client felt after the session, and how much were the risk behaviors (self-harm) controlled.

> T: How did you feel after the last session?

> C: I felt very bad.

> T: Can you describe how you felt?

> C: I was crying very much… I hadn´t cried for such a long time. I had some anxiety crisis. It brought a lot of emotions. I usually repress them… I remembered past issues and cried… one day I had a nervous breakdown… I felt really bad.

At this point, we could think that the effect was negative, but we need to explore more. The client seems to be more relaxed and emotionally connected.

T: And after this?

C: This happened three times.

T: Just after the session?

C: Yes.

T: And the days after that?

C: Afterwards, we were very sensitive, I cried for everything (smiling). I used to be harsher.

T: And what does this mean to you? Do you consider it positive or negative?

C: My husband says it is good, he says I communicate better with him, and I think he is right.

T: Did you harm yourself in any way?

C: No.

T: And how is this other part? How did he feel this week?

C: He is reluctant, because he doesn't want to do things as he did before, but at the same time, he doesn't want to see me suffering. He wonders what would happen if I continue with this. He wanted to protect me and felt powerless looking at me. When I was anxious, he was not in control, I was.

T (reinforcing the EP's new role): When a person is feeling bad, doing something is not always the best, being present and giving support is often more important. He can do that.

C: Yes.

We can observe that the most concerning issue, the self-harming behavior and suicide attempts were absent after the session. Collaboration and empathy between parts substantially increased. The client was more emotionally connected, and her ability to communicate with others improved.

In the tip of the finger strategy, a crucial aspect is the negotiation with the dissociative part that will be the focus of the procedure. To adequately process the dysfunctional element inside the dissociative part, the EP should agree. Sometimes this can be quite easy, but it may need a hard negotiation process on other occasions. We have observed the following obstacles:

1. EP's fear to lose their power and strength if the dysfunctional emotion, frequently rage, decreases or disappears. Psychoeducational work explaining that true power, strength, and control do not need to be based on rage but on serene decision-making can be very useful.

2. The part may fear to lose his hierarchic position in the internal system. To explain the function they will have when the pain is over may help them overcome this situation.

3. The part may distrust the therapist. In this case, we can propose the part to test "a little dosage" of BLS on the dysfunctional emotion. We explain that EMDR does not affect functional elements, only when the emotion is dysfunctional it would be affected by BLS. Only after being sure that the effect of BLS is interesting for the part, he can decide to continue or not with the procedure.

4. The part may be convinced that the pain will never end. This is a trauma-based belief, after living a long-lasting situation with no solution throughout their childhood, and may be approached in the same way as in the previous paragraph.

5. The part may think that, if he focuses on the emotion, all the pain will "burst out" and he would not be able to contain it. Proposing to focus on the part of the emotion that he can safely relieve and reassuring the part that we will be checking that he does not feel overloaded can help with this situation. This procedure is in line with the slow leak technique (Kluft, 1990).

6. The part may think he does not deserve to be okay. A part containing traumatic memories may also contain the shame and guilt associated with it. To recognize the importance of the mission that this part has performed during this time, and that precisely because of this he deserves to experience the "good side of life" and relieve the pain, may be useful in this situation.

When the dissociative part agrees with the processing, we ask him to focus on the part of the emotion/sensation he wants to relieve and, from this single element, we start with a few BLS movements, as it was described in the previous example.

It is very important to be attentive to two main aspects:

1. Appearance of an overwhelming emotion in the ANP, the EP who is directly working, or any other part in the internal system.

2. The associative process and the appearance of traumatic memories, which the client is not prepared to deal with.

In many of the cases we have applied this procedure, the dysfunctional emotion decreased. Associations may come and tend to appear after the arousal decreased, and it seems to be partially dose-dependent, being more probable with longer sets of BLS. To use a very tentative and careful approach, step by step checking how each part in the system experienced the procedure, is crucial to prevent this possibility, as in the case we described before.

The most important aspect of this intervention, as any other using bilateral stimulation during the preparation phase, is not to be too ambitious. We must stop the intervention earlier rather than later, especially when we are performing the procedure for the first time. The effect may be evident or not during the session. But even when the effect is apparently calming, the after-session effect may be intense. It is important to wait for the next session (reevaluation) to evaluate the changes after the intervention and to titrate the next one.

Not all clients have the same effect with this or any other intervention. In some clients, internal dialogue by itself generates positive changes without the need for bilateral stimulation. Other times, self-care interventions are more appropriate, or focusing on internal conflicts, or parts´ phobic reactions to each other. Each client works differently. For example, with the client from the case example, the TFS was the most stabilizing intervention. However, when working with self-care patterns, which is a more emotionally regulatory intervention in many other cases, she experienced very disturbing and overwhelming emotions and became more depressed the week after the session. When, how, and how much of each intervention proposed in this book we can use in each case depends on the clinical judgment of the therapist and the collaborative decision-making with the client and the system of parts.

How to Process Trauma in Structural Dissociation

The fact that the standard protocol is not appropriate for many dissociative clients, especially in early stages of therapy, is widely accepted. Different modifications have been proposed for the standard protocol in these cases. We could summarize these modifications in four main sections: progression, directivity, fractionation, and synthesis.

1. A Gradual Approach

We propose a progressive approach that follows the beginning steps in a gradual way. First, we start by processing small, specific elements, such as obstacles for self-care, in increasing amounts, starting from the early phases of treatment. Next, if that goes well, the client can begin processing dysfunctional emotions, such as shame, obstacles to treatment (e.g., parts´ fears of vulnerability or feeling overwhelmed), dissociative phobias, and peripheral emotions using the tip of the finger strategy. As the client demonstrates the ability to process obstacles to treatment, we can begin to process traumatic issues triggered in current life or even in therapy. Over this time, the client will generally experience de-sensitization of trauma-related feelings and sensations, indicating that he is now ready to slowly process aspects of the core trauma. For the progressive approach to be successful, reinforcing of adaptive information, restoring self-care patterns, enhancing high order mental functions, working with the internal system of parts, and developing a good therapeutic relationships should be reinforced throughout the therapeutic process. But the important point is that we do not have to wait until all of this is achieved to begin to introduce processing selected elements, as previously described. This sequence is flexible and can be modified according to each client´s specific characteristics. As we have commented before, the classic all-or-nothing perspective is changed for a progressive approach.

A nice example of a progressive protocol is the CIPOS (Constant Installation of Present Orientation and Safety) method by Jim Knipe (2008). In this protocol, reality orientation (one foot in the present) is installed with BLS. Then, reality orientation and contact with traumatic experience (one foot in the past) are constantly linked in a progressive protocol that ends with the processing of the traumatic experience with BLS, maintaining the client in the present (dual attention). We believe that this progression can be extended to the entire therapeutic process, using the interventions that each specific client has tolerated best earlier, and later on, increasing the amount of different procedures that are more challenging.

2. Directivity

In a standard protocol, there is not much intervention needed from the therapist, if any at all. The Adaptive Information Processing Model (AIP) makes the associations come fluently. But, in severe dissociative disorders, fragmentation, complexity, and internal conflict are so high that the spontaneous procedure may lead to chaos rather than to an effective processing.

The individual is asked to be present in the here-and-now (ANP) while we are processing the there-and-then (EP). This facilitates maintaining dual attention during processing, and it is one of the active elements in EMDR therapy (Shapiro, 2001; Lee, Taylor, & Drummond, 2006). But, in the dissociative client, rather than to maintain duality, we need, as Twombly (2008) pointed out, to maintain "quadrality," having in mind, during the session, not only the client's past and present, but also the parts present in the session and the internal system. Twombly points out the need for the clinician to constantly conduct, structure, and direct the EMDR protocol.

Allowing a severely dissociated client to follow a spontaneous processing often implies to leave him at the mercy of the same chaos at which he is usually functioning. This processing may consist of switches from one mental state to another, according to the presenting emotion or the element that the person must face. This situation reproduces exactly how the dissociative individual faces both internal and external events, by alternating among different dissociative parts of the personality. When stress or emotional arousal increase, the individual switches into a different compartment or part of the personality. But then, if processing continues and arousal increases, another switch will be needed, and another, and another. Though we may think we are processing trauma, in fact, we may be stirring up or triggering the same defensive responses that accompanied the trauma, which are now protecting the client from EMDR or any other trauma work he is not ready for.

For this reason, taking as a reference the usual channel of processing in a non-dissociative client will not be effective. We must have ways to structure, contain, and direct the protocol to help the client effectively process the elements we are working on.

3. Fractionation

The amount of traumatic material is so huge that we must divide the work into fractions in order to make it possible for the client to assimilate it without exposing him to retraumatization. This is one of the factors that make these cases more difficult to manage. In working with dissociative disorders, it is advisable to divide the therapeutic work in order to process manageable pieces of this material.

It might not seem to make sense that in a disorder determined by fragmentation, we choose to fractionate the work. It might even sound equivalent to worsening the problem. However, to divide interventions has long been recognized as a basic way to work with these dissociative disorder cases (Fine, 1993). Fractionation ensures that the amount and intensity of the stimuli offered to the client will not overwhelm his resources for staying present, maintaining dual awareness, and tolerating affect. As we have pointed out before, attention to these priorities allows us to avoid retraumatization, to maintain abreactions in a therapeutic window of tolerance (Siegel, 1999; Ogden, Minton, & Pain, 2006), to give a sense of control and mastery both to client and therapist, and to work with safety and stabilization during the different phases of the therapy.

This fractionation can be applicable to different elements: abreactions, phase 3 of the EMDR protocol (e.g., the choice of target), and the internal system of dissociative parts and associative chains.

3.1. Fractionating Abreactions.

For over twenty years, Kluft (1990) and Fine (1993) have emphasized the need to fractionate abreactions in order to avoid retraumatization. This implies breaking down the progressive elaboration of a traumatic situation into small pieces. Rather than pursuing a complete abreaction in a single session, since that might exacerbate the symptoms rather than de-sensitize, the targets chosen are concrete aspects of the traumatic memory that initially increase arousal but allow safe, gradual reconnection with feelings. Each partial abreaction is preceded and followed by a cognitive restructuration, in which other emotions and cognitions are being re-linked. Lazrove and Fine (1996) adapt this concept for EMDR therapy.

The concept of abreaction is not completely equivalent in EMDR to that of other approaches. The term abreaction is used differently by some experts to mean a flashback or re-living experience. In EMDR, the term abreaction is used to mean high emotional activation without loss of time or reality orientation. Anyway, the same structure proposed by Kluft and Fine can be used to guide the EMDR treatment. We could choose to select a limited element to be processed, desensitizing progressively, and helping the client to cognitively elaborate and assimilate the changes in his subjective experience, as it was described in the previous example of the tip of the finger strategy. Paulsen (2008) outlines the importance of using tools that allow us to maintain abreactions limited to one single aspect. An example could be the slow leak technique by Kluft (1988) that suggest that traumata or painful affects come into awareness at a pace that the client can tolerate, or the application of hypnotic techniques as containment strategies for EMDR processing (Paulsen 2008), in order to maintain the emotional intensity in the therapeutic window (Odgen & Minton, 2000; Ogden, Minton, & Pain, 2006).

As we have been suggesting, in the first stages of the therapy, very short sets of BLS can be used to process a peripheral traumatic element, such as shaking or a disturbing emotion. It could be only 6 sets of BLS on an undefined disturbing emotion in an EP.

For example, a teenage boy EP was having constant overwhelming flashbacks leading to cutting, which then caused chaos in the system. The therapist asked him to notice the flashes without "going there" and then turned on the light bar, asking him to imagine that the lights were taking the memories away back to the past. As they came up, the therapist would ask him to focus on the lights and let the lights "take away" the memory "back to where it belonged." He practiced this over and over again in the therapy session, until the flashbacks lessened and finally stopped. In this type of treatment, we first processed the overwhelming emotions but did not address the content of the flashback or the EP stimulating it. Longer associative chains and higher amounts of BLS may be further applied over more specific targets, using a progression from the best tolerated to the core traumatic, and highly disturbing, memories.

3.2. Fractionating Phase 3 Elements of the EMDR Protocol.

In the prior paragraphs, we described how to fractionate abreactions, but we can also fractionate Phase 3 components and process separate elements like an intrusive flashback, an isolated emotion, or a sensation. For clients with a low attention capacity, who tend to disconnect from distressing emotions, to remain in contact with the target for a long time, searching for an image, a sensation, and an emotion with its SUDs level, can be difficult or impossible. A detailed definition of negative and positive cognition can be experienced as an impossible challenge and might make the client feel insecure. The experience of relief and control during the first experiences with EMDR processing is more important than to complete all the habitual steps of the standard protocol. Perhaps the best way to think of this approach is that we introduce individual elements of the EMDR protocol one or two at a time, based on the client´s window of tolerance for both concentrated attention and affect tolerate. This progressive approach is the best way to do a complete and well structured processing of core traumatic memories in further stages of the therapy.

After processing these initial elements, we can try to link image, beliefs, emotions, and somatic sensations, which increases the integrative effect of EMDR. However, with some dissociative clients, we might begin by linking two of these together. The standard protocol is intended to promote synthesis and integration of past and present, emotions and cognitions, body sensations and perceptual awareness. In phase 3 of the protocol, we help the client identify different levels of one disturbing experience: perceptual elements (image), self-beliefs, emotions, and sensations. After breaking the memory down into its component parts, "building these blocks," allows synthesizing all of the memory´s elements.

To achieve the integration level in people with structural dissociation, we should decrease the amount of total disturbance. In severe traumatization, the SUD level can be experienced as much more than 10, because the maximum is more than anybody can ever imagine and much more than what they feel they can tolerate. Many dissociative disorder clients have such a severe phobia of emotion and sensation that a SUD of 3-4 may be experienced as if it were a 10+. In some cases, these clients have a very low SUD, indicating contained or dissociated emotions or chronic shutdown and numbing. A chronically low SUD can be a risk factor in dissociative clients. Processing can turn very quickly into very strong emotional activation, flashbacks, dissociation, or disconnection.

3.3. Fractionating the Internal System of Dissociative Parts.

One of our final goals with dissociative clients is the synthesis of different elements contained in different parts. But, sometimes, it is initially useful to work with each part separately, in order to decrease the traumatic burden contained in different parts. If the client has the ability to ensure that the internal system participates in the work, while the parts that are not processing remain apart and not activated, we can use EMDR processing directly. If this is not the case, we can keep the parts that were previously not involved in present work in their safe places and behind soundproof walls.

Case example: "Team work"

Reflections after a "no harm" agreement, after 2 aggressive EPs agreed to stop hurting the ANP, and the ANP agreed to not self medicate to "shut the voices":

> Client: I don´t know if…. after our last session I was thinking of what we talked about and it seems as if the "little dwarf" (EP), the colleague (EP), and myself (ANP) got to an agreement where I can live in peace.

> Therapist: Aha

> C: So I´m happy, I feel happy because even though I still have the voices in my head, they don´t attack me anymore, they are there reminding me that they are part of me, that I have to live with them but they don´t wish to destroy me anymore.

> T: This is great, they are keeping their part of the agreement, are you keeping yours?

> C: Yes, I am not hurting them either. But the big empty balloon is still there (an EP not yet identified, the one that keeps all the secrets).

> At this point we decide to install this "union" and ask the client to focus on a pleasant sensation that the 3 parts share. They pick "caring for the kittens."

> After BLS.

> C: They want the kittens to stay home.

> T: How was it for you to experience this sensation at the same time?

C: Weird, because usually one part felt disdain toward the others, or two parts towards one, or the 3 of them toward myself at the same time. So, to realize that there is something that unifies us gives them strength.

T: Okay, can you focus on this union and strength, all of you?

Client nods.

T: What do you notice?

C: I feel the union of the 3 parts, except for the balloon… the "little dwarf," the "colleague," and me feel united.

T: Stay with that for a little bit.

BLS.

T: Now ask each one of them how they felt doing this.

C: Okay… strength… wanting to fight (for getting better).

T: Could you tell them that this is what you can all feel in many more aspects and moments if you work as a team…

C: Okay.

T: Ask the "little dwarf" what he thinks about this (this EP usually felt left out so we made an agreement that we would also check for his sensations).

C: The "little dwarf," the colleague, and me are in agreement. The "little dwarf" is afraid of being left out.

T: Can you ask the little dwarf to focus on this sensation he is feeling now? If he agrees…

C: Okay.

T: Where does the little dwarf feel this sensation in his body?

C: Here (pointing to his stomach).

T: Okay, ask him to focus on that sensation and ask him if he wants you and/or the colleague to be with him or if he prefers to do it by himself.

C: He wants to do it alone, he thinks if he does this with somebody else he may be ruled out.

T: Okay, so he can focus on that.

BLS.

T: What does he notice?

C: Terror.

T: Ask him if he would like to work with this terror, to see if he can feel better.

C: Okay… He says he is afraid of disappearing.

T: Tell him he is not going to disappear.

C: Okay.

T: He is part of you; an important part, he is not going to disappear. Ask him if he wants to work a little more.

C: He says it´s enough for now.

T: Ok, tell him we will pay attention to him and that it´s okay for him to say no, this is good. He has been respecting the agreement and we will also respect what we had promised (to work step by step, at a pace they could all handle).

C: He says "okay" and he says that next time he will try to do a little more.

T: Okay, great, next time we will check again if it´s a good time.

C: Okay.

T: I think the 3 of you are doing very good, we have to be aware of this balloon and give him time, see what his needs are...

C: I am afraid this balloon will explode... I´m afraid this could make me do one of my "things" (suicide attempt, severe injuries...).

T: Okay, let´s do something about this... are you seeing the balloon now?

C: Yes.

T: What do you see?

C: I see the balloon with a brown frame all around.

T: Ok, could you place a protective coat around it?

C: Yes.

T: How would this protection be?

C: Like very light cement, this white cement, do you know what I´m talking about? It´s like clay, so it´s soft and we can take it out when it´s needed without breaking the content.

T: Okay, close your eyes and imagine how to place this protective coat around it, so in case it explodes, it has a container.

C: Okay.

T: Do it with lots of care... remember you want to protect this balloon, it´s not a restraint.

BLS.

T: What do you get?

C: He is placing small amounts of this clay and making it all even, he is being very careful but it´s still wet for now, it has to dry.

T: Who is doing this?

C: The colleague.

T: Okay, observe how he does this, and do whatever you need to do to finish this process… if you need to use a fan so it can dry sooner it´s okay.

BLS.

C: It doesn´t need a fan, it´s safer if it dries naturally…. now I see a white sphere that is over the balloon.

T: Ok, close your eyes…. Ask this part if it would be ok to add a window to this sphere, so the balloon doesn´t feel so restrained… so it can look outside.

C: Okay.

BLS.

C: If the window is small he agrees.

T: Ok, so let´s place that small window.

T: How is your inside now?

C: Much more relaxed, like he did something important and it seems he wants to keep working with me… the little dwarf is still a little nervous, he is observing and he is still afraid… waiting to have another moment for him and then it´s me, that I feel relaxed, I feel well.

T: Okay, the colleague did a great job, can you thank him?

C: Yes.

T: You also participated in this.

C: Yes.

T: So it would be important that the little dwarf participates too…. Could you ask him if he could do something? Maybe paint this cement… ask him if there is something he can do to feel part of this.

C: Paint it red (happy).

T: Okay, so let him do that… observe how he does that.

C: Okay, that is my favorite color!

Client takes time to do this.

T: How is he now?

C: Still afraid but more relaxed… because he has seen that he is allowed to participate and reach more things… He feels he did something... He says, "I don´t feel so useless or so fearful."

T: You are doing great team work... remember that if the balloon explodes, the content has a container to keep it safe...

Client nods (relaxed).

We need to know the internal system, but it is important to keep in mind that some parts, frequently the more dysfunctional and difficult to manage, can appear later in therapy. We may know many aspects that the client has told us, but untold issues frequently give us more relevant information later, as we have discussed in chapter 4 on dissociative language. To work with this system, we need a map, including hypotheses about untold aspects. However, this does not mean that we have to wait until the map is completed to proceed with processing. Although we know there is incomplete knowledge about the client, we also know that it will be developed during the therapeutic process, but we must remember to use a very tentative and progressive approach.

3.4. Fractionating Associative Chains.

When we begin to process dysfunctional elements, our goal is not to achieve a SUD = 0. A decreasing on the initial SUD, any significant association or realization, or even a change of subject can be a good result, and a general rule with structural dissociation is not to be too ambitious. If we do that and want to go beyond, sometimes we get into complicated issues, and the session cannot end with a good level of self-regulation and safety. As a general rule, "slower is faster" (Fisher, 2000).

We can take advantage of the effects of BLS to provoke specific effects. One example: The use of BLS produces, in some situations, an effect that can be called "sliding." The mental contents shift from one element to another, so we can work more easily on them.

Let´s see an example: We are negotiating a therapeutic contract with a hostile dissociative part. After some time communicating with this part, the client experiences an intense headache that does not go away. We propose to the client doing a brief attempt to see if the headache could get better. Using BLS with the headache as a target, the client begins to speak about a family problem. After two sets of BLS, we interrupt the processing, and we comment on the new situation with the client. The headache does not come back again. In this example, we have not used the full standard protocol, only the somatic sensation as the target. However, the BLS has led to processing of the underlying stressor activating distressing emotions among the EPs leading to the headache.

In summary, less is better. When clients have experienced that processing can decrease a disturbing emotion, help them to resolve a difficult issue, increase their perspective, awareness, or understanding of their situations, it will be easier to progressively introduce larger amounts of processing, until we can assemble a complete EMDR protocol on a traumatic memory. In essence, their experience of EMDR will be a positive one, motivating all parts to participate in processing increasingly challenging and painful memories.

4. Synthesis

In the preceding paragraphs, we remarked the importance of fractionating the processing to work on issues in ways that might be manageable for the client, in order to administer the therapy with safety, containment, and within the tolerance window. Now we shall remark the importance of the opposite process: synthesis. Dissociation is in essence fragmentation. Emotions, body sensations, cognitions, and behaviors (BASK model, Braun, 1988a,b) are disconnected, and reconnection is not an automatic process. We need to help the client synthesize the previously dissociated elements.

The theory of structural dissociation (Van der Hart, Steele, & Nijenhuis, 2006) remarks the importance of synthesis as one of the main elements of trauma therapy. They use the term "guided synthesis" to describe a highly structured method designed to re-link the traumatic elements stored in different dissociated parts, all related to the same traumatic scene, reconstructing that event with the collaboration of the different parts. This technique allows a true elaboration of the traumatic elements, often very fragmented and disconnected.

In a wide sense, we may also say that the main dimension of the work with a dissociative client is "to re-link those parts that have been split off." We may elaborate a lot of different interventions or protocol modifications according to the client's resources, the therapist's training and orientation, and the therapy moment. But synthesis will be one of the basic goals in working with this therapeutic group.

The basic protocol itself may be understood as a synthesis protocol. From the host or the apparently normal part of the personality (ANP), we are processing the emotional part of the personality (EP) or, in other words, the disturbing elements of the traumatic memory. This is the basis of dual attention (Shapiro, 2001). In Phase 3, we differentiate between different elements of the traumatic memory (perceptions, self-beliefs, emotions, and sensations) in order to achieve synthesis (the integrative phrase and other interventions).

But, in complex trauma or severe dissociative disorders, spontaneous association with positive memories, resources, or adaptive cognitions rarely occurs. This is due to fragmentation, even when such elements are present, for example, when the client has some positive memories, a safe environment, resources, and more adaptive self-beliefs. That is why the therapist must help the dissociative disorder client to introduce these positive aspects, resources, adaptive cognitions, and presence in the here-and-now.

Different authors have elaborated interesting protocols in this direction (Fine & Berkowitz, 2001). As Suokas-Cunliffe, Mattheβ, & Van der Hart (2008) point out, "it is important to inter-connect the traumatic states with internal resources, both at somatic and other levels." Quoting Peter Levine, they begin by saying, "The pendulum-like motion between resources (positive) and trauma (negative) dissolves dissociation directly and actively, and supports the patient's strength."

Synthesis may be more or less extensive. We can connect the ANP's resources to vulnerable or dysfunctional parts by stimulating the resource with BLS and asking EPs to experiment with seeing how it feels. Different EPs can collaborate with the ANP and process a shared memory. When the therapy is advancing, the tendency will be to increasingly introduce more synthesis until all the elements of the traumatic events can be joined and processed in conjunction. In a progressive approach, the sense of mastery and collaboration, even in the use of EMDR with the client, is an indirect form of reprocessing. Rather than being asked to experience overwhelming and frightening emotions without choice, the client collaborates in a gradual reconnection with dissociated parts and feelings that may be challenging but never overwhelming and never without a sense of choice.

Summary

Fig. 2: Onion layers

The processing of traumatic experiences is not just a protocol, is a main goal of EMDR treatment in structural dissociation. It covers the entire therapeutic process and not only the work on traumatic events. Using the metaphor of onion layers, we will start with the most peripheral elements, in order to progressively approach core trauma.

Chapter 13
The Meeting Place Procedure for EMDR Therapy

Anabel Gonzalez, Dolores Mosquera, & Roger Solomon

The Dissociative Table

The *dissociative table* is a useful procedure for working with dissociative parts, especially in the preparation phase of EMDR. These parts can also be referred to as *self states* or *ego states*. In the original articles describing the *dissociative table* (Fraser, 1991, 2003), the client imagines sitting at an oval table and inviting ego states to sit in the empty chairs around it. Different variations of this imaginary space have been proposed, like a conference room in a home (Forgash, 2009), a special room in the client´s home, the therapist´s office, or any other familiar place. Some authors propose adding elements like microphones, speakers, a TV or movie screen, etc. to facilitate communication (Forgash, 2008, pp. 42).

Different names have been used to describe the same concept. Caul (1984) uses the term "internal group therapy," and Watkins (1993) calls it the "hallucinated room." However, since some people do not like to meet around a table or a in a closed space and prefer instead to have a meeting place outside, in a meadow, or by the beach, we prefer to call it the "meeting place."

Several authors have written about how the dissociative table technique can be used in the preparation phase of EMDR, when treating complex trauma. Paulsen (2007, 2009) proposes the dissociative table as a good way to gain access to multiple aspects of self. She views the dissociative table as an intervention for the containment and stabilization phase, in her ACT-AS-IF model, and she uses it in the same way as in *ego state therapy* (Watkins & Watkins, 1997), without introducing bilateral stimulation. This is, as a phase 2 intervention, before phases 3-7 in the standard EMDR protocol. She also describes how the dissociative table can be used as an intervention to overcome blockages or looping during the desensitization phase. The client is asked to imagine a conference room where the ego states can gather. Any resistance or dynamic blocking the EMDR processing often becomes visible in some way in the internal conference room, as a part of the self that is not engaged in the process (Paulsen, 2009).

Forgash (2008) also utilizes the dissociative table technique for stabilization. She points out that this technique is not always effective with extremely dissociative clients whose amnesic barriers and self-structure may not permit visual accessing, especially early in treatment, or with a rare few who cannot visualize a conference room or meeting place. However, for many people, it enables rapid access to disowned aspects of the self without formal trance induction. Bergmann (2008) also proposes this technique to enhance internal communication and collaboration in Phase 2 (safety and preparation) of the EMDR protocol. Neither Forgash nor Bergman introduce BLS in the procedure.

Many interventions for working with dissociative parts have been developed by other approaches, such as ego states therapy (Watkins & Watkins, 1997; Forgash & Copeley, 2008; Paulsen, 2008, 2009), internal family systems therapy (Schwartz, 1995; Schwartz & Goulding, 2002), or the theory of structural dissociation of the personality (Van der Hart et al., 2006). In this chapter, we will describe different adaptations that can be introduced when using the meeting place procedure so it can be used safely throughout the therapeutic process.

The Meeting Place Procedure: A Modified Dissociative Table Technique for Working with EMDR in Structural Dissociation

What different meeting place procedures have in common is the establishment of an imaginary place to enhance communication with the internal system; a place where even the more disowned, rejected, or feared parts are invited to participate. This way, the client may start developing an integrative perspective of himself.

We will introduce several modifications to Fraser´s original design. Our main proposals are the work through the *adult self* and the use of BLS at different times. Different interventions presented in previous chapters of this book, such as the work on self-care patterns, the co-consciousness exercises, the processing of dissociative phobias, and the tip of the finger strategy, can be performed in the meeting place. Processing of dysfunctional elements is introduced from the early phases of therapy, preparing the structure for a safe and integrative way of working on specific traumatic memories.

The meeting place imagery offers interesting possibilities to promote a) *differentiation* between self and others, b) *personification* (recognizing all the different dissociative parts as parts of the self, and the memories as parts of the history) and c) *presentification* (learning to be in the here-and-now, keeping past and present in mind).

Bilateral Stimulation in the Meeting Place

In the progressive approach, bilateral stimulation is introduced to process dysfunctional elements from the very early phases of the therapeutic work. In the meeting place procedure, where a dynamic process of promoting empathy and communication among parts takes place, short sets of bilateral stimulation may be useful in:

1. Decreasing the intensity of a disturbing emotion or sensation in a dissociative part, which does not allow this part to make changes

2. Decreasing phobias among different parts

3. Facilitating the linking in of adaptive information and the assimilation of psychoeducational interventions

4. Promoting co-consciousness

5. Increasing realization and meaning

Setting Up the Meeting Place

We begin by using the term meeting place, giving clients the chance to choose the best way for them to imagine this space. Some people prefer a room or a closed area. Others need an open space, because they feel confined in closed ones, or they evoke traumatic associations.

We ask the client to imagine an internal meeting room or place where the *adult self* invites "different aspects" of himself in order to facilitate or initiate communication. Some clients have different parts and identify them clearly; others have difficulty explaining their inner world and recognizing their sensations, so they will need guidance. We can talk about "different aspects of the self," "different aspects," or "different parts," depending on the client's ability to identify and recognize the existence of different parts or self-states and the level of first-person perspective that they have. Instructions regarding meeting place characteristics and communication rules are given to the patient: "Imagine you are in a meeting place, this can look however you like. It has to be nice and pleasant in order to invite communication. Different aspects or parts of yourself may come into this place. You don't have to do anything else. Just imagine this and tell me what happens..." It may be important to add: "No part of you is forced to be there. This should be voluntary, not forced. We just want to invite everyone, everything, or each and every aspect; we want them to understand how important they are for you." This last comment is very important because many traumatized clients have been forced to do things they did not want to do. We want to convey a message of deep respect for the client and the entire system.

Parts who spontaneously present themselves in the meeting place at the beginning do not necessarily represent the entire system. At first, only those parts more acceptable to the ANP may be present, as we commented in prior chapters, but other rejected parts can show up along different phases of treatment. Perpetrator-imitator parts, those aspects that resemble the abuser's features, may be the last ones to show up because they represent aspects that are very difficult for the client to accept. It is sometimes useful to ask clients to imagine how many places or seats would be needed. Empty spaces tell us about the most rejected, feared, or disowned parts of the self.

It is important to adapt to the client's particular characteristics, but at the same time the therapist needs to be directive. The internal dissociative system is defined by chaos, fight for control, and constant conflict. Therefore, the therapist should provide clear rules from the beginning, as Fraser explains in his original article (1991): "I want to emphasize that is a safe room (place). In here, no one gets hurt. I don't hurt you and you don't hurt me. Those around the table don't hurt each other. This is a place to get to know each other better. We can talk, but we don't act out. The intent here - explains the author – is to set up a negotiation room and to indicate that this is not just another setting in which to carry on the chaotic relationships with preceded therapy." The therapist must carefully conduct any hostile or controlling interaction, especially in the early phases of therapy, when the new way of relating to each other is still not well established.

Working From the *Adult Self*

Some approaches, such as Fraser's, include the apparently normal part of the personality (ANP) in the meeting room, along with the other parts. One moderator is chosen by the "internal system" to modulate inner communication.

We propose something different, which is to intervene through the *adult self* (see chapter 4 about high order mental functions. By working in this way, we help the clients to look at the system of dissociative parts with an adult perspective, which becomes the seed for the future integrated self. We offer them a leading role in their recovery, giving them back the power others have taken from them and reinforcing their autonomy.

An important difference with other approaches is that we do not talk directly to the parts. Instead, we show the *adult self* how to talk to them, understand what they need, how they feel, and how to take care of them. In this way, clients are building their capacity for self-soothing and self-care and become more capable of functioning outside of the therapy session. These types of interventions decrease the risk of dependency from the client.

In secondary structural dissociation, the ANP will be the one who carries out the process, developing the ability to communicate with other parts, proposing interventions and changes, and adopting a reflective, integrative role with the therapist's guidance.

When a client has tertiary structural dissociation (DID), ANPs and EPs will be represented in the meeting room. We will work through the ANP that is present in the session, the one that is participating in therapy, without establishing an intense negotiation regarding which part will lead the processing, although this may be necessary in some cases. When a different ANP appears in the session, the work is developed with this part, but always considering the ANP as a variant of the *adult self*, containing different adult resources and capacities. The activation of emotional parts and the switching between parts are actively prevented.

It does not matter if different ANPs perform this leading role at different times or in different sessions, or if the ANP is not confident about his capacity to guide the process or take care of others. We are always seeing the capable adult within the client and his resources. Some parts, or the entire system, may feel insecure about the possibilities of change, and, as we stated before, the phobia of change is a common dissociative phobia. But we, as therapists, must be confident about the client's possibilities.

The more fragmented clients may be very chaotic, and they may spontaneously shift when they try to visualize the meeting room. These are clients with a low meta-consciousness level and a low capacity for being present and connected, while different parts are interacting in imagery. With this kind of clients, it is particularly interesting to "concretize" the meeting between parts using intermediary objects like puppets, figurines, drawings, etc. This representation of the internal system helps us to have a more direct idea of what is happening inside, and it helps the client to remain focused and be able to "think about his inner mental process" (meta-consciousness).

Promoting Healthy Self-Care Patterns

Another relevant point in our approach, present in each intervention as well as in the meeting place, is the promotion of healthy self-care patterns. After some parts come into the meeting place, we ask the *adult self* to look at each one of them and feel what they may need. The adult part is urged to look at the internal system in a different way than usual: without judgment. Quite often, the client expresses fear, rejection, or different negative emotions toward some parts, which are examples of the phobia of dissociative parts of the personality that can be processed (see chapter 8).

The *adult self* will function as a good enough caregiver, who with modeling and guidance from the therapist, helps repair attachment disruptions. When the *adult self* looks at an emotional child part, we ask the adult part to feel what this part needs and how to satisfy that need.

The therapist can explain and model how an adult can adequately care for parts, particularly younger parts. Psychoeducation is often needed, and it can be interweaved with other procedures, promoting the assimilation of healthy information by every part of the system. For example, the therapist may comment that having needs and trying to meet them is normal and good, or that a child taking care of an adult is a reversal of natural care-taking roles. Communication between the therapist and the *adult self* takes the form of a conversation between adults about how to deal with little children, like a first-time mother learning from a supportive and more experienced one. This style of conversation sends an indirect message, "You and me are at the same level, I am only more experienced in this topic. You are in charge of yourself and I am here supporting you."

We can see these aspects in the following example:

Therapist: What do you think that part needs?

Client: I don´t know, I can´t figure out what she needs. She looks like she doesn´t need anything.

T: Well... You know that some children that are experiencing difficulties need to appear strong.

C: But she was really strong.

T: Yes she was, she was very brave dealing with such difficult issues, your brother´s aggressive behaviors, your mother´s illness... But it had to be terrible that nobody could notice how she felt and what she needed. Your mother was very ill and she couldn´t do it, and this is very hard for a little girl.

C: I don´t know.

T: I am sure you can see it, you are an adult now. And you can figure out how a child of that age could feel in such a situation ... How old does she look?

C (showing understanding): She is very little.

T: Aha, and what can you see in her eyes?

C: She refuses to look at me.

T: However, you can understand many things from her attitude... when you see a child now, you can realize if the child is angry or sad, it doesn´t matter if she doesn´t look at you.

C: I think she is ashamed, she seems to feel guilty.

T: You are really perceptive... But we adults know that a little girl cannot take on the responsibility, don´t we?

C: But a girl can do bad things.

T: Really? Do you think that a child that is so little can do bad things? Do you know any child of this age?

C: Yes, my niece.

T: And if your niece does something wrong, do you think it´s her responsibility or is it the responsibility of the adults who should be taking care of her?

C: No, absolutely, the adults are the ones who are responsible for her.

T: And rules are the same for everybody, right?

C (doubting): It´s difficult for me to look at this little girl inside me the same way I look at my niece.

T: I know, it´s difficult, but it´s fair to do so. All children should have the same rights, what do you think?

C: Maybe.

T: So, we can try to do an exercise… We are working on a crucial issue. This little child inside you has the right to be attended to, to be important for somebody. And you have a good capacity to realize all these aspects in your niece and in other children. We can try to link both things. Do you agree with this?

C: I can try.

T: So, close your eyes and look at your niece in the eyes, and notice what is in her mind… (the therapist gives her time) what do you feel towards her?

C: I love her very much.

T: Okay, now look at that inner child with the same eyes.

C (experiencing sadness and compassion): She suffered a lot.

T: Okay, notice how you can understand how she felt….

Short set of BLS.

C: Now she is looking into my eyes.

T: And now you can realize what she needs, is this right?

C: She needs to be loved.

T: Now that you realize this, what would you tell her?

C: That she is important, that I´m here for her.

T: And can you let her know this?

C: Yes, I can.

T: Okay, so let her know and notice what happens (client smiles).

BLS.

T: How does she look?

C: She knows she is not alone anymore.

T: And how do you feel?

C: Really good.

The same process can be done with other parts in the same session or in future sessions. It is important that all parts know they will be acknowledged and looked after when we do not have enough time in one session to work with the entire system. Note that, in this example, short sets of BLS were applied to enhance compassion, empathy, and understanding between ANP and EP.

Modeling healthy self-care patterns is not a specific stage in the meeting place procedure, but a style of intervention. Each time the adult part interacts with a dissociative part in the meeting place, we can ask the *adult self* to "look at the part and notice what she needs and how to take care of her." We teach the *adult self* to recognize different needs in different parts, to care for them, and to help them take care of one another, establishing a respectful relationship with each and every one of them. Through the therapist´s modeling, the role of the *adult self* in leading the process is enhanced, which facilitates the internalization of healthy self-care patterns, returns the power to the client, and increases autonomy. These types of interventions also reduce the possible risks of the client´s dependency towards the therapist or therapy.

Time Orientation (Presentification): "The Danger of Childhood is Over"

EPs live in "trauma time" and, by definition, are not time-oriented. In order to promote co-consciousness, cooperation, and stabilization it is helpful to install present time orientation with each part of the system (Twombly, 2000). We do this by helping the part realize the "danger" of childhood is over and not happening right now, and by teaching the client a number of grounding techniques that allow him to know he is living in the present. Some of these grounding methods or orientation exercises can be moving around, looking at the size of "your adult hand," noticing that he lives in a different place now than in childhood, etc. The client, when oriented to the present, can focus on body sensations, and once the present orientation is acknowledged, we enhance it with short sets of BLS. Then, the therapist can ask the EP if it can understand that what happened in childhood is not happening in the present. When an EP has some realization of this, short sets of BLS can enhance awareness. Total realization may not come until further traumatic memory work is done.

 If there is still danger in the present, like when the abusive parent is still alive, the part, through the adult, can be asked, "Are there more choices regarding how to respond now that you are an adult than when you were a child?," or "How dangerous is X (the parent or abuser) now that you have grown up?" When a part realizes he is living in the present and, therefore, that the danger is over, short sets of BLS can be utilized to enhance this realization. Time orientation may need to be done with the parts many times during treatment and can be part of different interventions. For example, when thinking of a present stressful situation, we can ask a part to feel "what part of the distressful emotion actually is related to the present situation, and what part of this emotion comes from the past."

Focusing the work in the meeting place around the *adult self* helps the client to pay attention on the here-and-now. Continuing to introduce time orientation, reminding the client that he is an adult, that the danger is over and not happening anymore, and reinforcing a present time orientation, helps establish reality orientation. Once reality orientation has been established, we can progressively approach the work with traumatic material, maintaining the necessary dual attention (Shapiro, 2001).

The Screen Strategy

The screen strategy was proposed in Fraser´s original article (1991, 2003) as a way for ego states to share bits and pieces of their experience with others before any attempt of fusion. This strategy is also included in the standard EMDR protocol (Shapiro, 1995) as a way to gain some distance from the traumatic material. When there is structural dissociation, the screen strategy needs to be utilized because the capacity to take perspective is underdeveloped.

The ability to look at the traumatic image and describe a negative belief, emotion, and somatic sensation implies that clients are able to distinguish the event from themselves. In structural dissociation, each part may have different beliefs, emotions, and sensations, and the ANP can have difficulties getting in touch with different aspects held by different parts, or taking an overall, objective perspective of these reactions.

For example, it can be difficult to differentiate the person who was hurting them from an internal dissociative part(s) that imitates the abuser. In standard EMDR protocol, we typically work with past, present, and future. However, all these aspects are mixed up and frequently confused in severely traumatized clients. The past is present, and things happening here and now are experienced as reenactments of past events. The future is felt as foreshortened, and clients imagine that their futures will contain the same unbearable situations that were part of their traumatic past. Some parts are not time-oriented. In order to work on past/present/future, the client needs to learn to differentiate these concepts.

For this reason, it is useful to prepare the client to recognize these aspects, prior to working on traumatic memories with the standard protocol. The screen strategy is a useful tool to develop differentiation, synthesis, personification, presentification and time orientation, and promoting the integrative process. The meeting place can help to differentiate self from others, present from past, and to recognize as "me" previously disowned parts of the self.

Description of the Screen Strategy

The client can imagine a screen in the meeting place. The screen can be used to place images of the external world, other people, or past or future situations. Each element that is not part of the self in the here-and-now may be placed on the screen. Whenever any element from the outside world comes into the meeting place, we propose that the client places it on the screen and asks all parts to realize that this is not part of the person in the here-and-now.

At the beginning, we explain to the client that the meeting place is a specific place to meet with different aspects of the self. In spite of this, people who grew up in traumatic environments, including those with attachment disruptions, tend to confuse the inner and the outer worlds in different ways, as it was previously described .

They may include imaginary safe or idealized figures or people from their present or past life, like a parent, a partner, etc. in the meeting place. Sometimes, those figures are not parts of the personality that are reproducing the attachment figure, and this differentiation may not be easy for the client. It is important to explain that although the identified person may be very relevant in their life, this meeting place is entirely private, it is for parts of oneself, and no one from the outside should be included. For example, some clients may place their abusive partner in the meeting place. Whenever this happens, we ask the *adult self* to place the partner on the screen, help other parts to realize he is outside, and understand the different reactions that different parts may experience. Some parts may feel strongly attached to the partner, and others may feel a lot of rage against him for being abusive and disrespectful.

Some authors include safe attachment figures in the meeting place. We prefer not to do so, since we believe it is important to enhance the differentiation of the self. Even though safe attachment figures are extremely important for healthy development, we understand differentiation as a very basic element needed for the development of an integrated self.

Some dissociative clients are extremely dependent on the environment being able to meet their needs. They need too much external attention and care, and they are not confident about their internal resources. Or on the other hand, they remain isolated with the conviction of being unable to manage even minimal stressors. When this happens, we can ask the client to place problematic external situations on the screen. Then we can help the *adult self* to realize which parts have become activated by the situation, which resources are present or needed in each part, even when the part cannot be aware of them, and what adaptive function can each one perform. Dissociative parts are encouraged to propose a plan for solving the situation and different options are discussed among the internal system from a reflective perspective. Any adaptive and collaborative solutions can be enhanced with BLS.

For example, a client is dealing with current problems with her husband, and from the meeting place, she can identify different dissociative parts that seem to be activated. A part who loves the partner, and can understand what is good for the client in this relationship, may collaborate with another part, fixated on a fight action system, who is triggered when the partner uses a loud voice, even if it is not emotionally abusive. This brings up a memory of maltreatment from her abusive father in childhood, contained in a vulnerable, childlike part. A "maternal" part can take care of this little child and maintain her far from the present situation. A part fixated on attachment can be the part that connects with other people, and notices what is good in relationships; and a part fixated on defense-fight can identify when others are being inadequate or damaging. The first one can help the second one to verbalize things in a constructive way. The second one protects the system from retraumatization by standing up for herself. From a "team" perspective they can tell the partner, "It´s very distressing for me when you speak so loud, please lower your tone of voice… You know, my father was angry all the time, so I am very sensitive to loud voices."

Whenever there are dissociative parts imitating or reproducing abusive figures, we should introduce psychoeducation about how these parts resemble people from early traumatic scenery. For example, an ANP is fearful because her abusive father is present in the meeting room. We explain that, for different reasons, this EP is only a part of the system that is reproducing an aspect related to the father or some of his behaviors. We ask the *adult self* to place the image of the real father on the screen, and all the parts should help differentiate the external real abuser from the part of the self who resembles the abuser. Once differentiation has been achieved, short sets of BLS can be provided to enhance this awareness. This work is frequently difficult to develop, and sometimes it needs to be combined with different interventions during an extended therapy period.

The screen can also be used to distance the client and the system from the unwanted emergence of traumatic memories. We ask the client to place this memory on the screen, and we explain that we will not work on these issues right now, because he is not prepared for it at the moment. Once again, we would ask the client, or any specific part, to realize the difference between "who I am" and "what has happened to me," and some parts could be encouraged to help others. The image can be distorted (blurred, without colors, without sound, etc.), in order to make it more tolerable for the client and the system of parts. Adaptive information could be introduced and eventually installed. For example, we can say, "It was not your fault. Do you understand that a small child is not guilty of the bad things that other people do to him?" Or, "What do you think could have happened if you had defended yourself?" The goal of this intervention is to introduce adaptive information progressively and prepare the client for the change in core cognitions and beliefs.

When the system is ready for trauma processing, the screen strategy will be invaluable in helping to maintain dual attention and distance the client from the traumatic content we are working on.

The Meeting Place as a Procedure to Increase Communication, Collaboration, and an Integrative (Metacognitive) Capacity

Dialogue with the internal system is a difficult task for many dissociative clients. By proposing that the *adult self* can observe and relate to all parts or aspects of the self in the meeting place, the client can begin to develop a more integrated sense of self. Some of these parts are more easily accepted as part of the person. However, as we commented before, those that contain the worst memories or the emotions that are more difficult to deal with, tend to appear later.

Sometimes, we can encounter a strong phobia of mental actions (Van der Hart, Nijenhuis, & Steele, 2006) that does not allow the client to perform the procedure. It can manifest as an apparent inability to visualize or imagine the place or as an uncomfortable sensation when trying to design a meeting place for the internal system. This is not the only cause for this situation. For example, a weak therapeutic relationship and a lack of trust from the client can also interfere with this procedure. We should explore what is happening in the internal system, but without a good alliance with all the parts, we will only get the information from the ANP.

When the phobia of mental contents is an obstacle for the construction of a meeting place, we can use this phobia as a target to be processed, as we can see in the following example:

> Therapist: Today we will work with the MP procedure, as I mentioned in our last session. Are you ready?

Client: Yes, I am.

T: Then imagine a meeting place where you can meet with different aspects or parts of yourself.

C (uncomfortable): I can´t do it.

T: Are you feeling any negative emotion or physical sensation?

C: I am not sure.

T: Please, slowly scan all your body while you think about the meeting place, and notice if you feel some uncomfortable sensation.

C: I feel a little pressure on my chest.

T: Is it okay if we try to process it with EMDR? Please, scan your body again while you think about doing this.

C (after doing an inner scan for a minute): Yes, I want to do it.

T: Okay. Then focus on your bodily sensation while you try to imagine your meeting place, and let me know when you notice you are feeling this uncomfortable sensation.

Client nods.

T: Okay, go with that (short set of bilateral stimulation). How are you feeling now?

C: Better, the sensation is gone.

T: Okay, try to imagine the meeting place now.

C: I see a blurred room; there are undefined figures.

T: Go with that (short set of bilateral stimulation). What do you see now?

C: It´s the same place, but I can see it more clearly. There are some figures sitting on the chairs.

T: And how is your general sensation now?

C: Good.

Once we overcome this first obstacle, we can propose to the client, as *adult self*, to visualize an adequate place to establish contact and a constructive dialogue with the internal system of parts. The therapist should help the *adult self* to identify when the designed place is really safe and appropriate. We should not forget that, at this time, the *adult self* is mainly based on an ANP who still cannot realize many relevant aspects. For example, a client proposed the edge of a cliff as a meeting place. The therapist did not suspect that this could be dangerous, because the client (as ANP) was completely confident about it. But during an attempted dialogue with the parts, the ANP decided to "solve" a problem with one part by throwing her off the cliff.

When an adequate meeting place is set up, we will ask the client how many places he can see in the meeting room. Frequently, the ANP will name a specific number of seats, but not all of them are always occupied by a dissociative part. As we commented before, empty seats tend to be related to rejected, feared, disowned or fearful parts. The characteristics of the parts and their position regarding other parts can give us relevant information. Sometimes there are parts that look like the client at different ages. Others can be older than the real age of the client. When they do not represent real figures in his life, they can be symbols of wisdom, knowledge, or the premature adult that he was forced to be as a traumatized child. Some parts imitate attachment figures or abusers and, as we explained before, it can be difficult for other parts to differentiate them from the real parents or abusers. Sometimes the parts are like monsters or devils, but frequently inside they hide an angry or fearful child or adolescent. In other cases, unidentified parts can take a symbolic aspect such as "fog," "darkness," or "garbage."

We can consider this first approach to the meeting room not only as a stabilization technique, but also as an extremely rich source of information to add to the history taking. We can also gain further information regarding which phobias are present between dissociative parts and which ones are strongest. As we have described in the chapter on dissociative phobias, considering these phobic reactions as interoceptively generated DSI (dysfunctionally stored information), we can process them with BLS. But at the same time, as we remarked in the chapter on dissociative language, we should understand that these phobias are there for a reason, and all of the client's defenses should not be removed until we know he is prepared to tolerate the changes. Any procedure that we implement must come from a collaborative decision making process between the client's *adult self*, the system of parts, and the therapist. We search for a balance between helping the client to move forward and the need to be cautious and respect the client's timing and boundaries.

Bilateral stimulation can help to overcome obstacles in the process of change. We can process phobias between dissociative parts, or we can use the tip of the finger strategy to decrease an overwhelming emotion in some parts that do not allow them to change. There is not a set procedure for doing this because each system is different and the situation can be different at different times in the session. A dynamic dialogue is developed, introducing BLS when we realize that we are facing a blocking point, as it was described in previous chapters. It is important not to forget that BLS has powerful effects, even when using small dosages, and a tentative approach is always recommended. We must remember that less is always better than too much.

We can see how to combine different procedures in the following case-example:

The initial setting up of the meeting place takes place without difficulties, identifying the ANP and several EP. Difficulties arise when the ANP is invited to dialogue with a specific EP that she strongly rejects.

We start processing the ANP's rejection to talk with a specific EP, because this dissociative phobia is blocking the process. After this, the hate that this EP feels toward the ANP due to the association with the abuser's figure, which makes her think that all adults are dangerous, becomes more evident. With the EP's agreement, we can focus on this phobia and reprocess it. Psychoeducation about time orientation and differentiation is introduced to enhance stabilization.

We continue fostering the dialogue between these two parts without introducing BLS, while empathy and collaboration are improving. But after some time, another part appears, asking for the ANP and the therapist's attention. Noticing that this part is unable to think productively due to an intense emotional response, we propose the *tip of the finger strategy* to this part to relieve a portion of this disturbing emotion.

We can also apply bilateral stimulation in the meeting place to reinforce resources, achievements, insightful thoughts, or any positive element, always asking for permission from the internal system. BLS can be used to reinforce co-consciousness (see chapters 5 and 7), differentiation between past and present, and outer and inner worlds, as well as to enhance reality/time orientation in emotional parts and a positive self-care attitude, among other things. All these aspects will be interweaved with small fragments of processing, adapting to each client's needs and what takes place in each session.

When internal communication increases, different targets can be processed while several parts are collaborating. In structural dissociation, a progressive approach is recommended. We start by dealing with a current problem where the parts feel cooperative with one another, and we gradually target more delicate aspects in co-consciousness. When the client is able to effectively process more recent events, the traumatic past can be approached, in many cases starting from a fragment of the traumatic memory, to further reprocess entire core memories.

At some point, it can be useful to switch from working with the dissociative parts in the meeting place, to a standard EMDR processing of negative memories, because this can be useful to increase integration. We tend to alternate working with parts with a self-care approach from the *adult self*, as well as strengthen the achievements by enhancing the physical sensations associated with them.

We want to promote orientation toward the outside world from the beginning, since dissociative parts tend to be internally focused. This will increase a metacognitive position. If we only work from the meeting room, as therapists, we may end up becoming a part of the internal system, especially if the client experiences difficulties advancing toward a healthy future and relationships. Even when parts are not completely integrated, once many of the phobias between them have significantly decreased and some processing has been done, the client can be ready for standard EMDR processing. During the desensitization phase, we can see how different parts become spontaneously activated and partially or even completely integrated.

There can be blockages during the process and some interweaves may be needed, not only to deal with blockages, but also to keep the client present and maintain dual attention. If there is a blockage, or the client starts to become hyper or hypo-aroused, one option is to turn the attention back to the meeting place and ask if there is any part that is activated or has an objection. Sometimes new parts may emerge. If so, we identify the concerns and needs of the part and provide time orientation or other appropriate strategies and procedures.

Variations of the Meeting Place

The meeting place can be performed, not only with guided imagery, but also by using concrete representations of the systems´ aspects or parts. In fact, these concrete representations may help prevent loss of reality orientation, take perspective, and increase reflective, metacognitive thinking.

One possibility is to represent the meeting place in a drawing. This is an example of this procedure using drawings.

These are the steps that we followed in this example, and at the points where we decided to apply BLS:

1. Processing the Phobia of Mental Actions

We give this client a blank sheet of paper and ask her to draw "what she feels is inside her." Apparently, she presents difficulties in understanding the task and expresses that she is unable to draw. Understanding this difficulty as a phobia of mental actions, we process it with BLS.

2. Processing the Phobia of the ANP toward an EP

After BLS, the client is able to draw a small figure in the upper part of the paper (1). Looking at this part while we are tapping on her shoulders, the client draws a skirt and describes this initially undefined part as a little girl.

3. Increasing Awareness and Exploring the System

We ask the client to focus on the paper and to think if there are more parts present. She draws another figure (2) with two horns that she describes as a "demon." She associates this figure with a very critical and hostile auditory hallucination.

4. The Tip of the Finger Strategy

The dialogue with this part is very difficult, because it tends to engage in repetitive statements, answering, "I don´t need any help," "I know everything." After exploring the meaning of these messages, we consider the disturbing emotion in this part as an intense rage that is interfering with the possibility of effective communication. We ask this part if he wants to relieve part of the disturbance within him (she sees this EP as a male demon). The EP initially disagrees, arguing that he does not experience any disturbance. However, when we suggest that the part can decide after experiencing if BLS is positive or not for him, focusing on any sensation he would like to relieve, the EP agrees. After doing this, the client is able to draw a new figure (3).

5. Processing the Phobia between two EPs

We ask the client to focus on the drawing and to pay attention to what she is noticing in her body. She locates an unpleasant sensation in her stomach. We ask her to focus on that sensation and apply BLS (4-6 movements). After BLS, she draws a connection between parts 1 and 3, represented by number 4 in the drawing.

6. Processing the Phobia in the ANP toward Mental Actions and Dissociative Parts

Observing that the drawing was limited to just one area of the paper, we ask the client to focus on the rest of the paper and again to notice if there is any somatic sensation. She cannot describe it, but says it is there, so we ask her to focus on the body and apply a short set of BLS (4-6 movements).

7. Processing Unidentified Elements

After the BLS, the client says that there is "fog" on the left corner. We ask the client to focus on that and notice the body sensation, which at this moment is clearly disturbing. We apply BLS while she is focusing on the disturbance and its location in the body.

8. Exploring the Inner System of Parts

After some sets, she draws new figures, explaining, "There are many of them, and they are lost in the fog."

9. Installing a Meta-conscious, Integrative Perspective

Finally, a global, integrative view of all these figures as different parts of herself is suggested to the client as ANP, and after checking that the general sensation is not disturbing, this integrative view ("all these figures are me") is installed with BLS, promoting the developing of the *adult self*.

With the same purpose, we can use external figures as little toys or puppets. Each one of these modifications can give us different information, and it is useful to alternate between guided imagery, drawing, the use of figures, and other exercises, in order to decrease the tendency to get stuck in pathological structures that occurs in complex traumatization. Some clients are more capable of visualizing or drawing, but developing these symbolic capacities in people who are not prone to do so is useful in order to enhance high order mental functions, as described in chapter 4.

Summary

The meeting place is an integrative procedure that can facilitate moving through the different phases of treatment in severely traumatized clients. Many procedures to initiate, enhance, and reinforce integration can be implemented from the meeting place. During the preparation phase, it can help promote collaborative communication between dissociative parts and develop a meta-conscious perspective of different aspects of the self. Providing brief sets of BLS can enhance time orientation, cooperation, and collaboration among parts, and it can facilitate the processing of blockages and reduction of phobias that maintain dissociation. When we are working on traumatic targets, it can be helpful to structure trauma work and provide a basis for identifying and working through blockages.

This intervention may be used as a guided imagery exercise, as described by Fraser, but a similar procedure can be performed using different elements as drawings, figures, etc. These external elements can give us relevant information and offer specific possibilities of intervention.

There are several steps in the meeting place procedure, but these steps need to be implemented in a dynamic and progressive way. Consequently, the set up and implementation of the meeting place will be different for each client, depending on their needs, situation, and integrative capacity. Furthermore, it is important to use this procedure in conjunction with other interventions, depending on the client´s particular needs.

We should not forget that although these procedures are very useful with significant dissociative disorders, returning to the EMDR standard protocol is indicated when the main dissociative phobias and blockages have been overcome.

Appendix

.

Relational Problems Questionnaire (RPQ)

Dolores Mosquera, Anabel Gonzalez, & Andrew M. Leeds

This questionnaire is not designed for research purposes. It is proposed as a tool for therapists´ self-knowledge. All of us have pondered many of these questions, but for some therapists certain situations are more frequent or distressing. You can use the RPQ to identify your profile and to understand why this happens.

You can also use the RPQ to reflect on a specific client when the therapeutic process becomes stuck, when you feel there are problems in the therapist-client relationship, or when you want to supervise a case. It covers different aspects that can be influencing the therapeutic relationship.

Please, read the questions and mark with an X to the right whenever a) you consider that you frequently encounter this situation, b) you feel that you have difficulties managing these issues, or c) you consider that it is relevant in your practice.

Then, think about your own experience, your clients, and the way that you deal with each one of these situations. Which ones are more distressing or difficult for you? Which ones are more frequent in your daily work? Do you tend to find yourself being part of some of the kind of interactions described in the questionnaire?

After this reflection, choose one of the sections, the one you feel it is the most relevant to you. Think of how this part of the Questionnaire has to do with you. Do you find any link to your personal history?

Helpless Child vs. Idealized Omnipotent Rescuer	
Has any client told you how special you are for him?	
Do you remember any client telling you, "You are the only one who can help me, I am very disappointed with all my previous therapists, but I know you are different…" and after some time, saying, "You are just like the others… I thought you were different but I was wrong… Don´t you care about me?"	
Did you ever find yourself thinking or speaking about your good-for-nothing colleagues? Did you ever feel you were the "only one" who could save a client´s life or effectively treat him? And after some time, feeling useless or unable to carry the therapy through? Trying not to disappoint that client, who depends on you to survive or improve?	
Needy Child vs. Perfect Caregiver	
Do some clients seem so vulnerable that you are moved to do a lot of things for them?	

Have you found yourself doing things for a client and feeling that you were going beyond adequate limits? Or doing more and more for a client, so much so that you became exhausted and even then, you could not meet the client's needs?	
Did you ever go out of your way and do things you did not want to do, hoping this would make things in the relationship go better or trying not to disappoint a client?	
Did any of your clients end up as friends or having a work relationship with you?	
Have you had the experience of making a lot of concessions, as saving more time for sessions, extra sessions, favors... And, after some time, feeling unjustly treated by them, for not reciprocating your generosity?	
Have you found yourself disclosing personal information or your problems to a client?	
Did you let the client help you in any personal way?	
Submission vs. Domination	
Have you ever found clients extremely interested in pleasing you?	
Did clients ever tell you they were very relaxed or experienced a fast relief with EMDR, when you had a much different sensation... only to find out later that they became worse after the session?	
Did any clients offer or give you valuable gifts?	
What kind of clients do you prefer to treat? Do you prefer clients that tend to be compliant, do the homework, and agree with every proposal you suggest?	
Have you ever found yourself "challenged" by a client? Have you ever thought a client was not really motivated because he did not follow your instructions?	
Victimization vs. Aggression	
Have you been mistreated by a client? Unjustly accused of something? Physically assaulted?	
Have you felt manipulated? Fooled? Used?	
Have you ever achieved a strong alliance with a client, while a hostile dissociative part kept creating problems?	
Have you ever felt that "no matter what you would say or do" it would be used against you?	
Have you ever found yourself subtly challenged or threatened by a client?	
Did a client ever give you a compliment that sounded odd and felt like an attack?	
Have you ever thought, "I hope he does not come to session today"?	
Have you found yourself feeling angry with a client?	
Have you ever felt annoyed thinking, "He is theatrical, hysteric, a bad person, selfish"?	
Have you ever confronted a client in an extremely harsh way?	
Have you ever felt like saying rude things to a client? Have you ever felt like saying or doing "terrible things" to a client?	
Have you ever experienced negative visceral responses toward apparently nice clients?	

Seducer vs. Seduced	
Have you ever felt attracted by a client, to the point of having difficulties focusing during the session?	
Have you ever found yourself trying to look better or more attractive before seeing a certain client?	
Have you ever found yourself inquiring about sexual details that are not relevant for therapy?	
Have you ever thought about engaging in an intimate relation with a client?	
Have you ever felt a client was trying to seduce you?	
Has a client ever declared his love to you or expressed his wishes to be intimate with you?	
Have any clients described their sex life in detail, even when it was not related to what you asked?	
I do not Realize that Trauma has Happened to me vs. I Relive the Trauma	
Have any of your clients wanted to avoid reprocessing traumatic issues?	
Did any of them experience negative reactions during trauma reprocessing?	
Has a client ever asked you to work on a traumatic experience with EMDR, and when you are about to work on it, all you encountered were problems?	
Or has a client ever told you that he wanted to recover memories of his past, and when you agreed to try, he reacted negatively?	
Have you ever felt so much curiosity about a client's history that you acted in ways where you ended up feeling like an investigator?	
Have you ever delayed reprocessing a specific memory because you found it was too hard or intense?	
Have you ever felt distant or disconnected during a therapy session, not because you were tired, but because you "needed to distance yourself" or you "couldn't help it"?	
Have you ever thought in terms of "I hope the client doesn't bring me that memory to work on it today!" or "I am starting to think the abuse was not real, but is just the client's fantasy?"	
Have you felt exhausted by so many traumatic histories?	
Control vs. Out of Control	
Have you ever felt that the therapeutic process was out of control? That there were so many crisis and relapses that you could not work on the therapeutic goals?	
Have you found yourself performing a fire-extinguisher role?	
Do the crisis in the client's current life contrast with a rigid attitude from the client during the sessions?	
Have you sensed the client was trying to be in control during the EMDR reprocessing or trying to over-control their symptoms during the session?	

Have you ever thought, "Is the client controlling the session instead of me?"	
Have you ever said to a client, "If you don´t stop this behavior, don´t return to this consultation"?	
Have you ever applied one protocol after another, trying to help the client in taking control over his symptoms without results?	
Do you remember ever engaging in a power struggle with a client?	
The Holding of Hope vs. the Despair of Hopelessness	
Has your client expressed hopelessness or distrust repeatedly during the therapy session, and you felt you should encourage him to continue?	
And yet, at the same time as you were overtly encouraging him, you could not avoid feeling frustration or distrust about the client really wanting to improve?	
Have you thought, "This client is adopting an illness role" or "He doesn´t want to get better, he has no real motivation for therapy"?	
Have you found yourself thinking, "This client is so damaged that he will never recover?" or "All the work we are doing is useless. Is it worth making such an effort?"	
Extreme Guilt vs. Irresponsibility or Blaming Others	
Have you ever felt too concerned about some of your clients?	
Have you ever felt responsible for the client´s actions? When your client gets worse, do you tend to think you are not doing things the right way?	
Does your sense of responsibility increase as the client becomes more irresponsible?	
Have you thought of any of your clients in these terms: "He is searching for trouble, so in some way he deserve their problems," "He is always complaining about things that he caused,"	
Have you ever felt unjustly blamed by a client?	
Have you ever found yourself in a "judging" role rather than in a therapeutic one?	
Did a client ever apologize for not doing what was expected of him? Or for not progressing positively in therapy?	

References

Ainsworth, M.D., Blehar, M., Waters, E., & Wall, S. (1978). *Patterns of attachment: A psychological study of the strange situation*. Hillsdale NJ: Lawrence Erlbaum Associates.

Armstrong, D.M. (1979). Three types of consciousness. *Ciba Foundation Symposium,* (69) 235-253.

Baita, S. & Gonzalez, A. (2008). *Working through consciousness with adults and children*. Paper presented at the 25th annual meeting of the International Society for the Study of Trauma and Dissociation, Chicago, IL.

Barach, P.M. (1991). Multiple dersonality disorder as an attachment disorder. *Dissociation*, 4,117-123.

Bateman, A. & Fonagy, P. (2004). *Psychotherapy for borderline personality disorder. Mentalization-based treatment*. Oxford University Press.

Bergmann, U. (2000). Further thoughts on the neurobiology of EMDR: The role of the cerebellum in the accelerated information processing. *Traumatology*, 6 (3), Article 4.

Bergmann, U. (2008). Hidden selves: Treating dissociation in the spectrum of personality disorders. In C. Forgash & M. Copeley (Eds.), *Healing the heart of trauma and dissociation with EMDR and ego state therapy* (pp. 227-265). New York, NY: Springer Publishing Co.

Bernstein, E.M. & Putnam, F.W. (1986). Development, reliability, and validity of a dissociation scale. *Journal of Nervous and Mental Disease*, 174, 727-735

Bishop, S.R., Lau, M., Shapiro, S., Carlson, L., Anderson, N., Carmody, J., Segal, Z.V., Abbey, S., Speca, M., Velting, D., & Devins, G. (2004). Mindfulness: A proposed operational definition. *Clinical Psychology: Science & Practice*, 11 (3), 230–241.

Bob, P. (2007). Consciousness and co-consciousness, binding problem and schizophrenia. *Neuro Endocrinology Letters*, Dec. 28, (6), 723-726.

Bodovitz, S. (2004). Consciousness is discontinuous. *Medical Hypotheses*, 62 (6), 1003-1005.

Bodovitz, S. (2008). The neural correlate of consciousness. *Journal of Theoretical Biology*, Apr 22.

Bower, G. (1981). Mood and memory. *American Psychologist*, 36,129–148.

Bowlby, J. (1969). *Attachment and loss. Vol. I: Attachment*. London: Hogarth.

Bowlby, J. (1973). *Attachment and loss: Vol. 2: Separation: Anxiety and anger*. London: Penguin Books.

Bowlby, J. (1980). *Attachment and loss: Vol. 3: Loss: Sadness and depression*. London: Penguin Books.

Braun, B.G. (1984). Uses of hypnosis with multiple personality. *Psychiatric Annals*. 14 (1), 34-40.

Braun, B.G. (1988a). The BASK (behavior, affect, sensation, knowledge) model of dissociation. *Dissociation*, 1 (1), 4-23.

Braun, B.G. (1988b). The BASK model of dissociation: clinical applications. *Dissociation*, 1 (2), 16-23.

Brown, D.P. & Fromm, E. (1986). *Hypnotherapy and hypnoanalysis*. Hillsdale, New Jersey: Lawrence Erlbaum Associates.

Brown, D., Scheflin, A.W., & Hammond, D.C. (1998). *Memory, trauma treatment, and the law*. New York: Norton.

Caul, D. (1984). Group and videotape techniques for multiple personality. *Psychiatric Annals*, 14, 43-50.

Chu, JA. (1988). Ten traps for therapists in the treatment of trauma survivors. *Dissociation*, 1 (4), 25-32.

Chu, J.A. (1998). *Rebuilding shattered lives: The responsible treatment of complex post-traumatic and dissociative disorders*. John Wiley & Songs, NY.

Chu, J.A., Dell, P.F., Van der Hart, O., Cardeña, E., Barach, P.M., Somer, E., et al. (2011). ISST-D Guidelines for treating dissociative identity disorders in adults, third revision. *Journal of Trauma and Dissociation*, 12, 115-187.

Classen, C., Pain, C., Field, N., & Woods, P. (2006). Posttraumatic personality disorder: A reformulation of the complex posttraumatic stress disorder and borderline personality disorder. *Psychiatric Clinics of North America*, 29, 87-112.

Cleeremans, A. (Ed.) (2003). *The unity of consciousness: Binding, integration, and dissociation*. Oxford, England: Oxford University Press.

Cooke, L.J. & Grand, C. (2009). The neurobiology of eating disorders, affect regulation skills, and EMDR in the treatment of eating disorders. In R. Shapiro (Ed.), *EMDR solutions II: For depression, eating disorders, performance, and more* (pp. 129-151). New York: Norton Professional Books.

Coons, P. & Milstein, V. (1990). Self-mutilation associated with dissociative disorders. *Dissociation*, 3 (2), 81-87.

Corrigan, F.M. (2002). Mindfulness, dissociation, EMDR and the anterior cingulate cortex: A hypothesis. *Contemporary Hypnosis*, 19 (1), 8-17.

Corrigan, F.M. (2004). Psychotherapy as assisted homeostasis: Activation of emotional processing mediated by the anterior cingulate cortex. *Medical Hypotheses*, 63 (6), 968-973.

Courtois, C. (1999). *Recollections of sexual abuse: Treatment principles and guidelines*. New York: W.W. Norton & Co.

Courtois, C.A., Ford, J.D., & Cloitre, M. (2009). Best practices in psychotherapy for adults. In C.A. Courtois & J. D. Ford (Eds.), *Treating complex traumatic stress disorders: An evidence-based guide* (pp. 82-103). Guilford Press.

Crick, F. (1994). *The astonishing hypothesis*. New York: Scribner´s.

Damasio, A.R. (1994). *Descartes´ error*. Grosset-Putnam. NY.

Dell, P.F. (2002). Dissociative phenomenology of dissociative identity disorder. *Journal of Nervous & Mental Disease*, 190, 1-15.

Dell, P.F. (2006). A New Model of Dissociative Identity Disorder. Psychiatric Clinics of North America, 29, 1–26.

Dutra, L., Bureau, J. F., Holmes, B., Lyubchik, A., & Lyons-Ruth, K. (2009). Quality of early care and childhood trauma: A prospective study of developmental pathways to dissociation. *The Journal of Nervous and Mental Disease*, 197(6), 383-90.

Dworkin, M. & Shapiro, F. (2005). *EMDR and the relational imperative: The therapeutic relationship in EMDR treatment.* Taylor & Francis.

Ebrinc, S., Semiz, U.B., Basoglu, C., Cetin, M., Agargun, M.Y,, Alguil, A., & Ates, A. (2008). Self mutilating behaviour in patients with dissociative disorders: The role of innate hypnotic capacity. *The Israel Journal of Psychiatry and Related Sciences*, 45, 39-48.

Elofsson, U.O.E., von Scheele, B., Theorell, T., & Sondergaard, H.P. (2008). Physiological correlates of eye movement desensitization and reprocessing. *Journal of Anxiety Disorders*, 22, 622–624.

Engelhard, I.M., van Uijen, S.L., & Van den Hout, M.A. (2010). The impact of taxing working memory on negative and positive memories. *European Journal of Psychotraumatology*, 1 (0).

Erikson, E.H. (1950). *Childhood and society*. New York: Norton.

Erikson, E.H. (1968). *Identity: Youth and crisis*. New York: Norton.

Erickson, M.H., Rossi, E.L., & Rossi, S.I. (1976). *Hypnotic realities: The induction of clinical hypnosis and forms of indirect suggestion*. New York: Irvington.

Falk, D., Hildebolt, C., Cheverud, J., Vannier, M., Helmkamp, R., & Kronisberg, L. (1990). Cortical asymmetries in frontal lobes of Rhesus monkeys. *Brain Research*, 512, 40-45.

Fanselow, M.S. & Lester, L.S. (1988). A functional behavioristic approach to aversively motivated behavior: Predatory imminence as a determinant of the topography of defensive behavior. In R.C. Bolles & M.D. Beecher (Eds.), *Evolution and learning* (pp. 185-212). Hillsdale, NJ: Erlbaum.

Fine, C.G. (1991). Treatment stabilization and crisis prevention: Pacing the therapy of the multiple personality disorder patient. *Psychiatric Clinics of North America*, 14, 661-676.

Fine, C.G. (1993). A tactical integrationalist perspective on the treatment of multiple personality disorder. In R.P. Kluft & C.G. Fine (Eds.), *Clinical perspectives on multiple personality disorder* (pp. 153-153). Washington, DC: American Psychiatric Press.

Fine, C.G. & Berkowitz, A.S. (2001). The Wreathing Protocol: The imbrication of hypnosis and EMDR in the treatment of dissociative identity disorder and other dissociative responses. *American Journal of Clinical Hypnosis* 43:3, 4, 275-290.

Fisher, J. (2000). *Adapting EMDR techniques in the treatment of dysregulated or dissociative patients*. Paper presented at the International Society for the Study of Dissociation Annual Meeting. San Antonio, Texas.

Fonagy, P., Gegerly, G., Jurist, E.L., & Target, M. (2002). *Affect regulation, mentalization and the development of the self*. New York: Other Press.

Forester, D. (2009). Treating bulimia nervosa with EMDR. In R. Shapiro (Ed.), *EMDR solutions II: For depression, eating disorders, performance, and more* (pp. 151-64). New York: Norton Professional Books.

Forgash, C. (2009). *An EMDR treatment approach to addressing health problems of complex trauma survivors*. Paper presented at the annual meeting of the EMDR International Association, Atlanta, GA.

Forgash, C. (2009). Home base. In M. Luber (Ed.), *Eye movement desensitization (EMDR) scripted protocols: Special populations* (pp. 217-219). New York, NY: Springer Publishing Co.

Forgash, C. (2010). *Dissociation in the dental chair: Implications for the EMDR treatment of health issues*. Paper presented at the annual meeting of the EMDR International Association, Minneapolis, MN.

Forgash, C. & Copeley, E. (2007). *Healing the heart of trauma and dissociation with EMDR and Ego-States Therapy.* New York: Springer Publishing.

Fraser, G.A. (1991). The dissociative table technique: A strategy for working with ego states in dissociative disorders and Ego-State Therapy. *Dissociation: Progress in the Dissociative Disorders*, 4, 205-213.

Fraser, G.A. (2003). Fraser´s "Dissociative Table Technique" revisited. Revised: A strategy for working with ego states in dissociative disorders and Ego-State Therapy. *Journal of Trauma & Dissociation*, 4 (4), 5-28.

Frederick, C. & McNeal, S. (1999). *Inner strengths: contemporary psychotherapy and hypnosis for ego-strengthening*. Mahwah, New Jersey: Lawrence Erlbaum Associates.

Gelinas, D.J. (2003). Integrating EMDR into phase-oriented treatment for trauma. *Journal of Trauma & Dissociation*, 4 (3), 91-135.

George, C., Kaplan, N., & Main, M. (1985). *The Adult Attachment Interview*. Unpublished manuscript, University of California. Berkeley.

Gonzalez, A. (2008). *Work with parts in DID & EMDR*. Paper presented at the annual meeting of EMDR Europe Association, June. London, UK.

Gonzalez, A., Seijo, N., & Mosquera, D. (2009). *EMDR in complex trauma and dissociative disorders*. Paper presented at the annual meeting of the EMDR International Association, Atlanta, GA.

Gonzalez, A., Mosquera, D., & Seijo, N. (2010). *Processing dissociative phobias with EMDR*. Workshop presented in the II Bi-annual ESTD Conference in Belfast.

Greenwald, R. (1993a). Treating children´s nightmares with EMDR. *EMDR Network Newsletter*, 3 (1), 7-9.

Greenwald, R. (1993b). Magical installations can empower patients to slay their dragons. *EMDR Network Newsletter*, 3 (2), 16-17.

Hase, M. H. (2008). *EMDR and substance-abuse.* Presentation at the Pre-Congress on EMDR at the European Congress of Hypnosis, Vienna, Austria.

Hase, M. (2010). *EMDR in the treatment of addiction. Reprocessing of the addiction memory*. Keynote presented at the annual meeting of the EMDR Europe Association, Hamburg, Germany.

Hayes, S.C., Strosahl, K., & Wilson, K.G. (1999). *Acceptance and commitment therapy: An experiential approach to behavior change*. New York: Guilford Press.

Herman, J.L. (1992). *Trauma and recovery: The aftermath of violence. From domestic abuse to political terror*. Library of Congress Cataloging-in-Publication Data. Basic Books. New York.

Hofmann, A. (2010). The inverted EMDR standard protocol for unstable complex post-traumatic stress disorder. In M. Luber (Ed.), *EMDR scripted protocols. Special populations*. Springer Publishing Company.

Janet, P. (1903). *Les obsessions et la psychasthénie (Vol. 1).* Paris: Félix Alcan.

Janet, P. (1904). L´amnésie et la dissociation des souvenirs par l´émotion. Journal de Psychologie, 1, 417-453.

Janet, P. (1919). *Les médications psychologiques*. Paris: Félix Alcan. English edition: Psychological healing. New York: Macmillan, 1925.

Janet, P. (1928). *L'évolution de la mémoire et de la notion du temps*. Paris: A. Chahine.

Janet, P. (1935). Realisation et interpretation. Annales Medico-Psychologiques, 93, II, 329-366.

Kernberg, O.F. (1993). *Severe personality disorders: Psychotherapeutic strategies*. Yale University Press.

Kluft, R.P. (1982). Varieties of hypnotic interventions in the treatment of multiple personality. *American Journal of Clinical Hypnosis*, 24 (4), 230-240.

Kluft, R.P. (1984). Treatment of multiple personality disorder. *Psychiatric Clinics of North America*, 7, 9-29.

Kluft, R.P. (1988). Playing for time: Temporizing techniques in the treatment of multiple personality disorder. *American Journal of Clinical Hypnosis*, 32, 90-98.

Kluft, R.P. (1990). The fractionated abreaction technique. In D.C. Hammond (Ed.), *Handbook of hypnotic suggestions and metaphors* (pp. 527-528). New York. Norton.

Kluft, R.P. (1993a). The initial stages of psychotherapy in the treatment of multiple personality disorder. *Dissociation*, 6, 145-161.

Kluft, R.P. (1993b). Clinical approaches to the integration of personalities. In Kluft, R.P. & Fine, C.G. (Eds.), *Clinical perspectives on multiple personality disorder* (pp. 101-133). Washington DC: American Psychiatric Press.

Kluft, R.P. (1994). Countertransference in the treatment of MPD. In J.P. Wilson & J. Lindy (Eds.), *Countertransference in the treatment of post-traumatic stress disorder* (pp. 121-151). New York: Guilford Press.

Knipe, J. (1995). Targeting defensive avoidance and dissociated numbing. *EMDR Network Newsletter*, 5 (2), 6-7.

Knipe, J. (1999). Targeting defensive avoidance and dissociated numbing. *EMDRIA Newsletter*, 4 (2), 10-25.

Knipe, J. (2006). *EMDR toolbox: Video examples of methods of targeting avoidance, procrastination, affect dysregulation, the pain of being "dumped" by a lover, and a shame-based ego state in a client with a identity disorder*. Presentation at the annual meeting of the EMDR Europe Association, Istanbul, Turkey.

Knipe, J. (2008). Loving eyes: Procedures to therapeutically reverse dissociative processes while preserving emotional safety. In C. Forgash & M. Copeley (Eds.), *Healing the heart of trauma and dissociation with EMDR and Ego-State Therapy* (pp. 181-225). New York, NY: Springer Pub. Co.

Knipe, J. (2009). Shame is my safe place: Adaptive information processing methods of resolving chronic shame-based depression. In Shapiro, R. (Ed). *EMDR Solutions, Vol. II*, New York: Norton.

Knipe, J. (2009). Dysfunctional positive affect: To assist clients with unwanted avoidance defenses. In M. Luber (Ed.), *Eye movement desensitization (EMDR) scripted protocols: Special populations* (pp. 451-452). New York, NY: Springer Publishing Co.

Knipe, J. (2010). *Taller "La caja de herramientas"*. Workshop provided by the EMDR Spanish Association. Madrid.

Kohut, H., Ornstein, P.H. (Ed)., & Madison, C.T. (1978-1981) *The search for the self: Selected writings of Heinz Kohut: 1978-1981, Vol. 4.* Kohut, H.; Ornstein, P.H. (Ed). Madison, CT, US: International Universities Press, Inc. (1991).

Kong, L., Allen, J.B., & Glisky, E.L. (2008). Interidentity memory transfer in dissociative identity disorder. *Journal of Abnormal Psychology*, 117(3), 686-692.

Korn, D.L. (2009). EMDR and the treatment of complex PTSD: A review. *Journal of EMDR Practice and Research*, 3 (4), 264-278.

Korn, D.L. & Leeds, A.M. (2002). Preliminary evidence of efficacy for EMDR resource development and installation in the stabilization phase of complex posttraumatic stress disorder. *Journal of Clinical Psychology*, 58 (12), 1465-1487.

Krakauer, S.Y. (2006). The two-part film technique: Empowering dissociative patients to alter cognitive distortions and maladaptive behaviors. *Journal of Trauma & Dissociation*, 7 (2), 39-57.

Lang, P.J. (1995). The emotion probe: Studies of motivation and attention. *American Psychologist*, 50, 372-385.

Lanius, U. (2008). *The neurobiology of dissociation*. Presentation on the EMDRIA Conference. Phoenix, USA.

Lankton, S.R. (1987). *Central themes and principles of Ericksonian therapy (Ericksonian monographs, 2)*. New York: Brunner-Routledge.

Lazrove, S. & Fine, C.G. (1996). The use of EMDR in patients with dissociative identity disorder. *Dissociation*, 9 (1), 289-299.

Lee, C., Taylor, G., & Drummond, P. (2006). The active ingredient in EMDR: Is it traditional exposure or dual focus of attention? *Clinical Psychology and Psychotherapy*. 13, 97–107.

Leeds, A.M. (1991). *Eye movement desensitization & reprocessing: A rapid treatment modality for anxiety and trauma*. Presentation at the EMDR Network Conference, San Jose, CA.

Leeds, A.M. (1995). *EMDR case formulation symposium*. Paper presented at the 1995 International EMDR Conference: Research and Clinical Applications, Santa Monica, CA.

Leeds, A.M. (1997). *In the eye of the beholder: reflections on shame, dissociation, and transference in complex posttraumatic stress and attachment related disorders. Principles of case formulation for EMDR treatment planning and the use of Resource Installation*. Paper presented at the EMDR International Association, San Francisco.

Leeds, A.M. (1998). Lifting the burden of shame: Using EMDR resource installation to resolve a therapeutic impasse. In P. Manfield (Ed.), *Extending EMDR: A casebook of innovative applications (1st ed.)* (pp. 256-281). New York, NY: W. W. Norton & Co.

Leeds, A.M. (2001). Principles and procedures for enhancing current functioning in complex posttraumatic stress disorder with EMDR resource development and installation. *The EMDRIA Newsletter Special Edition*, 4-11.

Leeds, A.M. (2001). *Strengthening the self: Principles and procedures for creating successful treatment outcomes for adult survivors of neglect and abuse*. Santa Rosa: (Recording, Transcript and Manual available from Andrew M. Leeds, Ph.D., 1049 Fourth Street, Suite G, Santa Rosa, CA 95404).

Leeds, A.M. (2006). *Criteria for assuring appropriate clinical use and avoiding misuse of resource development and installation when treating complex posttraumatic stress syndromes.* EMDRIA conference. Philadelphia: Session 226.

Leeds, A.M. (2006). *Learning to feel good about positive emotions with the Positive Affect Tolerance and Integration Protocol.* Paper presented at the EMDRIA Conference, Philadelphia, PA.

Leeds, A.M. (2007). *Learning to feel good about positive emotions with the Positive Affect Tolerance and Integrative Protocol.* EMDRIA Annual Conference. Dallas.

Leeds, A.M. (2009). *A guide to the standard EMDR protocols for clinicians, supervisors, and consultants.* New York: Springer Publishing.

Leeds, A.M. (2009). Resources in EMDR and other trauma-focused psychotherapy: A review. *Journal of EMDR Practice and Research*, 3 (3), 152-160. doi:10.1891/1933-3196.3.3.152

Leeds, A.M. (2010). *Attachment theory and case formulation in the EMDR approach to psychotherapy.* 11th EMDR Europe Conference. Hamburg, Germany.

Leeds, A.M., & Shapiro, F. (2000). EMDR and Resource Installation: Principles and procedures for enhancing current functioning and resolving traumatic experiences. In J. Carlson & L. Sperry (Eds.), *Brief therapy with individuals and couples* (pp. 469-534). Phoenix, AZ: Zeig, Tucker & Theisen, Inc.

Linehan, M.M. (1993a). *Cognitive-behavioral treatment of borderline personality disorder.* New York: Guilford Press.

Linehan, M.M. (1993b). *Skills training manual for treating borderline personality disorder.* New York: Guilford Press.

Liotti, G. (2004). Trauma, dissociation and disorganized attachment: three strands of a single braid. *Psychotherapy: Theory, research, practice, training*, 41, 472-486.

Liotti, G. (2006). A model of dissociation based on attachment theory and research. *Journal of Trauma and Dissociation*, 7, 55-74.

Lipke, H. (1995). EMDR clinician survey. In F. Shapiro (Ed.), *Eye movement desensitization and reprocessing, basic principles, protocols and procedures* (pp. 376-386). New York: The Guilford Press.

Llinas R. (2001) Consciousness and the brain: The thalamocortical dialogue in health and disease. *Annals of the New York Academy of Sciences,* 929, 166-175.

Loevinger, J. (1976). *Ego development.* San Francisco: Jossey-Bass.

Main, M. (1996). Introduction to the special section on attachment and psychopathology: 2. Overview of the field of attachment. *Journal of Consulting and Clinical Psychology*, 64 (2), 237-243.

Main, M. (1999). Attachment theory: Eighteen points with suggestions for future studies. In J. Cassidy & P. R. Shaver (Eds.), *Handbook of attachment: Theory, research and clinical applications* (pp. 845-87). New York: Guilford.

Main, M. & Solomon, J. (1986). Discovery of an insecure disoriented attachment pattern: procedures, findings and implications for the classification of behavior. In Brazelton T. & Youngman M. *Affective Development in Infancy.* Norwood, NJ: Ablex.

Martinez, R. (1991). EMDR: Innovative uses. *EMDR Network Newsletter*, 1 (2), 7.

Mattheβ, H. (2008). *I Jornadas de Intervención en Catástrofes de la Asociación EMDR España*. Madrid.

McCullough, L. (1996). *Changing character: Short-term anxiety-regulating psychotherapy for restructuring defenses, affects, and attachment*. Basic Books.

McCullough, L., Kuhn, N., Andrews, S., Kaplan, A., Wolf, J., & Hurley, C. (2003). *Treating affect phobia: A manual for short-term dynamic psychotherapy*. New York: Guilford Press.

Metzinger, T. (2003). *Being no one: The self-model theory of subjectivity*. Cambridge, MA: MIT Press.

Miller, E.K., Freedman, D.J., and Wallis, J.D. (2002). The prefrontal cortex: categories, concepts, and cognition. *Philosophical Transactions: Biological Sciences*, 357, 1123-1136.

Missildine, W.H. (1963). *Your inner child of the past*. Simon & Schuster, NY.

Mosquera, D. (2004). *Diamantes en bruto II. Programa psicoeducativo para personas con trastorno límite de la personalidad*. Ediciones Pléyades. Madrid.

Mosquera, D. (2008). Personalidades narcisistas y personalidades con rasgos narcisistas. *Revista Persona. Institulo Argentino para el Estudio de la Personalidad y sus desórdenes,* 8 (2).

Mosquera, D. & Gonzalez, A. (2009). Relational Problems Questionnarie (RPQ).

Mosquera, D., Gonzalez, A., & Seijo, N., (2010). *Understanding dissociative language*. EMDRIA Conference. EMDR: From Trauma to Dissociation. EMDRIA. Minneapolis.

Mosquera, D. & Gonzalez, A. (2011). Del apego temprano al TLP. *Revista Mente y Cerebro (Investigación y Ciencia)*.

Mosquera, D., González A., & Van der Hart, O. (2011). Borderline personality disorder, childhood trauma and structural dissociation of the personality. *Persona, FUNDAP,* (44-73).

Multhaup, K.S., Johnson, M.D., & Tetirick, J.C. (2005). The wane of childhood amnesia for autobiographical and public event memories. *Memory,* 13 (2), 161–173.

Myers, C.S. (1940). *Shell-shock in France 1914-18*. Cambridge: Cambridge University Press.

Nauta, W. (1964). Some efferent connections of the frontal cortex in the monkey. In Warren & Akert (Ed.), *The frontal granular cortex and behavior* (pp. 397-407). Mc Graw Hill. NY.

Neff, K., Rude, S., & Kirkpatrick, K. (2007). An examination of self-compassion in relation to positive psychological functioning and personality traits. *Journal of Research in Personality,* 41, 908–916.

Newen, D. & Vogeley, K. (2008). The "sense of agency" and its underlying cognitive and neural mechanisms. *Conscious Cogn.* Jun, 17 (2), 523-534.

Nijenhuis, E.R.S., Van der Hart, O., & Steele, K. (2002). The emerging psychobiology of trauma-related dissociation and dissociative disorders. In H. D´haenen, J.A. den Boer, & P. Willner (Eds.), *Biological psychiatry* (pp. 1079-1098). Chicester, UK: John Wiley & Sons.

Ogawa, J.R., Sroufe, L.A., Weinfield, N.S., Carlson, E.A., & Egeland, B. (1997). Development and the fragmented self: Longitudinal study of dissociative symptomatology in a nonclinical sample. *Developmental Psychopathology*, 9 (4), 855-879.

Ogden, P. & Minton, K. (2000). Sensorimotor psychotherapy: One method for processing traumatic memory. *Traumatology*, 6 (3), Article 3 (October).

Ogden, P., Minton, K., & Pain, C. (2006). *Trauma and the body: A sensorimotor approach to psychotherapy.* New York: W.W. Norton.

Ostacoli, L. & Bertino, G. (2010). *EMDR and drawing: A tool to integrate post-traumatic dissociation and overwhelming emotions.* Paper presented at the annual meeting of the EMDR Europe Association, Hamburg, Germany.

Panksepp, J. (1998). *Affective neuroscience: the foundations of human and animal emotion.* New York, NY: Oxford University Press.

Parker, A., Relph, S., & Dagnall, N. (2008). Effects of bilateral eye movement on retrieval of item, associative and contextual information. *Neuropsychology*, 22, 136-145.

Paulsen, S. (1995). Eye movement desensitization and reprocessing: Its cautious use in the dissociative disorders. *Dissociation*, 8 (1), 32-44.

Paulsen, S. (2007). Treating dissociative identity disorder with EMDR, ego state therapy, and adjunct approaches. In C. Forgash & M. Copeley (Eds.), *Healing the heart of trauma and dissociation with EMDR and ego state therapy* (pp. 141-179). New York: Springer.

Paulsen, S. (2009). *Looking through the eyes of trauma & dissociation: An illustrated guide for EMDR clinicians and patients.* Bainbridge Institute for Integrative Psychology.

Phillips, M. & Frederick, C. (1995). *Healing the divided self: Clinical and Ericksonian hypnotherapy for post-traumatic and dissociative conditions.* New York: W.W. Norton & Co.

Pope, K.S. (1990). Therapist-patient sexual involvement: A review of the research. *Clinical Psychology Review*, 10, 477-490.

Pope, K.S. (1993). Licensing disciplinary actions for psychologists who have been sexually involved with a client: Some information about offenders. *Professional Psychology: Research and Practice*, 24, 374-377.

Popky, A.J. (1992). Smoking cessation protocol. *EMDR Network Newsletter*, 2 (3), 4-6.

Popky, A.J. (2005). DeTUR, an urge reduction protocol for addictions and dysfunctional behaviors. In R. Shapiro (Ed.), *EMDR Solutions: Pathways to Healing.* Norton & Company. NY.

Porges, S.W. (2001). The polyvagal theory: Phylogenetics substrates of a social nervous system. *International Journal of Psychophysiology.* 42, 123-146.

Porges, S.W. (2003). The polyvagal theory: Phylogenetic contributions to social behavior. *Physiology and Behavior,* 79, 503–513.

Porges, S.W. (2003). Social engagement and attachment: A phylogenetic perspective. *Roots of Mental Illness in Children, Annals of the New York Academy of Sciences*, 1008, 31-47.

Porges, S.W. (2008). Regulation of the stress response: Stress and parasympathetic control. In Larry R. Squire (Ed.), *Encyclopedia of Neuroscience.* Oxford: Academic Press.

Pribram, K.H. (1987). The subdivisions of the frontal cortex revisited. In Perekman (Ed.), *The frontal lobes revisited.* Hillsdale.

Prince, M. (1906). *The dissociation of a personality.* New York: Longmans, Green, & Co.

Putnam, F.W et al. (1986). The clinical phenomenology of multiple personality disorder. *Journal of Clinical Psychiatry*, 140, 867-872.

Putnam, F.W. (1989). *Diagnosis and treatment of multiple personality disorder*. New York: The Guilford Press.

Putnam, F.W (1997). *Dissociation in children and adolescents: A developmental perspective*. The Guilford Press.

Putnam, F.W., Guroff, J., Silverman, E., Barban, L., & and Post, R. (1986). The clinical phenomenology of multiple personality disorder: Review of 100 recent cases. *Journal of Clinical Psychiatry*, 47, 285-293.

Reinders, A.A., Nijenhuis, E.R., Paans, A.M., Korf, J, Willemsen A.T., & den Boer, J.A. (2003). One brain, two selves. *Neuroimage*, Dec., 20 (4), 2119-25.

Ryle, A. (1995). *Cognitive Analytic Therapy: Developments in theory and practice*. Wiley Series in Psychotherapy and Counselling.

Ryle, A. & Kerr, I.B. (2002). *Introducing Cognitive Analytic Therapy. Principles and practice*. John Wiley & Sons.

Sack, M., Lempa, W., & Lemprecht, W. (2007). Assessment of psychophysiological stress reactions during a traumatic reminder in patients treated with EMDR. *Journal of EMDR Practice and Research*, 1, 15–23.

Salter, A. (2003). *Predators: Pedophiles, rapists and other sex offenders. Who they are, how they operate and how we can protect ourselves and our children*. NY: Basic Books.

Schore, A. (2003). *Affect dysregulation and disorders of the self*. Norton.

Schore, A. (2005). A neuropsychoanalytic viewpoint. *Psychoanalytic Dialogues*, 15(6), 829–854.

Schwartz, R.C. (1995). *Internal Family Systems Therapy*. Guilford Press.

Schwartz, R.C. & Goulding, R.A. (2002). *The Mosaic Mind*. Trailheads Publications.

Segal, Z.V., Williams, M., & Teasdale, J.D. (2002). *Mindfulness-based cognitive therapy for depression: a new approach to preventing relapse*. Guilford Press.

Seligman, M.E.P. & Maier, S.F. (1967). Failure to escape traumatic shock. *Journal of Experimental Psychology*, 74, 1–9.

Seubert, A. (2009). The why of eating disorders. In R. Shapiro (Ed.), *EMDR solutions II: For depression, eating disorders, performance, and more* (pp. 109-13). New York: Norton Professional Books.

Shapiro, F. (1989). Efficacy of the eye movement desensitization procedure in the treatment of traumatic memories. *Journal of Traumatic Stress*, 2 (2), 199-223.

Shapiro, F. (1991). Eye movement desensitization & reprocessing procedure: From EMD to EMD/R--A new treatment model for anxiety and related traumata. The Behavior Therapist, 14(5), 133-135.

Shapiro, F. (1995). *Eye movement desensitization and reprocessing. Basic principles, protocols and procedures*. New York. Guilford Press.

Shapiro, F. (2001). *Eye movement desensitization and reprocessing. Basic principles, protocols and procedures*. Second edition. Guilford Press.

Shapiro, F. (2002). Paradigms, processing, and personality development. In F. Shapiro (Ed.), *EMDR as an integrative psychotherapy approach: Experts of diverse orientations explore the paradigm prism* (pp. 3–26). Washington, DC: American Psychological Association Press.

Shapiro, F. (2004). *Adaptive information processing: EMDR clinical application and case conceptualization*. EMDRIA Conference 2004. Montreal.

Shapiro, F. (2006). *New notes on adaptive information processing*. Hamden, CT: EMDR Humanitarian Assistance Programs.

Shapiro, F. & Forrest, M. S. (1997). *EMDR: The breakthrough therapy for overcoming anxiety, stress, and trauma*. New York: Basic Books.

Shedler, J., Mayman, M., & Manis, M. (1993). The illusion of mental health. *American Psychologist*, 48, 1117-1131.

Shepard, L.A. (1979). Self-acceptance: The evaluative component of the self-concept construct. *American Educational Research Journal*, 16 (2), 139-160.

Siegel, D.J. (1999). *The developing mind: Towards a neurobiology of interpersonal experience*. New York: Norton.

Siegel, D.J. (2010). *Mindsight: the new science of personal transformation*. Bantam Books. The Random House Publishing Group, New York.

Siegel, D.J. & Hartzell, M. (2004). *Parenting from the inside out*. Jeremy P. Tacher / Penguin.

Suokas-Cunliffe, A., Mattheβ, H., & van der Hart, O. (2008). *The use of EMDR and guided synthesis in the treatment of chronically traumatized patients*. Proceedings of the 1st Bi-Annual International European Society for Trauma and Dissociation Conference, Amsterdam, the Netherlands.

Steele, K. (2009). Reflections on integration, mentalization, and institutional realization. *Journal of Trauma & Dissociation*, 10 (1), 1-8.

Steele, K., Van der Hart, O., & Nijenhuis, E.R.S. (2001). Dependency in the treatment of complex posttraumatic stress disorder and dissociative disorders. *Journal of Trauma and Dissociation*, 2 (4), 79-116.

Steele, K., Van der Hart, O., & Nijenhuis, E.R.S. (2005). Phase-oriented treatment of structural dissociation in complex traumatization: Overcoming trauma-related phobias. *Journal of Trauma and dissociation*, 6 (3), 11-53.

Stern, D. (1985). *The interpersonal world of the infant*. New York: Basic Books.

Stone, M. (1993). *Abnormalities of personality. Within and beyond the realm of treatment*. Norton.

Strehler, B.L. (1991). Where is the self? A neuroanatomical theory of consciousness. *Synapse*, Jan., 7 (1), 44-91.

Suzuki, A., Josselyn, S.A., Frankland, P.W., Masushige, S., Silva, A.J., & Kida, S. (2004). Memory reconsolidation and extinction have distinct temporal and biochemical signatures. *Journal of Neuroscience*, 24, 4787–4795.

Teasdale, J.D. (1999). Metacognition, mindfulness and the modification of mood disorders. *Clinical Psychology & Psychotherapy. Special Issue: Metacognition and Cognitive Behaviour Therapy*. 6 (2), 146–155.

Teicher, M.H., Samson, J.A., Polcari, A., & McGreenery, C.E. (2006). Sticks, stones, and hurtful words: Relative effects of various forms of childhood maltreatment. *American Journal of Psychiatry*, 163 (6), 993-1000.

Tirapu-Ustárroz, J., Muñoz-Céspedes, J.M., & Pelegrín-Valero, C. (2003). Hacia una taxonomía de la conciencia. *Revista de Neurología*, 36, 1083-1093.

Tomkins, S. (1962). *Affect imagery consciousness: Volume I. The positive affects*. London: Tavistock.

Turkus J.A, & Kahler J.A. (2006). Therapeutic interventions in the treatment of dissociative disorders. Psychiatric Clinics of North America 29: 245-262.

Twombly, J.H. (2000). Incorporating EMDR and EMDR adaptations into the treatment of clients with dissociative identity disorder. *Journal of Trauma and Dissociation*, 1 (2), 61-81.

Twombly, J.H. (2005). EMDR for patients with dissociative identity disorder, DDNOS, and ego states. In R. Shapiro (Ed.), *EMDR solutions: Pathways to healing* (pp. 88-120). New York: W. W. Norton & Co.

Twombly, J.H. & Waltham, M.A. (2008). *Dissociative disorders: Diagnosis, stabilization, internal communication and cooperation, facilitated by EMDR*. Presentation in the I ESTD Conference, Amsterdam.

Vaillant, G.E. (1992). *Ego mechanisms of defense: A guide for clinicians and researchers*. Washington, DC: American Psychiatric Press.

Van der Hart, O., Steele, K., Boon, S., & Brown, P. (1993). The treatment of traumatic memories: synthesis, realization, and integration. *Dissociation*, 6 (2/3), 162-180.

Van der Hart, O., Nijenhuis, E., & Steele, K. (2005). Dissociation: An insufficiently recognized major feature of complex PTSD. *Journal of Traumatic Stress*, 18 (5).

Van der Hart, O., Nijenhuis, E.R.S., & Steele, K. (2006). *The haunted self: Structural dissociation and the treatment of chronic traumatization*. New York: Norton.

Van der Hart, O., Nijenhuis, E.R.S., & Solomon, R. (2010). In complex trauma-related disorders and EMDR: Theoretical considerations. *Journal of EMDR Practice and Research*, 4 (2), 76-92.

Van der Hart, O., Solomon, R., & Gonzalez, A. (2010). *The theory of structural dissociation as a guide for EMDR treatment of chronically traumatized patients*. Paper presented at the annual meeting of the EMDR International Association, Minneapolis, MN.

Van der Hart, O., Groenendijk, M., Gonzalez, A., Mosquera, D., & Solomon, R. (2013). Dissociation of the personality and EMDR therapy in complex trauma-related disorders: Applications in the stabilization phase. *Journal of EMDR Practice and Research*, 7 (2), 81-94.

Van der Kolk, B.A. & Van der Hart, O. (1989). Pierre Janet and the breakdown of adaptation in psychological trauma. *American Journal of Psychiatry*, 146 (12), 1530-1540.

Van der Kolk, B., Roth, S., Pelcovitz, D., Sunday, S., & Spinazzola, J. (2005). Disorders of extreme stress: The empirical foundation of a complex adaptation to trauma. *Journal of Traumatic Stress*, 18 (5), 389–399.

Watkins, H.H. (1993). Ego-State therapy: An overview. *American Journal of Clinical Hypnosis*, 35 (4), 232-240.

Watkins, J. & and Watkins, H. (1997). *Ego states: Theory and therapy*. Norton Ed. New York.

Weinfield, N.S., Sroufe, L.A., Egeland, B., & Carlson, E. (1999). The nature of individual differences in infant-caregiver attachment. In J. Cassidy & P. Shaver (Eds.), *Handbook of attachment: Theory, research, and clinical application* (pp. 68-88). New York: Guilford Press.

Whitfield, C.L. (1987). *Healing the child within: Discovery and recovery for adult children of dysfunctional families*. Health Communications Inc.

Wildwind, C.L. (1992). *Treating chronic depression*. Paper presented at the First Annual EMDR Conference, San Jose, CA.

Wilson, D., Silver, S.M., Covi, W., & Foster, S. (1996). Eye movement desensitization and reprocessing: Effectiveness and autonomic correlates. *Journal of Behaviour Therapy and Experimental Psychiatry*, 27, 219–229.

Winnicott, D.W. (1960). Ego distortion in terms of true and false self. In *The maturational process and the facilitating environment: Studies in the theory of emotional development* (pp. 140-152). New York: International UP Inc, 1965.

Wolstein, B. (1987). Anxiety and the psychic center of the psychoanalytic self. *Contemporary Psychoanalysis*, 23, 631-658.

Yang, Y. & Raine, A. (2009). Prefrontal structural and functional brain imaging findings in antisocial, violent, and psychopathic individuals: A meta-analysis. *Psychiatry Res,* November 30, 174 (2), 81-88.

York, C. (2000). *Affect tolerance, modulation and management: A behavioral model for using EMDR*. Workshop. Austin, TX.

York, C. & Leeds, A. (2001). *Gate theory: An accelerated information processing model for developing functional state change*. Presentation at the annual meeting of the EMDR International Association, Austin,TX.

Young, J., Klosko, J., & Weishaar, M. (2003). *Schema therapy: A practitioner´s guide*. New York: Guilford Publications.

Ystgaard, M., Hestetun, I., Loeb, M., & Mehlum, L. (2004). Is there a specific relationship between childhood sexual and physical abuse and repeated suicidal behavior? *Child Abuse & Neglect*, 28, 863–875.

About the Authors

Anabel Gonzalez, M. D., Ph. D.

Anabel Gonzalez works as a psychiatrist and psychotherapist in the Public Mental Health System and in Private Practice. She coordinates the Trauma and Dissociation Program in the Severe Mental Disorders Services of the University Hospital of A Coruña, and has a broad clinical experience with Dissociative Disorders and Complex Trauma. Trained in different psychotherapeutic approaches, she has been working with EMDR since 1999 and is an EMDR Therapist, Consultant, and Facilitator. Anabel Gonzalez is Vice-President of the Spanish EMDR Association and member of the ESTD Board. She is head of the ISST-D online training on complex trauma and dissociation and has presented several workshops and courses about EMDR interventions in dissociative disorders, personality disorders, and psychosis. She is author of several articles, presentations, and books

Dolores Mosquera, M. A.

Dolores Mosquera is a psychologist and psychotherapist. She is the director of the Institute for the Study of Trauma and Personality disorders (INTRA-TP), a private institution where she has worked with EMDR for many years on cases related to severe traumatization. She works in an offenders program and collaborates treating adolescents in a youth correctional facility. She has been trained in several psychotherapeutic approaches and is an EMDR Europe Consultant and Facilitator. She has extensive teaching experience, leading seminars, workshops, and lectures internationally. She has published many books and articles on personality disorders, complex trauma, and dissociation and is a recognized expert in this field. Dolores Mosquera is a member of the ESTSS board and a member of the Editorial Board for the ESTD Newsletter.